American Jewish Films

ALSO BY LAWRENCE J. EPSTEIN

George Burns: An American Life (McFarland, 2011)
*Political Folk Music in America from
Its Origins to Bob Dylan* (McFarland, 2010)

American Jewish Films

The Search for Identity

LAWRENCE J. EPSTEIN

McFarland & Company, Inc., Publishers
Jefferson, North Carolina, and London

ISBN 978-0-7864-6962-8
softcover : acid free paper ∞

LIBRARY OF CONGRESS CATALOGUING DATA ARE AVAILABLE

BRITISH LIBRARY CATALOGUING DATA ARE AVAILABLE

© 2013 Lawrence J. Epstein. All rights reserved

No part of this book may be reproduced or transmitted in any form or by any means, electronic or mechanical, including photocopying or recording, or by any information storage and retrieval system, without permission in writing from the publisher.

On the cover: a scene from *Exodus*, 1960, with Jill Haworth as Karen Hansen Clement and Sal Mineo as Dov Landau in the center (United Artists/Photofest); film background (iStockphoto/Thinkstock)

Manufactured in the United States of America

McFarland & Company, Inc., Publishers
Box 611, Jefferson, North Carolina 28640
www.mcfarlandpub.com

For Lily Ada Reiser
Our first grandchild
When I hold her, I hold all the past and all the future.

Contents

Acknowledgments	ix
Preface	1
One. What Is a Jewish Film?	7
Two. The Jewish Plymouth Rock: Films About the Lower East Side	16
Three. The Past Is Prologue: Films of Jewish History	35
Four. The Oldest Hatred: Anti-Semitism in Films	48
Five. The Invisible Jews: Films About Assimilation	80
Six. Assimilation with a Heart: Romance in American Jewish Films	116
Seven. The Borscht Belt Shtetl: Films About Jewish Resorts in the Catskills	133
Eight. Zion on the Screen: Films About Israel	147
Nine. The Dark Side: Jewish Criminals on Film	164
Ten. Faith on Film	174
Eleven. An American Jewish Identity	196
Chronology of Films	201
Chapter Notes	203
Bibliography	206
Index	209

Acknowledgments

Many very kind people helped me get to the point where I could write this book. What happens during a writing career is that all the help from interview subjects, librarians, scholars, and others adds up so that the intellectual debt is large and covers a long span of time. In fact, it really is impossible to identify all the help I've gotten and all the people who have influenced me. My study of film began in earlier books, and so the help I received for those helped in this one. For example, I learned enormously from interviews I had done earlier, including those with Jeanine Basinger, Leo Brooks, David Bullard, Mark Dawidziak, William F. Drew, Wes Gehring, Kristine Karnick, John Larrabee, Leonard Maltin, and Ali Stevenson. Others who helped along the way were Jeff Abraham, Joe Adamson, Michael Gerien, and Paul Wesolowki. The late, wonderful television personality Steve Allen gave me great advice. Robert J. Thompson, director of the Center for the Study of Popular Television at Syracuse University, knows a lot about popular culture and is always willing to share his knowledge.

I'm sure it is true of other authors as well, but I could not write without the help of librarians. They provide advice, track down obscure materials, offer unasked for and unmerited words of support, and have more knowledge than seems possible.

The National Center for Jewish Film, located at Brandeis University, has graciously provided materials for several of my books. This is the indispensable source for Jewish film materials.

I received help from David Schwartz, chief curator of film, American Museum of the Moving Image. The New York Library of the Performing Arts is a treasure chest, and its staff extremely helpful.

I have, for a long while, owed a personal debt of gratitude to Ned Comstock, archivist at the Cinema/TV Collections of the University of

Acknowledgments

Southern California. No one who researches motion pictures can fail to appreciate Ned's immense knowledge, his enthusiasm, and his professionalism. He searched the Constance McCormick Collection and the Hal Humphrey Collection for materials. Ned ended up sending me hundreds of pages of material and patiently guiding me through questions only he could answer.

While I taught at Suffolk County Community College I had the chance to work with many wonderful librarians. Susan Rubenstein DeMasi, then a media librarian at the Ammerman Campus, was the person I went to when I needed to locate some ridiculously obscure film unavailable on DVD or video. The people in the interlibrary loan area were wonderful as well. In particular, I owe a lot to Marilyn Ventiere and others.

The members of the English Department at the college were like an extended family for the thirty-four years I worked there. I appreciate them all and owe them my profound thanks. In particular, I can identify contributions to my film knowledge from Tony DiFranco, who was my office mate for most of my tenure there. Tony, a writer and filmmaker himself, had enormous insight into how films work, and what I might do in this book. Through the years I received help in my writing from others in the college and department as well, including Sandra Sprows, Doug Howard, Tony Martone, Ed Joyce, Gerry O'Connor, Steve Klipstein, Sarah Kain Gutowski, Liz Cone, Sam Robertson, Adam Penna, and many others.

This particular book was born in personal difficulty. I had a heart attack and ended up having an extremely difficult recovery. At one point my cardiologist stood in front of me and practically ordered me to write another book. That was fine, but I couldn't order anybody to do anything. What I could do, what I did do, was send an e-mail to my editor explaining the situation and outlining the book you are now reading. She responded affirmatively very quickly.

My friends have always been there for me. When it comes to film, Doug Rathgeb is without peer. We have been discussing and arguing film for about fifty years. He is a storehouse of knowledge and insight, and I always go to him when I am about to write about motion pictures. In the case of this book, Doug made suggestions about particular films and offered many astute observations.

Many other friends were there along the way to help. I'd like to thank Rich Tuckman and my extraordinary friend Assemblyman Mike Fitzpatrick for their support.

Acknowledgments

Don Gastwirth is my literary agent. The word "quit" is not in his vocabulary, but the words "unconditional support" always are there. I appreciate his help over the years. His brother, Joseph L. Gastwirth, has always provided much-needed support and kind words.

My cousins Toby Everett and Dr. Sheldon Scheinert have been extremely close family members and friends since childhood.

My in-laws, Harvey and Marsha Selib, and Judi Marshall, have always been most helpful and kind.

My late father, Fred Epstein, always supported my attempts at writing.

My late mother, Lillian Scheinert Epstein, was the one who passed on her love of movies. She knew stories about all the stars. She was always a kind audience for the outpourings of my wandering mind. Her indispensable loving kindness shaped my life.

My brother, Richard, is a careful reader of my work. How he remembers all the movies we saw as children is beyond me, but he does. His constant interest, his kind enthusiasm, and his perceptive comments and uncommonly good sense were vital to the book's completion. His wife, Perla, and children Adam and Sondra, as well as their children, have always been a source of support.

My own children have always been immeasurably important. My son, Michael, and his wife, Sophia Cacciola, know a lot about film, in part because they have made some, and so can engage in lively and informative discussions. My daughter Elana and her husband Justin Reiser listen patiently to my tales. Elana has been able to get materials for me. My daughter Rachel and her husband John Eddey are always extraordinarily supportive. Rachel, the author of a hilarious memoir titled *Running of the Bride*, has frequent and fascinating conversations with me about writing. John is vice-president at the largest American film and television production studio complex outside of Hollywood. He knows a thing or two about films. Lisa is my youngest daughter. She and her husband Florian Christen live in Switzerland, but that doesn't stop them from providing invaluable observations and advice.

The book's dedication—to Lily Ada Reiser, our first grandchild—speaks for itself. Lily is an unending delight. I just need to think of her in order to smile.

I especially enjoy watching my wife Sharon hold Lily. Sharon, it hardly needs to be said, is vital to my life. She is always there, on the good days

Acknowledgments

and the bad, on the days that my health seemed horribly precarious and on the days when there was more hope. She is endlessly willing to listen to me make observations about the films we watch.

Great films can make us appreciate those who are most important to us. My family does that every day.

Preface

In the movie theater, that darkened palace where the imagination ruled and the candy flowed and the inhibitions went to sleep, where the velvet black of the air blocked out the rest of reality, where the world was impossibly large and sparkling in its allure right in front of you, it was possible to believe the wildest fantasies. The person you loved in fact loved you back. The job you wanted, the one that would pay you a fortune and recognize you as the genius you were, was waiting for you. The painful life you led, the family that was a traveling psychodrama, the petty annoyances flying around your life like so many flies, would soon be transformed because everyone around you would come to their senses and reality would magically conform to your hopes and expectations.

Hollywood had devised clever ways to manufacture dreams and then make all the dreams seem palpable, fluttering before us like glittering prizes for us to grab. Hollywood found beautiful people we could pretend were real substitutes for us. Yes, we were that attractive, that brave, that clever, that blessed by Fate, which would clear a path in our lives as surely as it cleared a path for all those characters in all those movies.

America's Jews were among those deeply intrigued by the irresistible products of the Hollywood Dream Factory's assembly line. Perhaps that was because the Jews were so desperately in need of dreams. Away from the theaters, the Jews were poverty-stricken outsiders, escapees from persecution, religiously suspect, linguistically baffled, and confused about what kind of people they were in this new Golden Land and what America would permit them to do and to be. They gratefully and tearfully clung to prayers and hope, but they desperately needed guidance about how to navigate through their new surroundings. They, after all, didn't even know what chewing gum was. What a strange land. People got paid to vote. Doctors forced you to take off your clothes. You were supposed to be polite.

Preface

The Jews were baffled. Their culture was a closed one. No one else spoke Hebrew or understood that you didn't mix meat and milk products, that Saturday morning was for prayers, not work. And so the work, social, and romantic opportunities were severely limited for Jews. Their politics were framed by an Eastern European perspective. Even their intellectual horizons, broadened by the European Enlightenment and its Jewish counterpart, still didn't extend as far as for others.

It was film, an art form the Jews were instrumental in creating, that most forcefully provided passports away from the imaginations they inherited and toward the American imagination. Films gave them the answers to the questions they had about how to be a good American. But the answers were only of a certain kind. In a sense, American films were a series of images about appropriate etiquette, or rehearsals for reality, for Jews. They were not, and were not meant to be, serious reflections on what it meant to be an American Jew beyond the sociological meaning of the word. The films were great teachers of behavior but not great teachers of thought. As films defined what it meant to be an American, Jewish audiences saw in the glowing mythology that transfixed them on the screen a pleasing reality they could inhabit and role models to shape their emerging American selves. Suddenly, they thought, they too could find a more attractive romantic partner than the man or woman their family's marriage broker could provide. They too could get out from behind pressing the pants, out from behind the sewing machine, away from the horrific conditions of the sweatshops. They could dream of becoming doctors, lawyers, teachers, and other professionals. The films made them heady. This America was a great place, a land where today's dream could be tomorrow's reality.

But the very dazzling images that so enchanted the Jewish movie audiences also were bright enough to blind them to some aspects of both American and Jewish life. They saw only some of what they could get, and they didn't see what they were giving up to get it. In their eagerness to embrace all that was American, from that wild game called baseball to the idea of going out to a place called a restaurant where other people cooked for you and served you the food while you sat there like a king or queen, the Jews did not see the cost they were going to pay. Most especially, they did not grasp how much becoming American was going to alter their identity as Jews.

For if the American films defined what it meant to be an American,

Preface

they didn't quite define what it meant to be both American and Jewish. That conjoined identity was more elusive. To search for it on the screen, Jews had to create or view films that were filled with Jewish characters in America trying to understand what was happening to their Jewish selves.

This book is about those American Jewish films and what they had to say (and not say) about the Jewish search for identity in the Golden Land.

I was one of those American Jews on such a search. My mother had brought me up to love movies, and I saw them from an early age. In 1966, the year I turned twenty, I determined I would see as many films as I could in one year. I ended up seeing three hundred of them. But it wasn't until I began taking Judaism and Jewishness seriously a couple of years later that I concluded that one avenue of my exploration of what it meant to be Jewish would take me into the special palaces where movies were shown, there to seek out the brass ring of personal existence and understand my own identity.

And so, for the course of my life, I watched those films, some justly famous, some justly forgotten. Now I've had a chance to see the films several times, to think about them, to consider Jewish identity in America; and so now, I concluded, it was time to record some of what I had learned.

Sometimes the very act of thinking, the very obligation to make intellectual observations and decisions, makes us reach conclusions we had not expected. This might come about through research, talking to others, and re-viewing films we thought we psychologically owned. That's what happened to me.

I started out intending this book to be a simple celebration of Jewish movies. I had a strong personal motivating reason. After my heart attack, most of what I was able to do was read, watch a television screen with its shows on the air or on a DVD player and work on a computer. Therefore, for very practical reasons, the conclusion seemed inevitable: write a book about movies that I could watch. I had seen a lot of Jewish movies. I would, I decided, like to watch them again and watch those relatively few Jewish films I had missed. I didn't want to overburden myself, so I thought it would be fun and informative to write about Jewish films. I especially looked forward to seeing again many of the films I had seen and enjoyed decades earlier. I thought doing so would bring me back to some happier times.

And there were, in fact, many films I had enjoyed. But there was no pattern, no group name for them — like film noir for those wonderfully dark, cynical films of the 1940s and '50s. They were just Jewish films. They were points on a canvas that didn't make a portrait. I decided I wanted to try to connect all the films, to see an overall pattern if I could. I intuitively grasped that collectively they were trying, or should have been trying, to make a comment on what it meant to be Jewish in America, but that it wasn't, at the beginning, at all clear to me what these films as a group were saying about American Jewish identity. And so I began to look at the films not just as works of entertainment and not as isolated artistic products, but as part of a historical pattern, one that weaved together the fumbling attempt to understand what America meant for the Jews and how it changed them.

This book is the story of my search. Inevitably, as I watched and thought, my views changed or became sharpened. The unalloyed celebration soon devolved into a more realistic assessment of the Jewish films. I became increasingly uneasy, in fact, not so much with the films themselves (for they understandably varied quite widely in quality), but rather with the brute fact that most were inadequate for the task. True, it was a task I had assigned them. They mostly just wanted to entertain, to be fun, to let audiences escape the humdrum existence of life outside the theater. I wanted more than that, however. I wanted films to be serious artistic documents even as they provided entertainment. I wanted them to provide guidance about being Jewish. That proved to be a more elusive accomplishment.

I had a particular approach as I wrote about the films. I did my best not to duplicate material widely available in many other sources. I did not want, for example, to talk about a film with a substantial amount of the discussion devoted to a plot summary and then a rundown of the various principal critical reactions. When it was helpful I have included relatively brief discussions of the plot to clarify a point, and in certain cases, especially if a film is not well-known or more extended knowledge of the plot was needed, I included a more expansive summary. I've included dialogue from the film much more extensively for the same reason — not just to illustrate the film's content but to make a wider critical point. Most of the dialogue I've included is the most important dialogue in the film. Similarly, I didn't include a great deal about the making of a film. There is a lot of interesting background information available. When such information was vital I included it, but when I considered it trivial space filler I left it out.

Preface

I still intend this book to celebrate Jewish films. But more than that I hope it will lead to a discussion about what films have contributed to an understanding of American Jewish life and culture. I hope the book will be a fun house mirror, perhaps distorting the lives of readers a bit but nevertheless also providing a useful reflection from which to learn.

CHAPTER ONE

What Is a Jewish Film?

The very idea of a Jewish film is an imprecise notion. The first problem is how the adjective "Jewish" limits the broader subject of film. One approach is to be expansive, to include any film with a Jewish star, a Jewish writer, or a Jewish director, whatever the contents of the film happen to be. Given the role of Jews in Hollywood, that limiting idea is not very helpful because there are Jews involved in an extraordinary number of important motion pictures. They may not be the stars, but there were innumerable Jewish screenwriters, producers, directors, and others who helped create motion pictures. So this definition is entirely inadequate.

The second approach, the one taken in this book, is to define "Jewish films" to mean only American films with significant content and characters related to Jewish life, and that made an important statement about that life in America. This also has its problems because, for example, poor films with a Jewish content get discussed whereas excellent films that, say, had a Jewish director or screenwriter but no Jewish content are bypassed. Additionally, it is not even entirely clear what constitutes "significant" content. Relatively rarely, for instance, has Judaism been the subject of a film. And when the subject is Jews (a film about the Holocaust or about Israel), rarely is there a discussion about what it means to be Jewish. The job of the book is to sift through all this, to describe as many films as possible with at least some Jewish content, and try to figure out what they had to say about Jewish life.

There are therefore specific limitations, admittedly arbitrary in some cases, on the subject. Because of the narrowing of the discussion, the book focuses on artistic and fictional films that tell stories with some substantial Jewish subject matter. There is no discussion, for example, of some excellent documentaries with Jewish themes because audiences for documentaries are relatively small, and, by definition, the documentaries are not fictional.

American Jewish films that did reach a substantial audience did so because they were in part works of pure entertainment. If they had comments about American Jewish life, those comments were generally subtle and wrapped in an emotional story line. Documentaries proceed by argument, not story. *Zelig*, a film by Woody Allen, does use the documentary form and even interviews prominent Jews, but it is about a fictional character. Even in that case it is the stories and characters that bring audiences to the theater.

There are many wonderful and worthwhile Yiddish films that provide valuable viewing experiences, but they are not included in the book because they don't have a large contemporary audience and don't generally discuss the content of American Jewish life today. Additionally, the book does not include foreign films unless they had very wide distribution in the United States and had an impact on American Jewish life.

But this is just a decision; it doesn't go to a central question. That question involves the relationship between Judaism and images. Historically, the Jewish people and the Jewish religion have been very suspicious of images. The Jews, the "people of the Book," didn't focus on pictures. They relied on language. Words, primarily in holy texts, prayer, and song, formed the contours of living and examining what it meant to be Jewish. Indeed, the fourth of the Ten Commandments forbids Jews to make any graven images either of what is in Heaven, on Earth, or in the seas. A "graven" image is one that is deeply impressed on a person. Evidently, fleeting, ephemeral images necessary (indeed unavoidable) in life are allowed for practical reasons.

Jews avoided paintings, sculptures, and other means of artistic reproduction through much of their history. And so it might appear as a surprise that Jews were so taken by motion pictures, so instrumental in their creation, so admiring of their existence (becoming as avid a group of viewers as films had).

Why? What had changed? One element that changed was what was called the Jewish Enlightenment, the secularization of Jewish life, the embrace of modernity and the seeming acceptance as citizens by European countries and then especially in America. It was the time that light broke through the crack of tradition, the moment, a millennium in coming, when Jewish traditions no longer defined the emotionally protective borders of a Jewish life. It was a moment when European languages and literature were learned and studied — not just for practical purposes but for

One—What Is a Jewish Film?

intellectual pleasure and inquiry into the wider world. It was a time when education meant more than studying the Talmud and following the 613 commandments that the holy Torah purportedly contained. This secular knowledge the Jews obtained sometimes supplemented the classic Jewish education grounded in Torah and Talmud. But sometimes, and at an accelerating pace, the secular knowledge replaced traditional religious knowledge. A relatively small percentage of American Jews are literate in Hebrew or Yiddish. American English is their Jewish language. However, the rhythms of American English stem from particular traditions, and they aren't Jewish ones.

This broader change in Jewish life was sharpened by the American experience. The Golden Land particularly attracted the young and the most secular. The more religious were wary of the new country across the ocean, afraid that it was a land where religion went to die. And so, to their descendants' horrific misfortune under the Nazis and the Communists, the more religious stayed behind. America had the adventurous young willing to shave their beards and discard their traditions for the sake of liberty from oppression and immense economic opportunity.

These Jewish immigrants arrived from Eastern Europe in large numbers precisely at the time when film technology was just developing. Others may have been reluctant to enter the new business that some found morally questionable and financially uncertain. But Jews were willing to take a chance. Indeed, precisely because of its nature, film welcomed Jews ,and Jews, having at the time relatively few attractive alternatives, saw in film an escalator providing upward social mobility.

Despite the existence of so many Jewish film moguls—men like Louis B. Mayer, Samuel Goldwyn, Adolph Zukor, William Fox, Carl Laemmle, Jesse Lasky, Marcus Loew, the Warner Brothers, David O. Selznick, and Harry Cohn—there were surprisingly few specifically Jewish films made. Most of these creators of the film industry were eager to discard their Jewish specificity, to assimilate and be seen as assimilated. Whatever their private thoughts, they didn't want to draw attention to their Jewishness by making Jewish films.

It is worthwhile following one of their careers to see the effect of these moguls and how Hollywood shaped them. Mayer was the most influential, but Goldwyn remained the most independent. His career is instructive because, unlike the others, he went to the bank to finance each film. If the movie failed, he failed. Every film, therefore, had to be attractive to audiences. Goldwyn, in a way at least, had to care more than the others about the tastes of the audience because his career was always on the line.

Goldwyn was born in Warsaw, Poland, on August 27, 1882. His original name can be transliterated as Samuel Goldfisch. The young boy began work in an office at age eleven, but he was quick and immediately realized the confining limits life seemed to offer. He prized courage and used it to make a decision to flee Poland. He first went to England to live with an aunt and uncle. But the boy, stubborn, proud, and ambitious (without knowing exactly what the word meant), knew success meant getting to the Golden Land of America. He arrived at Castle Garden (the forerunner to Ellis Island) in 1896. He had barely walked out of the immigration stalls when a man approached him and offered him a factory job in Gloversville in upstate New York. Goldwyn became an incredibly successful glove salesman, and like many people who grasped life's possibilities, he saw in his developing abilities not just the skill to sell gloves but a profound insight into what people wanted. He saw desire and need. He grew to understand why and how people spent their money, and what he could sell them. It was that ability, one shared by the other moguls as well, that eventually transformed Goldwyn from a glove salesman into a movie salesman. Goldwyn wanted status and excitement, not the sort of payoff available through gloves.

In 1911 Goldwyn saw a two-reel western and was surprised at how much money was made by the very brief film. But Goldwyn also had an artistic side. He liked a good story, and he liked it well-told. In 1913 Goldwyn joined Jesse Lasky and Cecil B. De Mille to form the Lasky Feature Players Company. Goldwyn immediately sought to improve films, to make them five reels long (about an hour in length). The Lasky Company produced a western in 1914, and *The Squaw Man* made movie history. It was the first full-length feature that had been produced within the United States, and the first major motion picture that was made in Hollywood.

It was after a merger with another company, one headed by Adolph Zukor, that Goldwyn found he could not work within the emerging corporate structure. Goldwyn had his own vision. He was a forceful personality, and he wanted films done in the way *he* wanted them done. Looking for new partners, Goldwyn, then still Goldfisch, started a company with the Selwyn brothers. They took the first syllable of Goldfisch and the last syllable of Selwyn and called the company the Goldwyn Pictures Corporation. (The alternative syllables would have led to the Selfisch Corpora-

One—What Is a Jewish Film?

tion; this was not a good alternative.) And Samuel Goldfisch so loved the corporate name that eventually he took it as his own. After he broke with this corporation, Goldwyn knew he had no choice but to make films on his own. He formed a new corporation in 1923 and began to make movies in the way he thought best.

Interestingly, the very first of his pictures that was released (although it was made after an earlier film, *The Eternal City*) was about Jewish life. Goldwyn, like the other moguls, was proud to be Jewish but didn't want it to interfere in his life. He wanted to be thought of as a proud and patriotic American, not a poor immigrant Jew. *Potash and Perlmutter* was produced in 1923. It was about two partners working in the clothing business on the Lower East Side of New York. The two title characters are tailors. They take on Boris, a new employee, to be a fitter. Boris falls in love with Abe Potash's daughter who has already been promised to the business' unscrupulous legal counsel. Boris is arrested and accused of murder when a labor agitator is shot and dies. Potash and Perlmutter mortgage the business to pay for Boris to get out on bail. Abe suggests Boris head for Canada because he might not get a fair trial. But this is Hollywood. He stays, is vindicated, and wins the woman of his dreams. The film was successful enough to warrant two sequels.

The film is revealing in a number of ways, most especially in how most of vaudeville and Hollywood viewed ethnic stereotypes. Ethnic characters of all types, including Jewish characters, were widely recognized and applauded by audiences. They found great humor in these stereotypes. Goldwyn did not challenge them. Indeed, he played to them, using them to make money and laughter. He would not have thought there was some problem morally or in any other way with doing that. Everyone did it.

Goldwyn admired parts of the Jewish character: the concern for social justice, what he witnessed as the open and unembarrassed expression of emotions and passions, and the visceral attachment to freedom. These were not religious dimensions. As a businessman, Goldwyn, as did the other moguls, realized the public wanted Jews who were shifty lawyers or not always honest tailors rather than heroic figures. Goldwyn concluded, again like all the moguls, that the public dictated what popular culture consisted of—not the producer trying to peddle the product. Any good glove salesman knew you can't sell the public what they don't want.

Samuel Goldwyn went on to have a long and gloried career in Hollywood. He gave to Jewish charities, including those that supported the new nation of Israel. He produced a series of wonderful films, including *Street Scene*, which is covered in a later chapter of the book, *Dodsworth*, *Wuthering Heights*, *The Pride of the Yankees*, *The Best Years of Our Lives* and many others. But he never tackled the great underlying stories of Jewish life the way he did with American ones.

In that sense Goldwyn was the perfect model of the mogul. He knew films. Above all he knew audiences. And American Gentile audiences didn't want Jewish films. Ethnic stereotypes of all kinds were all right for comedies such as the *Potash and Perlmutter* films, but the Jewish experience was too far removed from American Christians for them to want to watch Jewish films. The Jewish religion, after all, was as foreign to non-Jewish Americans as the strange newcomers to America who brought those odd customs with them.

The story was different for Jewish audiences. They were attracted to films generally for the same reason as other patrons—the cheap entertainment. But for all immigrants, films (mostly accidentally) were pleasurable lessons about living in America. Jewish immigrants, like others new to the land, wanted to speak English and learn the bizarre, even outlandish customs of the new country. They were fascinated by the strange smells, the tasty foods, the new treats, the raucous noises of a new life. Additionally, at their deepest level, films helped all people think about their lives, not just about their social position.

Eventually, with an accumulation of films that bypassed the normative restrictions on Jewish content, there were American movies that illustrated and explored some aspect of American Jewish life and culture, such as identity questions (including the tensions between an American and a Jewish identity and between a Jewish identity and a broader human identity), religious questions (such as the nature of God, why a good God permits evil, and the nature of suffering and death), assimilation and acculturation, interfaith relations, Israel, marriage and family relations, the role of women, Jews and American politics, anti–Semitism (including the Holocaust), moral dilemmas associated with Jewish life, how American Jews perceived themselves and how they were perceived by others (including Jewish stereotypes), and so on.

Most importantly, the films were an ongoing record of a wider search, an American Jewish quest for identity. In the conflicts, the heroes and villains, the heartbreaking love stories, the images of war and injustice, and much more, American Jews saw in the films' images a mirror of themselves and simultaneously a projection of what they might become. This search for identity stemmed from the ongoing "Jewish Question"—the question not that Jews had but that nations and peoples had. The "Jewish Question" involved the role of Jews in society, the question of whether they could be integrated into Gentile societies, and if so, how much and, if allowed or encouraged to integrate, would they be loyal.

Against such a social background, Jews and Gentiles struggled for answers.

Of course, not all Jewish movies contained steps on the road to constructing identities or to answering questions surrounding Jews. That is, this book is not a complete history of American Jewish films but a focused examination of the major movies that provided tentative answers to the question of what it means to be Jewish in America.

To examine Jewish identity in Jewish films requires more precise definitions of the terms. A personal identity refers to the aspects of someone's self-definition that persist over time. Such an identity is how individuals conceive of themselves across the days and years, and across various situations. There are certainly different parts of a person's personality, and these parts in one way or another communicate. Such communication does not mean the parts of a personality are harmonious. Harmony is elusive.

A Jewish identity, therefore, refers to how people perceive themselves as Jewish. This identity may be religious, cultural, ethnic, social (as in belonging to a people), national, or some other kind.

An American Jewish identity involves multiple integrations. First, a person has to have a personal identity. Then added to that there must be a complex Jewish identity determined and integrated. With that done, this identity must be integrated into an American identity. It is a complex and difficult process indeed.

Jewish identity comes from within each person, from within the Jewish community, and from forces, friendly or hostile, outside the Jewish community. While the focus of the book is on the self-perception of being Jewish, inevitably all these sources of identity are considered.

In one sense, "identity" is a modern question in the Jewish community. A Jewish identity, by tradition, is simple to define. A person is Jewish if the person's mother was Jewish or if the person converted to Judaism via Jewish law. Jews living in segregated communities followed the rules that tradition had established, observing the Sabbath or keeping kosher, for example. People didn't struggle with their Jewish identity; they were just Jewish.

But with political freedom came identity confusion. Jewish religious law no longer had the sway over Jews that it once did. The borderlines of Jewish identity became permeable. Questions arose. Is a person born of a Jewish father and Gentile mother Jewish? Is a person whose mother was Jewish but who was brought up and identifies with another religion Jewish? Is a person who had Jewish parents but doesn't believe in God, ever attend synagogue, and keeps no Jewish customs or rituals Jewish? And what, in a secular world, even constitutes Jewishness beyond a formal definition?

But why look at "Jewish" identity? Why not examine another part of a person's identity such as their gender? Jewish identity is worth studying precisely because it is so powerful. For many Jews it is the gateway identity, the reflexive response to the question "Who are you?" It is the identity that explains much of the person's self-perceptions and actions. It shapes who they are, who they choose as friends and marital partners, and much else.

A Jewish identity, rightly or wrongly, can be a powerful explanatory factor in a person's life. Consider this. Through two thousand years of their history, the Jews were a small, defenseless people with no weapons and varying, though mostly insufficient, economic power. They couldn't defend themselves. This existential situation caused them to learn how to interpret others and please others, two skills necessary for survival. Having to interpret other people gave Jews intellectual skills. Lacking weapons, they relied on what was portable because they might at any moment have to move. They relied on music and education and intelligence and language. Having to please others depleted their ego, but that was balanced by a belief in their own chosenness. This led to a decay of personal identity but not ego. This led to a reliance on externally-imposed identities.

Given such an interpretation, it is not surprising that Jews became adept in America at being comedians and songwriters, novelists and critics. This was their inherited strength, but that strength was accompanied by an inherited weakness. Without an ego, there was depression (think of the songwriter Leonard Cohen). With the inherited ability to interpret where the culture was headed, Jews, using music and language, could appear prophetic (think of Bob Dylan).

These and other identity tensions are played out in Jewish films, though the most popular subjects by far, both in Jewish novels and Jewish films, are anti–Semitism, what it means to be hated, and romantic entanglements between Jews and Gentiles.

One way of looking at the American Jewish identity is to consider its sense of mission rather than definition, to conceive that it is less important what Jews should believe than what they should do. This, of course, is just a matter of emphasis, because action requires thought and vice versa.

American Jews have the normal Jewish mission to preserve and transmit the Jewish heritage, the entirety of Jewish civilization. Also, given the allure of America and the modern world, American Jews have perceived their mission negatively — not to assimilate into the American melting pot and disappear.

American Jews have also focused on Jewish learning — to study — but in America this has been translated as a study especially of non–Jewish subjects. Additionally, Jews have focused on social action as a core definition of their selves.

The entire spectrum of Jewish efforts at self-definition can be seen in the history of American Jewish films. As this history unfolds, it will be clear that American Jewry lacks a clear definition of mission and therefore a clear self-identity. One tentative conclusion that will have to be tested against film history is this: The diversity of identity shows that the unique American Jewish mission is to explore the borders of a Jewish identity. But is such an effort worthwhile? Just how expansive are those borders anyway? Is it successful? Can it maintain the Jewish people, or will such a broad effort simply lead to an assimilatory disappearance of the Jews, a de facto elimination of their cultural and political significance in America? Can seeking the borders of an identity be the moral center of Judaism? Is such a mission too diffuse?

These are the questions this book will try to answer by its end. But first it is time to enter the alluring darkness, to sit down and eagerly await the flickering images of the alternate reality that are motion pictures.

CHAPTER TWO

The Jewish Plymouth Rock: Films About the Lower East Side

Jewish actors were not great successes in silent films. The Jewish emphasis on language would have to wait until technology provided the virtual death knell for silent pictures by offering audiences sound. Nevertheless, there were many silent movies about Jewish subjects. Some just poked fun at so-called Jewish traits in the manner of ethnic stereotyping popular in the humor of the day. Early one-reelers that featured Jewish characters made sure audiences knew that those characters were Jewish. They did this by giving the Jewish characters long beards and mustaches. They made the characters pawnbrokers, tailors, con artists, and cowards. There wasn't an ethnic stereotype they didn't gleefully employ.

There were some Jews who made their way onto the silent screen, mostly as comedians. The Jewish vaudeville team of Weber and Fields, for example, starred in a variety of films. Max Davidson, who will be discussed in regards to the film *The Rag Man*, was a popular star as Izzy Davidson, a lazy Jewish character. Sammy Cohen was a comic actor with a prominent nose. George Sidney, who had been born Sammy Greenfield, was the most important Jewish comedian in silent films. He spent some time in vaudeville and then began his silent film career in 1915. Eventually he became famous for the character of Busy Izzy, which was the title of Sidney's first film. He then made the Samuel Goldwyn films *In Hollywood with Potash and Perlmutter* and *Partners Again, with Potash and Perlmutter*. His most famous appearance was in *The Cohens and the Kellys*. That movie appeared in 1926 and was so popular it spawned six sequels. Sidney played Jacob Cohen, who, again conforming to stereotype, was overweight, wore a suit that didn't fit him, constantly moved his hands, had a large nose, and didn't shave. Additionally, he was awkward in social situations, and he cheated people in business.

But silent films did this with all ethnic minority groups. By definition, silent films could not include spoken humor. All the laughs had to rely on physical appearances and funny physical movements. Verbal humor was the Jewish strength, but that was simply not yet possible.

When films began to talk, Jewish comedians began to appear. George Jessel, Smith and Dale, Jack Benny, Milton Berle, George Burns, Fanny Brice, Bert Lahr, and Ed Wynn all made their appearance in film comedies, though none was remarkably successful, and none of the movies made a lasting impact.

But there were serious films of the day as well. The most important of these focused on Jewish life on the Lower East Side of New York City. While many Jews had already arrived in America — Sephardic Jews whose ancestors came from Spain and Portugal, and German Jews being the most prominent — it was the wave of Eastern European immigrants who arrived from 1881 to 1910 who most swelled the American Jewish population. 1,562,800 Jews arrived in the United States during those thirty years, fleeing poverty and persecution, sensing a need for refuge from the Old World.

Many of these new immigrants found their way to the Lower East Side in New York. They did find freedom. But, to their dismay, the roads weren't paved with gold. They weren't paved at all. It was the Jews and other immigrants who had to pave them. The Lower East Side was disease-ridden. It was so crowded that deft nurses had to walk across the rooftops to reach patients because the streets were so overflowing with pushcarts and shoppers and children and criminals and, it seemed, just about everyone else.

The new immigrants worked in sweatshops for low wages. They tried to avoid the prostitutes on Allen Street, the opium dens, the dead horses, the pickpockets, the gamblers, the men hired to make outrageous claims and lure them into shops—in short, the world that walked the streets of the Jewish ghetto. The immigrants walked up dark stairs to their tiny apartments in crowded tenements, often sleeping on the floor or taking turns in a makeshift bed made up of some discarded crates and a lumpy mattress. They scrambled for success. And some found it. Irving Berlin, Fanny Brice, George Burns, Eddie Cantor, and many others grew up there.

They shopped among torch-lit pushcarts on Hester Street on Thursday nights. They sought escape in Yiddish theater, vaudeville, and, when they emerged, movie houses. Eventually, there were movies about the Lower East Side.

Hungry Hearts (1922) was made by Samuel Goldwyn. He was taken with the success of a novel about the Jewish Ghetto in New York. The novel, titled *Hungry Hearts*, had been written by twenty-five-year-old Anzia Yezierska. Her emotionally powerful novel is centered on the Lower East Side, but its anguished sensibility, its palpable portrayal of unfulfilled longings and dreams that died in the night, caught the much wider reading public's attention. In the novel, the character Hanneh Levin wants to improve her life. She finds a symbol of her despair, the kitchen, and decides to paint it white to provide brightness and cheer and cleanliness. The transformed kitchen, for Hanneh, represents a success that has eluded her

Millions of Eastern European Jews came to the Lower East Side, the Jewish Plymouth Rock. Here Rosa Rosanova (left) as Hanneh and Helen Ferguson as Sara in *Hungry Hearts* (Goldwyn Pictures, 1922) realize that poverty and hunger have followed them to the Golden Land.

Two—The Jewish Plymouth Rock

wider life. Still, in this she succeeds. But the success is short-lived. Seeing the new kitchen, the landlord raises her rent. Her despair so boils over she takes an axe to her room.

Sara is the name of the lead character in the film, which opens on a cruel Cossack, a forerunner of the New York landlord yet to appear in the film. Sara, though, is optimistic. "It must be always sunshine in America," she declares.

But America is a shocking disappointment, with its dirty laundry and dark room. The film details how emotionally difficult it is to live in such poverty. Unfortunately, there aren't a lot of exterior shots of the Lower East Side. By focusing on the apartment, viewers get a strong sense of being trapped in a small world. We do see a factory, pushcarts, shops, and a night school to get a sense of the life.

And, like the novel, the landlord, Rosenblatt, is a villain of sorts. He disdains people and even fights with his nephew David, who loves Sara. In a sense, the film is really a love story, with the environment providing obstacles. David becomes the mother's attorney after she destroys the kitchen, and he gets the case dismissed. Happiness is the result, but despite this, the film can't help but depict the despair of the Jewish ghetto.

If Jews were looking for a safe, secure, comfortable substitute for the Jewish village (a shtetl in Yiddish) they had left while seeking freedom from Cossacks and economic opportunity, this film gave no hope that such a place could be found on the Lower East Side. Still, it is clear from the movie that love can be found within the Jewish community, as well as personal fulfillment. Obstacles can be overcome. Optimistically, the film's ending suggests that it is possible to leave the Lower East Side for the lush houses found in America and remain Jewish.

This adaptive model is a foundation for an American Jewish identity. Look for a community. If it doesn't work, it's still possible within the Jewish peoplehood and within Judaism to find happiness. Just a nicer place is needed. America is indeed the Golden Land. Here Jews can have it all. It was going to be difficult for Jews to realize the obstacles they truly faced.

Goldwyn had brought Yezierska to Hollywood to work on the film. However, she was strong-willed and independent; she was unable or unwilling to conform to the various suggestions Goldwyn made to make the movie more attractive to audiences. She left Hollywood, accepting instead a life of poverty and literary silence.

American Jewish Films

The Rag Man (1925) starred Jackie Coogan, who had become famous starring with Charlie Chaplin in *The Kid* (1921). In this film Coogan is paired with the underappreciated Jewish comedy actor Max Davidson. Coogan stars as Tim Kelly, an obviously Gentile boy who runs away when the orphanage he was living in burns down. A policeman chases him, but the boy hides in Max Ginsberg's wagon. Ginsberg, a rheumatic Jewish junk dealer, is the rag man. Tim proves his honesty and worth by returning Ginsberg's coin purse. Tim declines the nickel reward and asks for a job. Ginsberg eventually relents, and the two, who desperately need each other, form a warm, sweet, and deeply moving attachment.

Eventually the rag man tells the boy of a sad incident. Ginsberg had been working in a factory and created a new product, but two lawyers cheated him. They made a fortune while the poor rag man became poverty-stricken. There is a lawyer attempting to help Ginsberg, but there is no proof of the rag man's assertions.

Tim tracks down Bernard, one of the lawyers, and charms the man's wife. She gives Tim some older clothes that belonged to her husband. What she doesn't know is that one piece of clothing holds a letter written to Bernard. It is by his legal partner, now dead, and in the letter the dying partner expresses regret over cheating Max Ginsberg and begs his partner to correct their moral error.

But Tim doesn't realize what the letter means and stuffs it in a hole in their horse's feedbag. Tim learns about the importance of the letter, but it is now in unreadable pieces. Tim goes to see Bernard but can't convince him to be honest. Dejected, Tim returns and removes his name from the wagon sign. Tim says he must return to the orphanage. Ginsberg is profoundly saddened.

Suddenly Bernard appears. He announces that Tim had made him realize his error, and he intends to right the wrong done to Max Ginsberg. Bernard offers to give the rag man $200,000, but a dissatisfied Tim says that his partner deserves interest as well, and Bernard promises to provide that too.

Tim discovers that the letter was not destroyed after all and saves it in case it is ever needed.

The film ends as the two become antique dealers—the biggest in the city—and enjoy their success by playing golf.

The close attachment between the Jewish rag man and the Gentile boy is a statement that Jews can form such emotional attachments, but it is telling that in this case the bond is with a relatively helpless child. The

Two—The Jewish Plymouth Rock

Jews were still tentative about bonding with adult peers. The film is one of many that pairs Jews with someone Irish, as though an immigrant bond transcended the many religious differences that might otherwise have kept them apart.

One of the wonderful things about *The Rag Man* is that, unlike *Hungry Hearts*, the camera captures extraordinary city images.

His People (1925) was produced by Carl Laemmele. The film tells the story of the Cominsky family. The mother in this film is played by Rosa Rosanova, the tormented mother in *Hungry Hearts*. The film's plot focuses on the family's two sons, Morris, who studies law, and Sammy, who, as "Battling Rooney," struggles to be a boxer.

Morris moves out of the Lower East Side and, taking the physical departing one step further, steps toward romantic assimilation, not just geographic mixing. Morris becomes engaged to his boss' daughter. Feeling shame about his background and his family, Morris lies, claiming to be an orphan. Sammy brings Morris home to reconcile with his ill father.

In case the audience misses the difficulties of Lower East Side life, the film's titles make the situation clear: "In the heart of every large city, another city lives and has its being—the Ghetto." A title announces that the Jews were "scattered for centuries," but they have come to New York, "each bringing a dream of prosperity and happiness, but finding only the reality of hard work, suffering, and privation."

The Jewish mother is presented as warm, supportive, and loving, very far from the later tradition of the Jewish mother as suffocating. The brother story—built on the Jacob and Esau story in the Bible—is moving. The beloved son engages in betrayal, and the dismissed son ends up bringing the family together.

Thematically, the film doesn't expand the identity question. But it is important because it contains so many of the moral struggles featured in movies about the Lower East Side. There is romance and then marriage between a Jewish man and an Irish woman. There is the pain of living in the ghetto and the desperate desire to escape. There is the internal struggle between keeping tradition and fleeing from it. There are emotional difficulties between brother and brother, and parent and child.

Still to come, though, was the most crucial picture about the Lower East Side, a movie important in general film history and, partly because of that, important in Jewish film history.

The Jazz Singer (1927) was the first full-length sound motion picture.

Jackie Coogan as Tim Kelly in *The Rag Man* (Metro-Goldwyn, 1925), showcasing the cooperation between Jews and other immigrant groups and the warmth of substitute families. The film is particularly interesting because of its depiction of scenes on the Lower East Side.

Two—The Jewish Plymouth Rock

That made it historically one of the most important films of all time. Yet however technically important it was, however wonderful lead actor Al Jolson's voice was and how animated was his acting, however emotionally compelling the story told in the film, it did not include Jewish themes that hadn't been covered in previous films.

The Jazz Singer had limited innovations. It was mostly a silent film. The Vitaphone sound system was only used for some musical numbers and, seemingly almost by accident only caught a bit of Jolson's dialogue. But those small bits of sound were thrilling to audiences. With rare exceptions, audiences wanted sound films after that. (The best single exception was Charlie Chaplin's *City Lights*, a brilliant picture made totally against the artistic current in 1931.)

The film's technological innovations had another effect. Anxious to

The great Al Jolson as Jakie Rabinowitz sings to Eugenie Besserer, playing his beloved mama, Sara Rabinowitz, in the groundbreaking partially-sound film *The Jazz Singer* (Warner Brothers, 1927). The film was a landmark not just because audiences could hear Jolson singing but also in the depiction of Jews successfully assimilating into American life while they struggled with their parents' old-world values.

see the new invention, crowds flocked to the film, whereas they may not have if they had read it was about a Jewish family, with the father a cantor in a synagogue and his son seeking fame as a jazz singer. Watching the movie, they were introduced to the new immigrants, and identified with their struggles, particularly the love of a son for his father. That was a universal theme. The film helped introduce Jews to America and, in doing so, set them on the long and sometimes difficult path of acceptance in their new homeland.

Ironically, but typically, Jewish producers were reluctant to film the story. The Warner Brothers were concerned that America wasn't ready for so Jewish a tale, but Darryl Zanuck, a Gentile producer, convinced them that the family struggles were not just Jewish and that audiences would respond to the movie.

Because of its vast historical importance it should be a matter of record to provide an extended summary of the film's plot.

The story begins on the Lower East Side in New York at the beginning of the 20th century. It is the moment when Jews were most congregated in New York, the time when they were still an undispersed community, by and large, when they continued to keep their customs and traditions. The struggle between age-old traditions and the new attractions of America is played out in the film in a struggle between father and son. The father is a Cantor, someone (then always a man) who chants the prayers in synagogue. Cantor Rabinowitz wants Jakie, his thirteen-year-old son, to follow in this holy task, this family tradition. Thirteen, of course, is a crucial age, for little Jakie is between childhood and adulthood. Bar mitzvah, after all, literally means the "son of the commandments." It is the moment when a Jew is obliged to keep the 613 holy laws. In particular, Cantor Rabinowitz wants Jakie one day to take his place on the holiest day of the Jewish year, Yom Kippur, the Day of Atonement. Seeing Jakie leading the prayers constitutes the father's hopes and dreams. But, as Sara, Jakie's mother and the Cantor's wife, knows, Jakie doesn't share his father's great dream. Sara thinks her son, who has a beautiful voice, wants to put it to use in places outside the synagogue. Indeed, we see Jakie in a saloon singing his heart out. Unfortunately, Moishe Yudelson, a man who knows the family and enjoys gossip, spots the young man and dashes off to tell Cantor Rabinowitz. The Cantor drags the boy back to the family apartment and whips him. Jakie can only seek solace in his mother's arms. Poor Sara is broken-hearted, torn as she is between her husband and her son.

Two—The Jewish Plymouth Rock

It should be noted that by the Cantor's behavior, the audience is being thoroughly manipulated to side with the boy, even if their feelings were more genuinely mixed. That is, this film, as other thematically-related films, was firmly on the side of jettisoning the traditions carried across the ocean from the Old Country. Jakie sees no choice but to run away from home.

Many years later we see Jakie in San Francisco performing in a restaurant. He sings "Dirty Hands, Dirty Face" and then "Toot, Toot, Tootsie." Mary Dale, who is a dancer in vaudeville, is sitting in the audience, fascinated by his voice and performance. She encourages him, saying that what sets him apart is that he has a tear that can be heard in his voice. Other singers, she says, just sing. Mary arranges for Jakie to join the vaudeville troupe. Jakie, now Jack Robin, one day finds himself in Chicago and goes to hear the well-known Cantor Josef Rosenblatt. Jack is deeply affected by the traditional tunes. He thinks of his family, of course. He has been sending letters home regularly, talking about his expanding career, but he remains distant from his father.

Unsurprisingly, Jack falls in love with Mary and is therefore disappointed when she leaves vaudeville for a Broadway show. His spirit brightens, however, when he learns that he, too, has a job waiting for him on Broadway. He is eager to return home and see his mother.

The time is now 1927 (the year the film was made). Cantor Rabinowitz is to celebrate his 60th birthday, and so Jack returns home as a surprise. Sara Rabinowitz is overwhelmed at the sight of her son. He says he wants them to move out of the Lower East Side and go to the Bronx. Jack begins to sing, but Cantor Rabinowitz becomes enraged at the American sounds in his religious home. Father and son have a terrible argument. The Cantor calls his son a "jazz singer," and that prompts Jack to leave.

Yom Kippur arrives, but Cantor Rabinowitz is too sick to sing. Still, after all that has happened, he retains his long-standing dream that Jakie will take his place. Moishe Yudelson goes to the theater where Jack and Mary are starring in a show and asks Jack to sing in the synagogue. Jack struggles with the request but realizes that his life is in the theater and his obligation is to the show, so he refuses Yudelson's request. But Yudelson does not give up. He goes back to the Rabinowitz apartment and returns with Sara who begs Jack to reconsider and sing as his father wishes. Jack again refuses, and Sara, realizes where his heart is when she sees him performing on stage.

Jack finishes his song. Mary tells him that his mother has accepted his decision, but perhaps his own singing has prompted some deep emotion in him for he then rushes home. Jack goes into the synagogue and sings. The Cantor hears his son performing the moving prayer Kol Nidre and dies, at peace with himself and his son.

Eventually, Jack is back on Broadway and appropriately sings "Mammy" as his mother, along with Yudelson, beams as she sits in the front row. Mary, watching from the wings, is happy for the man she loves. That is, it takes the literal death of tradition for a full measure of happiness.

In a way, this story of Jakie Rabinowitz who becomes Jack Robin, the successful popular singer, is the perfect symbol of American assimilation. There is a struggle, to be sure, with a supportive, warm mother and a disapproving father who wants his son to stay within the inherited tradition. But *The Jazz Singer*, again because of its fame as a film, did what had been done before, but did it emphatically and with wide notice. The film made the decision clear. If Sammy in *His People* literally had to battle his way out of the ghetto and, with final parental approval, marry a Gentile to thrive in a Gentile world, Jack Robin was the character America, and America's Jews, all saw. *The Jazz Singer* was the cinematic decision in the boxing match between tradition and assimilation. Assimilation was the winner. After this film, parents who resisted their child's romance with a Gentile were hopelessly old-fashioned and unable to adapt to the realities of their new country. Tradition, although it didn't know it, was in trouble after *The Jazz Singer*. As one of the film's titles put it, Jack's father "stubbornly held to the ancient traditions of his race." This stubbornness, the film concluded, did not jibe with American values, which called for immigrants to surrender their separateness and melt into Americanism.

Beyond the fact it broke no new thematic ground, Al Jolson's extensive use of blackface is one of the reasons the film has lost favor. The blackface tradition, going back to the minstrel shows, was traditionally used to mimic and mock African Americans. Ironically, many Jewish performers who used it (such as Eddie Cantor and Sophie Tucker, besides Jolson) transformed the tradition to make the black characters more fully human. Indeed, it is easy to see the Jewish performers, scared or reluctant or for some other reason unable to express their anguish at American society as Jews, chose to express it through an even more oppressed American minority. Still, because the blackface tradition was so clearly racist, any performer who relied on it as heavily as Jolson did eventually suffered in entertainment history.

It is also possible to see the mama in *The Jazz Singer* as the first hint of the stereotypical suffocating Jewish mother, a horrible stereotype that would emerge four decades after the film. Sara Rabinowitz does do a lot of crying and pleading in the film, but Jack profoundly loves her and doesn't in the least feel manipulated or put upon, as later Jewish males would. Still, it's an interesting character to consider, one that began the slow, painful downward portrayal of Jewish mothers.

The most famous example of the treatment of mothers in the film occurs after Jack sings a rendition of the Irving Berlin song *Blue Skies*. Then the dialogue begins:

> JACK: Did you like that, Mama?
> MOTHER: Yes.
> JACK: I'm glad of it. I'd rather please you than anybody I know of. Oh, darlin', will you give me something?
> MOTHER: What?
> JACK: You'll never guess. Shut your eyes, Mama. Shut 'em for little Jakie. Ha. I'm gonna steal something. [He kisses her, and she titters.] Ha, ha, ha, ha. I'll give it back to you some day, too, you see if I don't. Mama darlin', if I'm a success in this show, well, we're gonna move from here. Oh yes, we're gonna move up in the Bronx. A lot of nice green grass up there and a whole lot of people you know. There's the Ginsbergs, the Guttenbergs, and the Goldbergs. Oh, a whole lotta Bergs; I don't know 'em all. And I'm gonna buy you a nice black silk dress, Mama. You see Mrs. Friedman, the butcher's wife, she'll be jealous of you.
> MOTHER: Oh, no–
> JACK: Yes, she will. You see if she isn't. And I'm gonna get you a nice pink dress that'll go with your brown eyes.
> MOTHER: No, Jakie, no I-I-I-I...
> JACK: What? Whatta you mean, no? Who is— who is telling you? Whatta you mean, no? Yes, you'll wear pink or else. Or else you'll wear pink. [He laughs.] And, darlin', oh, I'm gonna take you to Coney Island.
> MOTHER: Yeah?
> JACK: Yes, I'm gonna ride on the Shoot-the Chutes. An' you know in the Dark Mill. Ever been in the Dark Mill?
> MOTHER: Oh, no. I wouldn't go...
> JACK: Well, with me, it's all right. I'll kiss you and hug you. You see if I don't. [Mother starts blushing.] Now Mama, Mama, stop now. You're gettin' kittenish...[1]

In this scene the mother is reduced (as too often occurred in real immigrant life) to the onlooker, the audience, the cheerleader, a person who had to invest all in her son because she couldn't succeed in the culture. Minnie, mother of the Marx Brothers, was a real-life example of such a woman. *The Jazz Singer* probably unintentionally captures that fate.

Street Scene (1931) does not focus exclusively on a Jewish family but uses a tenement filled with a stereotyped ethnic mix of people to show that Jews were just part of the mix. Indeed, to underscore the point, one of the Jewish characters notes in the film that "the Jews are no better than anyone else." The movie, based on Elmer Rice's Pulitzer Prize–winning play, is set almost exclusively on the steps of a slum tenement. All the residents of the building meet on the street. The film attempts to depict lives suffocated by the environment and the social conditions under which the characters live. Still, the static setting, the unspectacular acting, and the stereotyped characters prevent the movie from making a major contribution to the story of Jewish identity.

However, one interesting aspect of the film is an older Jewish man named Abraham Kaplan who has communistic ideals. In this picture, such radical notions are viewed positively, especially because the other characters mock them, evidently without realizing, in the writer's view, that such ideals provide an answer for their sad lives. But in giving such views to a flat Jewish character, and being sympathetic to them, the film inadvertently contributed to a wider American perception of a tie between American Jews and communism.

Symphony of Six Million (1932), the first fully-orchestrated talking film, is yet another urban drama; the number in the title refers to the residents of New York. What's interesting about the movie is that it represents an ongoing conflict about assimilation and renders more muddy the seeming clarity offered by *The Jazz Singer*. The film is about the Klauber family, especially Felix (played by Ricardo Cortez, a Jewish actor born Jacob Krantz, who becomes a wealthy doctor. This picture is in the tradition of *His People*. It delivers a large dose of nostalgia, and pursues the theme that the Jewish heritage is feeling, warm, and moral, while a headlong pursuit of money and fame distances people from that heritage in negative ways. The most dramatic example comes when a little boy dies because Felix, so caught up in his wealthy practice, has forgotten the appointment. In true sentimental style, the boy dies calling out the doctor's name.

But the film is cleverer than such a simple idea that leaving the ghetto is wrong, that poverty is ennobling. In Felix' case, it is true that poverty carries its own moral rewards. But for his sister it becomes possible to carry the heritage away, to maintain the close sense of family, the traditions, and the moral code. Therefore the film was able to have it both ways. One character's success as a doctor reminded him of the pull of tradition, while another character could become successful while keeping faithful to Judaism. It was a valuable if mixed message to audiences. They could acknowledge their guilt at wanting success but then see real success in social mobility. Such was the sort of satisfying psychological tension a film could provide.

Counsellor-at-Law is also about success, in this case a lawyer instead of a doctor. It was adapted from an Elmer Rice play, as was *Street Scene*. That may explain why it, too, has a Jewish political radical, a rare character in films of the time, and a discussion of the ethnic melting pot.

The film is about a successful Jewish attorney named George Simon, who, like the characters in the previous movies, had emerged from the Jewish ghetto. Simon is played by John Barrymore because producer Samuel Goldwyn believed a Jewish actor wouldn't work in the part. Paul Muni had starred in the stage play, and it's tempting to claim he would have been a perfect actor for the part. And yet the Gentile John Barrymore, always a superb actor, is terrific in this role.

Simon's return to his birthplace comes about when he bails out Harry Becker, a communist the police have mistreated. Simon has become a defender not of men such as Becker, but of wealthy clients. His secretary, "Rexy" Gordon, loves him, but Simon is married. His wife, Cora, doesn't like his attachment to his Jewish heritage and wants him not to take a case against one of her friends from high society. A series of complications follow, leading to Simon's increasing depression, which is compounded by Harry Becker's death.

Learning that his wife is having an affair, Simon contemplates jumping from his office window. Rexy's unexpected return and her scream stops him. A new case arises, and he and Rexy leave to examine the case.

Counsellor-at-Law rounded out all the options, it seemed, for films about the Lower East Side. By the early thirties, American Jews were beginning to assimilate, although the Great Depression and anti–Semitism delayed a full integration for several decades. Still, it seemed to many American Jews that they had fully left the ghetto, that they didn't want to be reminded of their origins and they didn't want to remind American Gentiles of their origins.

It would take decades and acceptance for nostalgic films about the Lower East Side.

Hester Street (1975) was created in a generation very distant from the Lower East Side and very intent on recovering its roots, which included a nostalgia for the Plymouth Rock — the landing place — for millions of American Jews and their descendants.

Hester Street retains the push and pull of the immigrant generation and its root question: Should we remain Jewish or should we assimilate? Jake has come to America ahead of his wife and child. After his arrival, Jake has embraced America, especially its yearning for money and romance. It is 1896, and his wife Gitl (played by Carol Kane, who received an Oscar nomination for the role) arrives wearing her traditional wig and with clothes as old-fashioned as her ways.

To earn money, Jake and Gitl take in a boarder, Mr. Bernstein, who is a scholar stuck in a sweatshop. Gitl is impressed, but Bernstein is wise to the ways of the New World. "When you get on a boat," he tells her, "You should say, 'Goodbye Oh Lord, I'm going to America.'"

Slowly, to her horror, Gitl comes to realize that Jake has irretrievably changed. He is no longer a mensch, no longer the good man she married. Eventually the two get divorced, a clear symbol that a choice is required between tradition and assimilation. Unlike some of the earlier films, *Hester Street* has a clear point of view. Jews can't have it both ways in the film's world.

Carol Kane as Gitl wears a less-than-stylish hat in ***Hester Street*** (Midwest Films, 1975). The story of immigrant Jews challenged by love and tradition is a mythic tale of the origins of twentieth-century American Jewish life.

Two—The Jewish Plymouth Rock

Joan Micklin Silver adapted and directed the movie, based on *Yekl*, a novella by the immigrant journalist and writer Abraham Cahan, who gained fame as the editor of the influential Yiddish-language newspaper the *Jewish Daily Forward*, as well as the novel *The Rise of David Levinsky*. Cahan was a socialist, and his ideology infused all of his work. He therefore opposed capitalism and the entrepreneurial efforts of the immigrants, such as Jake, who seems to be in mad pursuit of money. It is not that Jake should have remained religious, as Mr. Bernstein did. Cahan didn't like the capitalism of the New Country or the religion of the New Country. He wanted a new world, one run according to socialist values.

But such a political approach would have undercut the film's nostalgic power. The focus was on lost virtues not on a discredited political system. And so the socialist message was, except in mocking Jake's values, removed. We are left with immigrant memories of a time when Jews studied the Talmud, found love by clinging to their heritage, and flourished without surrendering to the coarser values of the culture. They remained happy while remaining true to their Jewish selves.

Growing up on the Lower East Side provided a great training ground for a large number of Jewish entertainers. They eventually left the Lower East Side physically, but they carried it around inside them for the rest of their lives. There are many films about such entertainers, and it is difficult to pick out one that is precisely representative. However, *The Sunshine Boys* (1975) is an interesting example. The film stars George Burns and Walter Matthau. Burns was born on, and shaped by, the Lower East Side. His entire personality developed there, imprinted sadly and most forcefully by the death of his father. Burns grew up to be one of the most famous entertainers in America, and he, along with his wife and comedy partner Gracie Allen, conquered one entertainment medium after another.

Jack Benny was Burns' best friend. Benny was originally set to star in *The Sunshine Boys* but unfortunately died prior to the film being made. Irving Fein, Benny's manager, also managed Burns and convinced Herbert Ross, the movie's director, to consider Burns. The part was an aging Jewish vaudevillian. It is difficult to imagine anyone in America (apart from Jack Benny) who had lived the part more than George Burns. Because of his reading difficulties, he memorized the entire script prior to the audition. This, needless to say, deeply impressed everyone.

The film was about a comedy team named Lewis (George Burns) and Clark (Walter Matthau), who, like many comedy teams, worked like magic onstage and disliked each other intensely off-stage. The comedy of Lewis and Clark is based on a real-life vaudeville comedy team: Smith and Dale. Joe Smith and Charlie Dale were best known for a sketch called "Doctor Kronkheit and His Only Living Patient." "Kronkheit" is the Yiddish word for illness. In the skit, Dale played the doctor and Smith the wary patient.

However, real life was very different from the movie. Smith and Dale were and remained close friends. Dale died in 1971. In a moving sign of affection, Smith asked that a single tombstone be erected for both of their graves. The inscription simply reads: "Smith and Dale."

As the film begins, these old-timers had not spoken to each other in two decades.

They disagree about the very fundamentals of what they were trying to do:

> AL LEWIS: You know what your trouble is, Willy? You always took the jokes too seriously. It was just jokes. We did comedy on the stage for 43 years. I don't think you enjoyed it once.
> WILLY CLARK: If I was there to enjoy it, I would buy a ticket.

But, despite this mutual animosity, Willy Clark's nephew Ben plans to produce a variety show. He wants the team to reunite for the program and tries his best to make that happen.

In a sense, the film shows the other end of the Lower East Side story, or at least part of it. It tells of the life of struggle that never ends, the inability to reconcile, the sustained testy personalities. It's a funny bookend to the Lower East Side story but a sad one.

Crossing Delancey (1988) offers another kind of bookend. The film was also directed by Joan Micklin Silver and so is therefore unsurprisingly a bit of an updated *Hester Street*. Once again, even after decades have passed, the burning question remains: Should Jews assimilate? Amy Irving plays Izzy, a woman struggling with romance, here a stand-in for assimilation. Izzy is the modern version of Gitl — smart (smarter than the men around her), alert to life's possibilities, and Jewish. Unlike Gitl, however, Izzy is attracted to the Gentile world in the form of its intellectual men. Izzy, that is, has left her roots in a way Gitl never did. The moral struggle at the heart of *Crossing Delancey* is whether or not Izzy should return to those roots.

She is in a very Jewish environment as can be seen in this exchange:

> ISABELLE "IZZY" GROSSMAN [*objecting to a surprise appointment with a matchmaker*]: Excuse me, but I don't know what you think you're doing.

Two—The Jewish Plymouth Rock

BUBBIE KANTOR: First you'll listen, then you'll talk.
HANNAH MANDELBAUM: Very nice, very nice girl. She lives by her parents?
BUBBIE KANTOR: Naaaah, they live in Florida with Red Buttons. All the social security checks under one roof—you can have it.
HANNAH MANDELBAUM: So, Isabella, you got your own apartment?
BUBBIE KANTOR: Naaaaah, she lives alone in a room, like a dog. A dog should live alone, not people ... a dog.
ISABELLE "IZZY" GROSSMAN: It is not a room, it's an apartment, a very nice apartment. You know, you've been there, there's a bedroom, a bathroom...
BUBBIE KANTOR: Sure, with bars on the windows like a prison. Someone should crawl in at night I'm always thinking.
ISABELLE "IZZY" GROSSMAN: Stop thinking.

Izzy's struggle comes to life in the form of Sam, who runs a pickle establishment and prays in the traditional manner. He is all that Izzy had left behind, all that American Jews of Izzy's generation had left behind. The film focuses on how Izzy—and, through her, the audience—comes to see Sam as right for her. But this romantic choice has much wider implications even than love. The choice is one of identity.

Ultimately, Silver wants to claim that to assimilate into America is a wrong choice for Jews. The honest choice is to cling to tradition. This is a film about coming to terms with the Jewish heritage, an important psychological moment for all American Jews, and its message is to walk the path that leads to faith, morality, community, and love.

It's a good message, but the romantic statistics about American Jews indicates that a large number of Jews have abandoned the pickle men in their lives. In that sense this is not just a sweet, sentimental film, it is also a warning. If it has a failure, it is the failure of all films with its message: how to deal with the reality of intermarriage specifically and assimilation generally.

There aren't a lot of movies made about Jewish life on the Lower East Side anymore. That is too bad because immigrant life was the first and therefore the paradigmatic American Jewish identity. As immigrants, Jews were strangers, outsiders, forced to rely on other Jews.

But, sadly, there is a reason that, beyond the emotional yearning involved in nostalgia, such films aren't made. Attempting to replicate the sort of separate Jewish community that was the Lower East Side simply won't work any longer. Ultra-Orthodox Hasidim is trying this, but for the overwhelming majority of American Jews the separate community model simply won't work. America has too many glittering prizes, too many attractive potential romantic partners, too many opportunities to test oneself to find success, too much to see, too much to do.

American Jews have crossed Delancey, and they are not turning around. Indeed they crossed it a long time ago.

CHAPTER THREE

The Past Is Prologue: Films of Jewish History

Attachment to tradition can come in a variety of ways. The simplest is to follow the customs of the Jewish religion: light Sabbath candles and keep the Sabbath rules, eat according to kosher dictates, pray, study, keep the ritualistic customs, and so on. It is when this obvious method of Jewish identity no longer suffices that alternatives are needed.

Zionism — the creation of a Jewish nation — is the most obvious modern example of an effective way to maintain a Jewish identity without necessarily maintaining Jewish religious rules, although many Jewish residents of Israel are, in fact, very strict about maintaining those traditions. But secular Jews can live there and feel completely Jewish. America, however, is not the equivalent of a Jewish nation. The Lower East Side provided one identity model: stay in a small, set-off community. American Jews didn't want that.

Another way to cling to a Jewish identity apart from religious ritual is to find a story in the Jewish past that is heroic or funny or tragic or illuminating or all of these.

History through motion pictures can be especially attractive. Unpleasant facts can be pushed aside. Heroism can be manipulated, as can every other emotion. Film can emphasize ideological positions. But, perhaps most of all, film can provide an emotional release comparable to the release. Historical films can remind us of the unpleasant past.

Disraeli (1929) was about the British prime minister of Jewish ancestry. There is an emphasis in the film on Disraeli's efforts to purchase the Suez Canal. Those efforts are hindered by his political opponent, William Gladstone, so Disraeli returns to his country estate, "bound to furnish [his] antagonists with arguments, but not with comprehension." Mrs.

Travers, a Russian spy, discovers Disraeli's desire to purchase the Canal. Disraeli cannot get credit through the Bank of England, but Hugh Meyers, a Jewish banker, provides funding. The Canal seems to have been purchased until Disraeli learns that Meyers' firm is bankrupt. Disraeli gets the Bank of England's Sir Michael Probert to honor the check used to purchase the Canal. But Probert notes, "I'm an Englishman. I'm not to be ordered about by an alien, a Jew." Disraeli, used to such language and faster than almost anyone with his tongue, replies, "The alien, the Jew, happens to be a better citizen. Moreover, he happens to be the Prime Minister." England gets the Suez Canal, and, with it, an expansive empire.

The film is filled with sharp dialogue and excellent acting, especially by George Arliss in the title role. Arliss won the Academy Award for Best Actor for the part.

Disraeli emerges as a great hero, except for the considerable fact that his family formally left Judaism and he was baptized a Christian. This vital biographical situation prevents Disraeli from providing a model for Jewish identity. His being British rather than American also provides some emotional distance from his usefulness for American Jews. Still, there is much inspiration to be drawn, and biography remains an important well from which to draw for forging an identity.

The far less pleasant historical past is covered, for example, in *The Yellow Ticket* (1931). As with a number of other historical films, the history is mixed with an attack on anti–Semitism. *The Yellow Ticket* is about Marya Kalish. It is 1913, and Marya, a young Jewish schoolteacher, wants to travel to St. Petersburg. Her father is ill in prison there. However, Marya is unable to obtain a passport because Jews are forbidden to travel. Marya sees a Jewish prostitute traveling with a yellow ticket (which enables prostitutes to travel around the country). Marya pays a madam and obtains the yellow ticket.

Marya arrives to see her father, but he has died. Later, in a park, Baron Igor Andreeff (played by Lionel Barrymore), the chief of police who enjoys women, prevents his nephew from attacking Marya. Then, on a train, Marya meets Julian Rolfe, an English journalist (played by Laurence Olivier) who stops a man from harassing her. Marya, vowing revenge for her father's death, provides information to Rolfe, who writes a series of shocking articles about prostitution in Russia, governmental corruption, and the mistreatment of Jews.

Julian wants to marry Marya, but her yellow ticket makes her so ashamed that she refuses. Marya encounters Andreeff, who orders Rolfe to be exiled to Siberia. Andreeff says he will rescind the order in return for Marya's favors. Instead, infuriated, she shoots him. Marya and Rolfe escape.

The film is overacted and filled more with a seething desire to expose Russia's political system than to portray Jewish life. There is not much in the film on which to build a Jewish identity. Marya, after all, ends up loving a Gentile. She leaves her native community for a non–Jewish world. She has suffered and revealed the sufferings Jews underwent, but she offers no Jewish emotional release from the suffering, only a romantic one. It is as though Jews can escape their situation and their suffering by exposing it for what it is and finding a warmer Gentile society to enter. In that sense, the film is an argument for assimilation more than an exposé of anti–Semitism. It is not an argument that Jewish history can provide a story to maintain a current Jewish identity.

The House of Rothschild (1934) also starred George Arliss in a biographical drama. Indeed, Arliss was instrumental in the film's production. While he was at Warner Brothers he asked the studio to purchase the play by George Hembert Westley on which the film was eventually based. Warners did acquire the rights, but the picture was not produced there. Arliss then convinced Darryl F. Zanuck to buy the rights from Warners for 20th Century Pictures, and the film was eventually made there.

As in *Disraeli*, the movie might have been American and the characters Jewish, but the setting is in Europe, not the United States.

The Rothschilds, an internationally famous banking family, are presented sympathetically here. But the attempt to display them as victims of anti–Semitism may have unintentionally also carried another message. As film critic Patricia Erens put it:

> When young Nathan dashes in to report that the tax collector is on the way, the money and documents are immediately hidden behind the fireplace, the food removed from the table, and Mayer transformed into a poor merchant. When the collector arrives and rudely commands, "Open up, Jew," Mayer is duly humble.... When Mayer receives the tax bill, he feigns horror and then proceeds to bribe the man.... In short, the scene reaffirms the old notion of the Jew as conniving schemer — a deceiving Jew. It further emphasizes the importance of money.... This scene, taken out of context, was incorporated in a 1942 Nazi film ... to support the claim that Jews, through subversive tactics, dominated world banking.[1]

American Jewish Films

The film *Der Ewige Jude* (*The Eternal Jew*, 1940) used the material by violating *The House of Rothschild* copyright and, as Erens suggests, was extremely misleading. Still, the reaction is revealing. It is awkward at best to deal with Jews and money, although it shouldn't be. The Rothschilds were genuinely helpful to the Jewish people, and at various points in the film it is clear that the Jews had no weapons at all, literal or otherwise, except money. Their role as moneylenders was forced upon them. They learned to value it because, beyond their religion, family, and community, it was all they had to deal with the Gentile world. And yet money becomes ultimately unsatisfying as a source of identity and for that, for its approval of intermarriage, and for the other reasons mentioned earlier, the film does not advance an American Jewish identity.

The Life of Emile Zola (1937) starred Paul Muni as the French writer who bravely confronted anti-Semitism during the Dreyfus Affair. But the very anti-Semitism that motivated the false accusation of Dreyfus for treason is underplayed here. There is a miscarriage of justice to be sure (as Zola says in the film, "What does it matter if an individual is shattered if only justice is resurrected?") He does make rousing speeches, such as this one:

> At this solemn moment, in the presence of this tribunal, which is the representative of human justice, before France, before the whole world, I swear that Dreyfus is innocent! By all that I have won, by all that I have written to spread the spirit of France, I swear that he is innocent. May all that melt away; may my name perish if Dreyfus be not innocent. He is innocent.

And Zola is suitably heroic, especially because in his later years he was famous and did not need to have his fellow citizens question him. But Dreyfus as a Jew is not emphasized. As film critic Lester Friedman noted:

> Unfortunately, the movie lacks any conscience of its own. It almost totally ignores the blatant anti-Semitism that destroys Dreyfus's career. Though [director William] Dieterle claims he did use the word and it was cut out by the studio, "Jew" is never heard in the movie. So in 1937, two full years after Hitler proclaimed the ... "Nuremberg Laws," Warner Brothers produced a universally-acclaimed film about the famous Dreyfus case that failed to emphasize why he was singled out, how he could be so unjustly accused, and why people were so willing to believe him guilty.[2]

The film missed a great opportunity. Theodor Herzl, the Austrian journalist who founded the Zionist movement that eventually led to the creation of Israel, covered the Dreyfus Affair and was present when military leaders publicly removed Dreyfus' military medals. Herzl was deeply influenced by what he saw, and his presence as a character in this film would have provided profound historical resonance. Instead, there is a general anguish at injustice.

The context of the film in Hollywood is important. By 1937, the rise of Hitler was obvious, as was his murderous hatred of the Jewish people. Muni, in particular, was glad to get the role of Zola as a way to speak to the world metaphorically about Nazism. But, as will become clear in the chapter on anti–Semitism, Hollywood couldn't bring itself to confront the Nazis directly. Jews as characters were eliminated from films, as were Jewish stories. Even attempts like *The Life of Emile Zola* were only very indirect and had minimal effect, despite the fact that the movie won the Academy Award for Best Picture.

Once again, other than striving for general matters of justice, a call that was stirring and welcomed already by American Jews, there was no contribution to the question of what it meant to be Jewish in the story of Zola.

After the three biographical films discussed above, historical films with a Jewish content were absent from the screen except for Biblical pictures, although they made a rousing comeback decades later.

Fiddler on the Roof (1971) is another wildly popular Jewish historical film.

There are many crucial hinge moments in Jewish history. The Exodus was certainly one of them. For American Jews especially, one of those moments came when millions of their recent ancestors left Eastern Europe and became new immigrants. Many left because of poverty or a sense of persecution. On the face of it, it appears odd that such a difficult moment be memorialized in a Broadway musical and then a musical film. But, based on the good-humored stories of the great writer Sholem Aleichem, the music invites audiences to recognize a joy in the face of difficulties, a method of resigned acceptance in the face of hate, that symbolically represents the Jewish spirit. The rueful humor can be seen in one of the most famous bits of dialogue in the film:

> TEVYE: And in the circle of our little village, we've always had our special types. For instance, Yente the matchmaker, Reb Nachum the beggar.... And most important of all, our beloved Rabbi.
> LEBISCH: Rabbi! May I ask you a question?
> RABBI: Certainly, Lebisch!

American Jewish Films

LEBISCH: Is there a proper blessing ... for the Tsar?
RABBI: A blessing for the Tsar? Of course! May God bless and keep the Tsar ... far away from us!

Fiddler on the Roof is a good film to talk about chronologically as foundational in any discussion of an American Jewish identity. But its folkways stop not long after these villagers, and especially their children, become Americans.

Tevye, the main character, bears many burdens. He must support his family and find husbands for his five daughters, none of whom has a dowry. He sighs at his reality and expects more out of life. He makes it through life by having an ongoing conversation with God. His good heart, and his struggle-filled relationship with God, his wife, and the world around him make him, a paradigmatic Jew of his era. He wants, for example, to be in charge of the family, but his wife will have none of it:

The joys and the horrors of small village Jewish life in nineteenth-century Russia are embodied in Tevye, played by Topol, walking down a dirt road with his horse and wagon in *Fiddler on the Roof* (Mirisch Corporation, 1971). No father raising daughters suffered so much or so loved his God and his family.

Three—The Past Is Prologue

> GOLDE: Oh, you're finally here. Come, let's go home now.
> TEVYE: I want to see Motel's new machine.
> GOLDE: You can see it some other time. Let's go home now.
> TEVYE: Quiet, woman, before I get angry! Because when I get angry, even flies don't dare to fly!
> GOLDE [with sarcasm]: I'm very frightened of you. After we finish supper I'll faint.
> TEVYE [angrily]: Golde, I am the head of the house! I am the head of the family! And I want to see Motel's new machine NOW! [Tevye looks inside and then closes the door.]
> TEVYE: Now, let's go home.

Or as Tevye tells a potential suitor for one of his daughters:

> PERCHIK: Your daughter has a quick and witty tongue.
> TEVYE: Yes, the wit she gets from me, as the good book says...
> GOLDE: The good book can wait, it's time for Sabbath.
> TEVYE: The tongue she gets from her mother.

The love Tevye and Goldie share is not the normal kind of love understood by American audiences. The two of them had an arranged marriage. There was a contract. The question was not whether or not they found each other attractive or congenial but whether or not they could find a way to live together to meet each other's needs, which, as the exchange indicates, they did. An undervalued part of the film is its keen insight into how the very nature of love has changed in Jewish life. The film is an accurate historical and sociological portrait of the evolution (or devolution, depending on one's point of view) from love as a practical arrangement to a personal, voluntary decision based on such factors as appearance, attractiveness, personality, and so on. Even such a listing misses the emotion of love, the overpowering sense of wanting to be with the person. This is what happens to Tevye's daughters in the film. They understand love in the modern way, not in the traditional one.

In a sense, the film can be compared to *Hester Street*. When seen side by side, *Hester Street* becomes even more interesting than it first appeared. It was about a poor woman, traditional in her outlook and ways, who is betrayed by her husband, who wants to be only an American. He wants wealth. The poor wife, though, finds happiness with the scholarly boarder. That is, *Hester Street* uniquely finds a way around the dilemma posed by *Fiddler on the Roof* in which there is an unbridgeable gap between tradition and modernity. You either have to choose the old-fashioned sort of love or you have to become modern and romantic. *Hester Street*, in contrast, offers the possibility of both. It, too, wants to give up the old-fashioned arranged marriage. But in its place it offers a marriage based on affection as well as practical elements, but not strictly in the way the modern temperament suggests of solely depending on the emotional attraction of one person for another. Unfortunately, as will be seen in an examination of romances, this approach is completely bypassed in favor of the familiar arc of tradition yielding to modern love. Still, this blending is worth exploring in other films.

There are elements of such an approach in *Fiddler on the Roof*, but the practical is understood as the political rather than the day-to-day real needs of the partners:

> PERCHIK: There's a question ... a certain question I want to discuss with you.
> HODEL: Yes?
> PERCHIK: It's a political question.
> HODEL: What is it?
> PERCHIK: The question of ... marriage.
> HODEL: Is this a political question?
> PERCHIK: Well, yes. Yes, everything's political. Like everything else, the relationship between a man and a woman has a socioeconomic base. Marriage must be founded on mutual beliefs. A common attitude and philosophy towards society...
> HODEL: And affection?
> PERCHIK: Well, yes, of course. That is also necessary. Such a relationship can have positive social values. When two people face the world with unity and solidarity...
> HODEL: And affection?
> PERCHIK: Yes, that is an important element! At any rate, I ... I personally am in favor of such a socioeconomic relationship.
> HODEL: I think ... you are asking me to marry you.
> PERCHIK: Well ... in a theoretical sense ... yes. I am.
> HODEL: I was hoping you were.

Hodel will later have a conversation with Tevye about this kind of love. The film presents it as being strongly in love, as being faithful, as being a good kind of love to have. But, without realizing it, the movie betrays romantic love as being unnecessarily blind to realities.

At the beginning of the film, Tevye compares his situation to a very precarious existence. He finds the perfect Jewish image:

> A fiddler on the roof. Sounds crazy, no? But here, in our little village of Anatevka, you might say every one of us is a fiddler on the roof trying

to scratch out a pleasant, simple tune without breaking his neck. It isn't easy. You may ask "Why do we stay up there if it's so dangerous?" Well, we stay because Anatevka is our home. And how do we keep our balance? That I can tell you in one word: tradition!

The title is derived from a Marc Chagall painting titled "The Dead Man." The picture shows a funeral scene and includes a man on a rooftop playing the violin.

At the beginning of the film Tevye explains the environment of the Jewish world in which he lives. He emphasizes that only Jewish traditions let him stay up on that roof.

> TEVYE: Because of our traditions, we've kept our balance for many, many years. Here in Anatevka, we have traditions for everything — how to sleep, how to eat ... how to work ... how to wear clothes. For instance, we always keep our heads covered, and always wear a little prayer shawl that shows our constant devotion to God. You may ask, "How did this tradition get started?" I'll tell you! [pause]
>
> TEVYE: I don't know. But it's a tradition. And because of our traditions ... every one of us knows who he is and what God expects him to do.

But this very reliance on tradition, on accepting a constantly precarious life, has its limits for American Jews. Shorn of nostalgia, even of admiration, Tevye would not fit in well in modern American Jewish life. Few American Jews constantly converse with God, are ready to give up a relationship with a child because she intermarries, or, for that matter, closely adhere to the very traditions Tevye finds not only meaningful but also indispensable. They want much more stability than is found in Tevye's life. That is, Tevye's warm humanity is more a reminder of how far we have spiritually fallen rather than a model of what we are or what we can return to being.

There is one aspect of Tevye that deserves more attention than it has received: his role as a Jewish father. When it comes to parenting, almost all attention has been focused on the Jewish mother. She has been portrayed in a variety of ways, usually as warm and supportive, or, more recently, as guilt-inducing or stifling. In either case, the mother is mostly portrayed as playing the key parenting role. Fathers in Jewish films (consider, for example, *The Jazz Singer*) are seen as rigid and unfeeling. Tevye, in contrast, is the center of the family. He manipulates his wife as best he can. He comes to terms with his daughters' romantic partners, including one he thinks of as a nebbish, a political radical, and even, to some extent at least, a Gentile.

For the last, he has stopped speaking to the daughter who intermarried, but as the family is ready to leave for America, he whispers for another daughter to tell the intermarried one to "Go with God." This strong male figure, more in keeping with the Jewish tradition as seen in films like *The Ten Commandments*, is much-needed in American Jewish films.

The Jewish values the film projects—the warmth, the compassion for others, the unbreakable sense of community, and many others—are all there to be woven together. We need a contemporary Tevye with these values to speak on behalf of tradition. *Fiddler on the Roof*, like so many American Jewish films, at its heart has a struggle between that tradition and assimilation. Assimilation is almost always presented as the more tolerant and humane approach because it is so often couched in the language of love or social acceptance. Tevye takes the side of tradition, but he does so with an embracing warmth and good humor. He is a great character.

But Tevye can be seen in another way — as, despite his attachment to tradition, ultimately accepting assimilation. Lester Friedman makes this argument, claiming the film "sides with love rather than tradition":

> Because he ultimately accepts love over principle, Tevye represents the assimilationist ethos.... But by juxtaposing negative events with these triumphs of love over tradition, the film creates an implicit cause and effect relationship between the breakdown of religious prohibitions and the arrival of destructive events.... Underneath its assimilationist exterior [the film] shows a real concern for traditions.... To miss this level of the film is to ignore its insistent though understated message: a place for tradition must be found in contemporary life.[3]

It is this message that makes the film so vital and so important. Somehow, in some way, in forging an American Jewish identity, the religious traditions need to have some place beyond simple nostalgia.

One attempt to examine religious traditions was to examine it through a feminist lens. Barbra Streisand did exactly this. *Yentl* (1983) had its origin in Isaac Bashevis Singer's story "Yentl the Yeshiva Boy." The film is a good companion film to *Fiddler on the Roof.* Both movies carefully, even lovingly, recreate the Jewish shtetl, the kind of small Jewish village that was sprinkled throughout the Eastern European Jewish world. There is, in both films, perhaps too much nostalgia, too much a sense that such places had a warm community that American Jews so sorely lack.

Beyond that, Streisand adapts Singer's small tale about a young Jewish

Three—The Past Is Prologue

Barbra Streisand as the title character in *Yentl* (United Artists, 1983), a young woman so thirsty for religious knowledge that she dresses as a boy because only males are allowed to study.

girl who disguises herself as a male in order to study Jewish sacred literature, traditionally forbidden to women, as this exchange illustrates:

> BOOKSELLER: You're in the wrong place, storybooks for women are over here.
> YENTL [holding a book]: I'd like this one, please.
> BOOKSELLER [taking the book away]: Sacred books are for men.
> YENTL: Why?
> BOOKSELLER: It's the law.
> YENTL: Where's it written?
> BOOKSELLER: It doesn't matter where it's written, it's the law.
> YENTL: Well if it's the law it must be written somewhere, perhaps in here. I'll take it.

The message is important; Streisand is clearly and usefully passionate about delivering the message. It's also a message about the Jewish community's ability to welcome women as serious students. As Yentl hears from her father:

YENTL: If we don't have to hide my studying from God, then why from the neighbors?
FATHER: Why? Because I trust God will understand. I'm not so sure about the neighbors.

There is, however, always a danger of creating a movie with a message. It can get in the way of the story.

In films, themes need to emerge naturally from the harmonious interplay of plot, characters, setting, and cinematic techniques. When the theme, the message, becomes insistent it reduces the artistic value of the film.

And that is too bad, because *Yentl* is so well-meaning, so correct in its message, so lushly filmed, that it is unfortunate that its message isn't blended in better. As Yentl says,

"Why is it people who want the truth never believe it when they hear it?" The movie is meant to make sure the audience hears it. But the message gets muddled because it's mixed with gender and sexual role confusion. Perhaps these are important issues, and certainly the cross-dressing can't be omitted (it's at the heart of the story). But the very authenticity Streisand worked so hard for and got is achieved at the cost of the very warmth that would make Yentl more believable.

The film ends with Yentl heading for America, determined to live both as a woman and a religious Jew. As the films of Jewish immigration show, this is not a likely outcome once in the Golden Land, filled as it is with its worldly temptations. In the Singer story Yentl goes on to another yeshiva. Singer disliked the film, arguing in the *New York Times* that "Miss Streisand was exceedingly kind to herself. The result is that Miss Streisand is always present, while poor Yentl is absent."[4]

Whatever the artistic qualities of the film — and critics were deeply divided — it's an important picture for its beautiful and admirably precise rendering of the environment of Eastern European Jewish life, and its courageous willingness to ignore traditional Hollywood barbs about Jewish films being inappropriate for wide audiences.

And *Yentl* does truly have a vital message for Jewish identity. The emerging ability of Jewish women to study the Talmud and other sacred literature is one of the great stories of contemporary Jewish life. The feminist perspective has added a tremendous amount to the study of Jewish life, and much else.

In that sense, the film really adds a lot to the American Jewish identity, for it forces all of us to conceive that identity outside of maleness. This is not a matter of political correctness or even feminism. It is a matter of deepening an understanding of what it means to be Jewish by welcoming and incorporating the contributions of half of the Jewish people. Insofar as *Yentl* invites its viewers to consider that, it is a vital Jewish film indeed.

CHAPTER FOUR

The Oldest Hatred: Anti-Semitism in Films

It is possible, though misleading, to assert that an identity can be shaped exclusively by hatred. According to such an interpretation, the anti-Semitism that has punctuated Jewish history, culminating in the Holocaust, forced Jews to retain their identity as a people. This approach is misguided, however, because religion is the bedrock of Jewish identity, and all other descriptors ultimately are parasitic on that basic definition. That is, having any outside force as defining Judaism rests on the premise that there is no internal force, despite the fact that there is one.

Jewish identity started with the Jewish apprehension of a moral God, one who wished to form a partnership with individuals and simultaneously the entire Jewish people. This covenant required Jews to be moral and serve as moral examples to others.

Hatred of the Jews has existed for a long while for many reasons. In the pagan world it perhaps existed because the Jews were different, or perhaps for religious reasons—that their beliefs directly challenged pagan beliefs. Hatred of the Jews accelerated during the Middle Ages when Judaism was seen to be in direct religious competition with Christianity, and Jews as a people were blamed for the killing of Jesus. Later hatred of the Jews changed from exclusively religious reasons—to "racial" reasons, that the Jews were a competing race of people who were inferior.

The term "anti-Semitism," now often spelled antisemitism, was used first in 1860 by Moritz Steinschneider, a Jewish scholar who attacked the writer Ernest Renan's beliefs that the "Aryan races" were superior to the "Semitic races." But the term did not enter popular usage until Wilhelm Marr, a German journalist, published a pamphlet in which he used the term "Semitismus" and "Judentum" in the same way. From the overlapping of the two emerged the idea of opposing Jews and (incorrectly) limiting the notion of "Semite" just to them.

By Marr's time the religious persecution that accompanied the Crusades and other attacks on Jews had changed into "racial" persecution. In a way this was even more insidious that religious hatred because, in principle, people could change their religions, but they could never change their "race" even if they wanted to do so.

American films reflected these various kinds of anti–Semitism. They portrayed Jews in ways that sometimes drew criticism. For example, D.W. Griffith's great 1916 film *Intolerance* included a Crucifixion scene that made it plain to viewers that Jews were responsible for Jesus' death. B'nai Brith, a Jewish organization, complained, and Griffith re-shot the scene. Cecil B. DeMille, producer and director of *The Ten Commandments*, had directed the film *King of Kings* in 1927 and ultimately agreed, after complaints, to remove dialogue that seemed to some viewers as anti–Semitic.

Note that these weren't films about anti–Semitism. Those films came about only slowly.

There had been a large number of Jewish actors and films, though relatively few about Jewish subjects. There had been, as discussed, stock comedic Jewish characters. And actors like the Marx Brothers and Eddie Cantor had thrown in their share of Yiddishisms in the films they made. All that changed in the 1930s after the rise of Nazism in Germany. As Patricia Erens puts it, "Beginning in the thirties, Jews were pushed off center ... although they remain as identifiable minor characters in many films up through 1933. From 1933 to the end of the decade even these types disappear. Thus from 1933 to 1940 few stories about Jews and Jewish life are filmed."[1]

Erens does not claim this reduction in Jewish characters was the result of a deliberate studio decision. There are various possible explanations for the reduction. One, the most benign, is that Jewish studio executives, noting the clear evidence of anti–Semitism in Europe and the United States (as made evident by Henry Ford and Father Charles Coughlin), did not want to exacerbate that anti–Semitism by having prominent stories about Jews or Jewish characters. There were even reports of a meeting of Jewish moguls to make such a decision, but there is no concrete evidence that such a meeting took place. It is a matter of film history that other ethnic stereotypes—Irish police and Italian organ grinders, for example—continued while Jewish stereotypes disappeared.

American Jewish Films

Another explanation is that the corporations that had gained control over studios previously owned by individuals made the business choice to seek the widest possible audience and so strained out Jewish material.

There are, however, other, more offensive possibilities. By the mid-30s the Hollywood studios were getting 30 to 40 percent of gross revenues from overseas distribution. According to this explanation, Hollywood executives didn't want to annoy the Nazis and endanger their overseas revenues.

William Randolph Hearst went directly to Hitler, seeking to protect those interests. This worked up to a point. By 1940 only three studios were still allowed to export their films to Germany. Permission to do even that stopped in September 1940.

The Hayes Office, enforcing a Code beginning in 1934, wanted, for both domestic and foreign reasons, to reduce any potential controversy in films. From September 15, 1939 (exactly two weeks after the Nazis invaded Poland and began World War Two) to January 1940, the Hays Office explicitly disallowed the making of any anti-Nazi films. The State Department supported American neutrality and supported this ban.

The emerging vicious anti-Semitism in Europe that would soon turn murderous to a degree beyond comprehension, and the very real anti-Semitic discrimination in housing, higher education, employment and elsewhere in American life, were met in Hollywood by silence. There were those who saw in Warner Brothers films allegorical attacks on Nazism, but viewers would have to have had quite a poetic sensibility to grasp them if they were intended. For example, Errol Flynn as Robin Hood, was, some thought, *really* fighting the Nazis.

The timidity of Hollywood can be put in relief by this fact: Moe Howard of the Three Stooges was the first American actor to portray Hitler. He did so in three films, starting with *You Nazty Spy* in 1940. But, of course, audiences for the Stooges were young and politically, socially, and culturally without power. Additionally, because the Stooges were often characterized as sadistically physical comedians, their efforts were dismissed.

The Great Dictator (1940) was the first film made in Hollywood to attack Nazism. Charlie Chaplin, the great star, writer, and director of the movie, was warned many times during the production of the picture not to make it. Chaplin was not Jewish, although at the time of the film's making his wife was a Jewish actress named Paulette Goddard. In the film Chaplin plays a dual role, a Jewish barber and a terrible dictator named

Adenoid Hynkel. By the film's conclusion the two characters have changed places.

It may seem odd to have a comedy about Hitler and Nazism, as was done by the Three Stooges and as would be done by Jack Benny. Humor is noted for making people laugh, but its real power emerges because it is subversive towards what it mocks. There were many ways to attack Hitler, and in 1940 one way was to reduce peoples' fears of him and reduce his seeming power. *The Great Dictator* accomplished his goal by mocking him. Indeed, Hitler banned the film and made it unavailable for screening in Nazi Germany. All this was done before the full horror of the Holocaust was known. Later in life, in his autobiography, Chaplin noted that had he been aware of the full extent of the horror he would not have deflated Hitler through comedy.

Given all that, it might be wondered why the film contained the word "great" when, even while it was being made, Hitler was hardly considered great by anyone in the West. The original title of the film was *The Dictator*, but, as it happened, Paramount already owned the rights to that title. Chaplin registered various potential titles, including *The Great Dictator*. The "great" ultimately was meant to be ironic. Indeed, the film underwent many changes. The famous Jewish stage star Fanny Brice was originally supposed to play the dictator's wife, but that idea was eventually abandoned.

The long speech that ends the film is among the various artistically controversial parts. Some critics thought it naïve or pretentious, but it was clearly heartfelt, and if Chaplin lacked political sophistication, his political intuitions were better than more sophisticated social thinkers. Here is part of that famous final speech from *The Great Dictator*:

> I'm sorry, but I don't want to be an emperor. That's not my business. I don't want to rule or conquer anyone. I should like to help everyone if possible: Jew, Gentile, black man, white. We all want to help one another. Human beings are like that ...
>
> We think too much and feel too little. More than machinery, we need humanity. More than cleverness, we need kindness and gentleness. Without these qualities, life will be violent and all will be lost.... To those who can hear me, I say, do not despair.... The hate of men will pass, and dictators die, and the power they took from the people will return to the people.... Fight for liberty! In the seventeenth chapter of St. Luke, it is written that the kingdom of God is within man, not one man nor a group of men, but in all men! In you! You, the people, have

the power, the power to create machines, the power to create happiness! You, the people, have the power to make this life free and beautiful, to make this life a wonderful adventure. Then in the name of democracy, let us use that power...

The clouds are lifting! The sun is breaking through! We are coming out of the darkness into the light! We are coming into a new world — a kindlier world, where men will rise above their hate, their greed, and brutality.... The glorious future, that belongs to you, to me and to all of us. Look up.... Look up!

It seems, in retrospect, obvious that Hitler should have been attacked. But at the time that Chaplin spent $2 million of his own money to make this film, it was precisely the historical moment when all other filmmakers shied away from the subject and tried desperately to stop him. Charlie Chaplin, therefore, deserves great credit for making this movie. And Chaplin's very courage puts the cowardice of the Jewish Hollywood moguls in sharp relief.

There is another, political, element to the decision. Chaplin was a man of the political Left. On August 23, 1939, the Soviet Union and Nazi Germany signed a non-aggression pact. This agreement led many pro–Soviet leftists in the United States to oppose any American intervention in Europe and to avoid attacking Hitler. In response, Chaplin continued making *The Great Dictator*. He broke, that is, with some of his former allies on the Left.

Hollywood had another chance to reward Chaplin. The film was nominated for Best Picture but lost. Hollywood really wasn't ready to alert the world to Hitler.

Chaplin may at least in part have been prompted by the uncanny connections to Hitler. Not only did their moustaches appear similar, but Chaplin had been born on April 16, 1889, just four days before Hitler's birth.

But it is what distinguishes them, not what is similar, that is most telling, most crucial. Indeed, as critic Omer Bartov notes about the two characters Chaplin plays, "Far more disturbing, however, is the discovery that no one can tell who is who: Where does Hynkel end and the 'Jew' begin? Essentially what distinguishes one from the other is not their appearance but their moral qualities."[2]

Here at last is a focal point for Jewish identity that can work. It is the Jewish barber's ethical compass that defines his character, not how he looks. Here is a guideline for an American Jewish identity. The guideline is muddled because it is connected to anti–Nazism and set in a (fictional but obvious) foreign country. Most particularly, the moral premise has serious problems because of its link to Hitler. As Bartov notes:

> The film unintentionally suggested precisely that uniquely Jewish trait of changing one's exterior (looking like the Fuhrer) while remaining the same on the inside (propagating racial equality).... In terms of linking motivation and phobia, this means that while some social psychologist would propose that a little Hitler lurks in everyone, the anti–Semitic fantasy would proclaim (both apologetically and aggressively) that in every Hitler lurks a little Jew.[3]

That is, in order to understand morality as a defining component of Jewish identity it needs to reside in some way exclusively in the Jew on the basis of a moral belief system and a religious connection, a covenant, with God. Such a representation would have made it impossible to confuse the barber and the dictator morally, for every Hitler exactly lacks these qualities.

Still, we have a hint of what that Jewish identity might look like. Grafted on to the religious identity mentioned earlier was also an ethical identity grounded in the religion.

The Great Dictator stood alone in its courage during the pre-war years.

The Mortal Storm (1940) does have the distinction of being the first explicitly anti–Nazi Hollywood movie and appearing before America entered the war. The film opens in a dramatic way with a narrative voice-over. The voice comes as white clouds appear on the screen and rapidly change into storm clouds:

> When man was new upon the earth, he was frightened by the dangers of the elements. He cried out, "The gods of the lightning are angry, and I must kill my fellow man to appease them!" As man grew bolder, he created shelters against the wind and the rain and made harmless the force of the lightning. But within man himself were elements strong as the wind and terrible as the lightning. And he denied the existence of these elements, because he dared not face them. The tale we are about to tell is of the mortal storm in which man finds himself today. Again he is crying, "I must kill my fellow man!" Our story asks, "How soon will man find wisdom in his heart and build a lasting shelter against his ignorant fears?"

The film begins its story in a small university town in Germany in 1933, the year Adolf Hitler was appointed Chancellor. There is a birthday celebration going on for Professor Viktor Roth, who seems to be very widely admired. His Jewishness is never mentioned by his students or anyone else. Roth's daughter Freya and a family friend (who loves Freya) named Martin Breitner react uneasily to the news of Hitler's rise. However, Roth's two stepsons, Otto and Erich Von Rohn, as well as Freya's fiancé, Fritz Marberg, are delighted with the news. Soon enough the Nazi thugs in the town begin to attack their enemies.

The two stepsons decide that they can no longer live in the house. Freya breaks off her engagement and realizes that it is Martin she loves. But Martin helps a friend escape Germany and by doing so finds himself in Austria, unable to return safely. Roth, meanwhile, refuses to go along with Nazi ideology. Specifically, he will not state what he knows to be false, that so-called "Aryan" blood is different from so-called "non–Aryan" blood. He loses his job as a teacher and is put in a concentration camp. His family makes a desperate attempt to locate him, and finally there is a brief visit, which is followed by his death. Freya and Mrs. Roth want to go to Austria, but they are stopped because Freya is taking along one of her father's manuscripts. Freya is told she must stay in Germany. Martin returns to rescue her, and the two plan a daring escape, skiing through a mountain pass. They are almost to Austria when a patrol of Nazis, led by Fritz, spots them. The two reach the border, but Freya is shot and dies.

The film's story is stirring and disturbing; its emotions are genuine. James Stewart and Robert Young excel in their parts, as does Margaret Sullivan. But, unfortunately, even shockingly, the film ignores anti–Semitism in Germany in any explicit way; the word "Jew" is never spoken in the film.

To Be or Not to Be (1942) was filmed in 1941—before the United States entered the war—making the filmmakers more daring than if they had simply been supporting the war effort. The famed radio comedian Jack Benny was cast as Joseph Tura, a vain Polish actor of questionable abilities. His troupe puts on an anti–Nazi play, but their timing is such that just as they prepare the production the Nazis invade Poland. The film's opening is shocking because audiences see the troupe rehearsing, and it at first appears that Benny is playing a Nazi. The Nazi uniform and his repeated yelling out of "Heil Hitler" so surprised Benny's father that when he saw it he left the theater after the first minute.

Jack Benny's father was not the film's only critic. Because it was seen later than when it was produced, the humor seemed to be grounded in horror. The film appeared to some to be (putting it mildly) in bad taste.

Four—The Oldest Hatred

At one point in the picture Benny, in order to fight the Nazis, pretends to be a Gestapo leader named "Concentration Camp" Ehrhardt and says, "We do the concentrating, and the Poles do the camping." Of course, the widespread incidence of concentration camp sadism and murder was not widely known at the time of filming, but a retrospective viewing of the movie is chilling.

In a further sad twist, Carole Lombard, who starred as Benny's wife in the movie, was killed in an airplane crash just prior to the picture's premiere. (The line "What can happen in a plane?" had to be deleted from the film.) Audiences were not prepared to laugh at this movie.

The film's plot revolves around a young man (Lieutenant Stanislav Sobinski) who has a crush on Lombard's character, Maria Tura. The lieutenant waits for her husband Josef to begin his Shakespearean soliloquy

Carole Lombard (seated) as Maria Tura, Maude Eburne as Anna, and comedian Jack Benny as the Hamlet-clad actor Joseph Tura in *To Be or Not to Be* (Romaine Film Corporation, 1942). The dark comedy about Nazis came out just as America entered the Second World War. The laughter proved hollow, although time has been kind to the film's scathing satire.

with the line "To be or not to be." The lieutenant uses that line to get up and walk out to meet Maria backstage. Later, Maria and her admirer try to convince Josef that Maria must have dinner with a Nazi to obtain crucial information:

> JOSEF TURA: Wait a minute. I'll decide with whom my wife is going to have dinner and whom she's going to kill.
> MARIA TURA: Don't you realize Poland's at stake?
> LIEUTENANT STANISLAV SOBINSKI: Have you no patriotism?
> JOSEF TURAa: Now listen, you ... first you walk out on my soliloquy and then you walk into my slippers. And now you question my patriotism. I'm a good Pole and I love my country and I love my slippers.
> MARIA TURA: Well, I hope your country comes first.
> LIEUTENANT STANISLAV SOBINSKI: So do I.
> MARIA TURA: This is an emergency! War!
> JOSEF TURA: Look, look, look, I don't know much about the whole thing ... but is this Siletsky a real danger to Poland?
> LIEUTENANT STANISLAV SOBINSKI: A catastrophe!
> MARIA TURA: He must be taken care of!
> JOSEF TURA: Then he will be taken care of.
> MARIA TURA: Well, who's gonna do it?
> JOSEF TURA: I'm gonna do it.
> LIEUTENANT STANISLAV SOBINSKI: But how?
> MARIA TURA: Where?
> JOSEF TURA: I'm gonna meet Herr Siletsky at Gestapo headquarters. And after I've killed him I hope you'll be kind enough to tell me what it was all about!

Like *The Great Dictator*, *To Be or Not to Be* invites a discussion of how comedy can or should be used to deal with tragedy, especially since it involves the worst tragedy of the century. Annette Insdorf argues that "the fact that the Gestapo constitutes a source of humor rather than horror becomes fairly horrifying itself, for [director Ernst] Lubitsch invites an awareness of our own responses through the juxtaposition of moods."[4]

This is an interesting argument, and certainly decades after its release, *To Be or Not to Be* has become a model for the limits of comedy's intrusion into the dark realities of the human mind and history. We can now see its subtle strengths. It is a direct assault on Nazism when such an approach was still unpopular in Hollywood.

But there is another aspect of the film that coheres better with American beliefs than Jewish ones. As Omer Bartov notes, "The film strives to undermine all racial and national prejudices by creating a comedy of mistaken identities, an endless masked ball in which the representatives of the Master Race and their allegedly subhuman subjects can never be told apart. Lubitsch thus slams directly into the rhetoric of essential difference, whereby the external appearance of human beings reveals their value and thus determines the manner in which they ought to be treated."[5]

The problem with this approach, as with Chaplin's, is the underlying humanistic assumption that all people are the same, that external differences mislead. But surely the very horror of the Holocaust undermines this comfortable Enlightenment value. A darker vision of the human being emerges. Some humans, like Hitler, cannot, even in principle, be seen to be like other human beings. Such a view challenges the value system of many (including many Jews, such as Ernst Lubitsch).

But if a Jewish identity is to have any meaning, it can't simply be able to melt into a wider human identity. It must have its distinctiveness, grounded in religion and ethics. Judaism is not humanism, and humanism is not Judaism. We have seen too much evil to accept such a naïve notion anymore.

More troubling, American values are built on the very notion of utter equality, an idea given voice in the film. But political, economic, and social equality are not the same as moral equivalence. The American view is that everyone should be given an equal chance. When this is confused with the idea that everyone is entirely interchangeable with everyone else in how they behave, then moral innocence has entered. We need to be able to say that there is a fundamental difference between the Nazi and Anne Frank, between a Ku Klux Klan organizer and an African American worker, between a criminal and a victim.

What this means is that without locating a distinctive, separate identity, films, even films about Jewish subjects or about Jews (there is only one clearly identifiable Jewish subject in *To Be or Not to Be*), do not contribute to an understanding of Jewish identity.

Gentleman's Agreement (1947) is the most important film right after the war to deal with anti–Semitism. Note that seemingly obvious subjects, such as the fate of Jews during the Holocaust, were still too fresh, the images too raw, to deal with in movies. It would take decades until audiences were ready to watch such films.

In a way, it is odd to talk about anti–Semitism as a part of a discussion about Jewish identity. After all, anti–Semitism existed and exists to erase Jewish identity and, at its extremes, to erase Jews. Anti-Semitism has punc-

The many stars of *Gentleman's Agreement* (Twentieth Century–Fox, 1947) include (left to right) Gregory Peck as Philip Green, Dorothy McGuire as Kathy Lacy, John Garfield as Dave Goldman, and Celeste Holm as Anne Dettrey. The film, with Peck as a Gentile reporter pretending to be Jewish to expose anti-Semitism, was only partially successful. It doesn't discuss the Holocaust.

tuated parts of Jewish history, and so obviously belongs in a discussion of Jewish materials broadly defined. But what is its contribution to a study of Jewish identity?

Jean-Paul Sartre, the French philosopher, asserted that it was anti-Semitism that gave Jews their identity, that without it Jews would have assimilated into the broader culture. Taken to its logical limit, this theory is clearly wrong because Jews stayed together because of their religious beliefs and traditions. There were and are increases in assimilation when societies in which Jews live are open, but there is no disappearance of the Jews. This is even true in the contemporary United States, where there is a Jewish intermarriage rate of about 50 percent among non–Orthodox Jews. Still, in a recent study of New York Jews, the Jewish population was growing. But it was getting more Orthodox because the non–Orthodox were in fact assimilating: intermarrying and having a negative birth rate.

Four—The Oldest Hatred

But Sartre's observation, however incorrect, remains interesting because ongoing hatred of the Jews has, in fact, shaped Jewish identity. It has made Jewish pride in remaining Jewish part of the identity. Its other effects are discussed below, but the crucial matter is anti–Semitism does need to be discussed as part of a wider discussion of Jewish identity.

Hollywood's Jews and Jewish leaders were reluctant to discuss anti–Semitism in films, even after the war. But Darryl Zanuck of Twentieth Century–Fox, a Gentile heading the only studio not owned by someone Jewish, refused to back down. He had witnessed anti–Semitism in a way Jews hadn't—the casual remarks, the statements made without self-censorship because they weren't being spoken to a Jew.

Gentleman's Agreement, adapted from the Laura Z. Hobson novel, has a clever premise: to expose the prejudice against Jews in New York and a wealthy Connecticut suburb, a Gentile reporter named Phil Green (wonderfully played by Gregory Peck) simply pretends that he is Jewish and observes how people react. And he has to explain what he's doing to his son, Tommy:

> TOMMY GREEN: What's anti–Semitism?
> PHIL GREEN: Well, uh, that's when some people don't like other people just because they're Jews.
> TOMMY: Why not? Are Jews bad?
> PHIL: Well, some are and some aren't, just like with everyone else.
> TOMMY: What are Jews, anyway?
> PHIL: Well, uh, it's like this. Remember last week when you asked me about that big church, and I told you there are all different kinds of churches? Well, the people who go to that particular church are called Catholics, and there are people who go to different churches and they're called Protestants, and there are people who go to different churches and they're called Jews, only they call their churches temples or synagogues.
> TOMMY: Why don't some people like them?
> PHIL: Well, I can't really explain it, Tommy.

This premise includes the now familiar notion that Phil is exactly the same man whether a Jew or a Gentile. As he tells his mother his plan for the article, he seems to understand suddenly himself that there are no real differences:

> Ma, I've got it! I've got the idea, the angle, the lead. I'll be Jewish! Why, all I've got to do is just say it! No one around here knows me. I can live with myself for six weeks, eight weeks, nine months. Ma, this is it! ... I

can just tell them I'm Jewish and see what happens.... Dark hair, dark eyes. Just like ...a lot of guys who aren't Jewish. No accent, no mannerisms.

This seems like a vital way for Jews to become accepted: have Americans believe there is no difference in any way between them and American Jews. Indeed, University of Pittsburgh psychologists found that students who had seen the film had a much more favorable attitude toward American Jews after seeing it than students who hadn't seen it.[6]

Phil Green comes to understand anti–Semitism not as some virulent Nazi-like brute and deadly force, but as neglect of American values. His fiancée has trouble with his actions. She wants their lives to go on as normal.

The welcome change in attitude as reflected in the film can be effective in leading to wider acceptance, but underneath is a more insidious action going on. Jews, to accept this, must also come to accept that they have no distinctive contributions to make, religiously or culturally, to American life, that they truly are no different at all from other Americans.

Gentleman's Agreement won the Academy Award for, among other categories, Best Picture. Despite the fear of the Jewish movie moguls, there was no backlash at all. There was only applause for the film. It incited tolerance, not prejudice.

But it is worth noting that the film was produced after much of the victory of anti–Semitism had taken place. There was plenty of prejudice in America against Jews and lots of other groups. But there was no government sanctioning of hate, no original stain of hatred against Jews as there was, for example, with slavery or the murder of Native Americans.

Jews suffered from incidents of anti–Semitism; Jews "as a class" were expelled from parts of Tennessee, Mississippi, and Kentucky under General Order No. 11 by then–Major General Ulysses S. Grant on December 17, 1862. Grant was trying to fight a black market for cotton produced in the South, and he believed Jews controlled the trade. There was a lot of protest against the Order, and President Abraham Lincoln revoked it a few weeks later. Even Grant, running from his own mistake, claimed a subordinate had written it, and that he had signed the General Order without first reading it. As President, Grant tried to make amends by attending the dedication of a synagogue.

Incidents of anti–Semitism (such as the Leo Frank case, in which an innocent man accused of the murder of a young woman was taken from a jail and hanged) have mostly focused on prejudice, such as restrictions on Jewish entrance into colleges, and not allowing Jews into hotels or country clubs or stores. But all these had been greatly reduced by the widespread repulsion toward Nazism and its hate, and more open American attitudes after World War II.

Certainly anti–Semitic stereotypes exist, as do incidents of anti–Semitism, such as the painting of swastikas, Holocaust denial, desecration of Jewish sites, and so on, but the Jewish community in the United States is not in physical danger. That fact should be juxtaposed against *Gentleman's Agreement* precisely because it is the most famous and most influential movie about anti–Semitism.

Anti-Semitism won't work as the foundation for an American Jewish identity. It's vital as a reminder of what was, a necessary cautionary note to remain vigilant by continuing to fight anti–Semitic individuals, organizations and ideas, and a prod to help those around the world who still suffer from any hatred of the Jews. It is not, however, a realistic potent identity force.

In fact, though, the focus on anti–Semitism does define the identity of some American Jews. And that explains why there are so many films in this category; viewers, both Gentile and Jewish, identify being Jewish with being a victim. Doing so when they are victims is welcome, needed, and appropriate. But doing so when they are not distorts a genuine Jewish identity.

Indeed, even with that, as Lester Friedman notes, *Gentleman's Agreement* does not truly focus on the problem. It does not "see the problem as a deep, pervasive issue of religious, psychological, and cultural indoctrination."[7]

Friedman goes on to suggest that Hollywood can't make films about social problems because of their

> inability to present the issues squarely, or for that matter, even to follow the sentiments expressed within films to their logical conclusions.... The films persuade the audience of their message by making their victims such certifiable white knights that we feel outraged at the circumstances they are forced to endure. The outrage, however, is for the wrong reasons.... The anti–Semitism does not disturb us, but rather the fact that it is directed against such worthy figures.[8]

This is an important concept, for its truth in some sense undermines the entire cinematic enterprise. It renders film not entirely able (after all, this is the most successful film about anti-Semitism) to deal with a fundamental social problem Jews might face.

But, to be fair, as Kathryn Bernheimer notes, "*Gentleman's Agreement* took a tough stand against the vicious, if often invisible, attitudes that exist even in polite society, where 'gentlemen' have a tacit understanding that Jews are to be restricted from entering the hallowed halls of high society."[9]

Crossfire (1947) is often paired with *Gentleman's Agreement* for its post-war portrayal of anti-Semitism. Interestingly, *Crossfire* also received a Best Picture nomination, the first "B" picture so honored. It is a classic police procedural, filled with the obligatory dark shadows and darker motives. Grafted onto the question of who killed the Jewish victim is the more significant message of the film, that hate is un–American. This message is delivered most directly by Robert Young, playing a homicide detective. As he finally says:

> My grandfather was killed just because he was an Irish Catholic. Hating is always the same, always senseless. One day it kills Irish Catholics, the next day Jews, the next day Protestants, the next day Quakers. It's hard to stop. It can end up killing people who wear striped neckties.

And also:

> This business about hating Jews comes in a lot of different sizes. There's the "you can't join our country club" kind. The "you can't live around here" kind. The "you can't work here" kind. Because we stand for all these, we get [the killer's] kind. He grows out of all the rest.... Hating is always insane, always senseless.

Unsurprisingly the film was attacked, sometimes by Jewish observers who, as always, feared it would spur further anti–Semitism or confirm for existing anti–Semites that they were not alone, that if they acted on their beliefs the actions would appear on the big screen.

The filmmakers defended their product, and did so successfully, for the movie does exactly what they intended — to put the focus on a man who hated Jews and present him for what he is. If the film is small, its message is clear, though it has exactly the same faults as *Gentleman's Agreement*.

In some ways, in fact, *Crossfire* is a better film. Its focus is only on anti–Semitism. Its darkness is more appropriate for the subject. The consequences of hate are deadly. Certainly, since neither film mentioned the

Four—The Oldest Hatred

Holocaust, the murder in *Crossfire* was closer to reality, if not an American reality. The hatred and the violence get at the anti–Semite, though, far better than *Gentleman's Agreement*'s more delicate prejudices of exclusion or mockery.

Additionally, *Crossfire*, in connecting an American murder of a Jew even obliquely to the psychopaths who carried out genocide in Europe, forced audience members to see such a connection Still, the simple answer of seeing Jews as just like other Americans misses the uniqueness of Jewishness and therefore employs a useful fiction instead of digging deeply to get at the problem of hatred. Only slowly did Hollywood films come to deal not just with prejudice or even the murder of one man, but also with the grotesque horror that had taken place in Europe.

The Search (1948) is a very moving film about a young boy who has survived Auschwitz. He and his mother search for each other in post-war Europe. Montgomery Clift stars as the American private who helps the boy, a nine-year-old who at first will not talk.

The film, directed by Fred Zinnemann, has the feel of a documentary. Indeed, much of it was shot on location in Germany.

The movie opens with a train carrying many dozens of war orphans arriving at a United Nations Relief and Rehabilitation Administration camp. The camp has been set up as temporary housing for the children, most of whom were found as they wandered alone, abandoned in the bombed wreckage of the war's cities or in the countryside, or because they were rescued from one of the Nazi's concentration camps.

The children understandably are very afraid. They fear the very people trying to help them. They have no trust in any authority. The children are cleaned off and given a meal. Then, under the direction of Mrs. Murray, they are interviewed in an attempt to discover their names and, if possible, any family members. One child speaks French as he tells of his father being killed and his mother being forcibly removed from him. Two Polish children talk of their parents who were murdered in a concentration camp. A young Hungarian girl had been given the job of sorting all the clothes that came from those in the camps who had been killed. The girl talks of finding her mother's blouse in the pile of clothes.

It is Karel Malik, a young Czech boy, who is among the most traumatized of the children. He only recalls seeing Hanna, his mother, in Auschwitz. Karel speaks, in German, but will only say, "I don't know."

When the children are being taken to another camp in ambulances, they suddenly panic, fearing they are being taken away to the gas chambers. They break out of the ambulances. Most of the children are quickly recovered, but some of them escape. Karel and another young boy jump into a river to make their escape, but the other boy is overcome by the water and drowns. Karel, whose name is still unknown, is presumed drowned as well when his cap is seen floating in the river.

It turns out Hanna, Karel's mother, has survived Auschwitz and is looking for her family. She learned that both her husband and daughter are dead, and so focuses all her hopes and all her efforts on finding Karel. She goes from one children's camp to another, always looking at the children, but she is not successful. In one moment of dashed hopes she is told her son is in a Catholic orphanage, but the boy believed to be her son is a young Jewish boy who has taken Karel's name when it was called during a roll and no one was there to answer.

Karel keeps wandering throughout Germany but is found one day by Steve Stevenson, an American soldier. Steve cares for the boy, feeds the hungry child, provides him a home, and begins to teach him English.

Hanna eventually gets to the camp where Karel was taken. Mrs. Murray recalls the found cap in the river and shows it to Hanna to provide evidence that Karel has drowned. Hanna, who has come so far, will not simply accept the evidence of a hat. She does not believe her son is dead, and she is determined to continue searching until she finds him. After a while, Hanna comes to accept that she is not going to find Karel. She determines, though, to help other children and so takes a job in the camp working with Mrs. Murray.

Steve believes Karel's mother is dead and develops plans to take Karel back to the United States.

The children in the camp leave for the Land of Israel, and on the day afterwards Hanna decides her job is over and plans to resume searching for her son.

It is only a few moments after Hanna leaves the camp that Steve brings Karel there so that he can get Mrs. Murray's permission to take the boy to America. Mrs. Murray immediately recognizes Karel and dashes to the train to prevent Hanna from leaving. She arrives too late; the train has pulled out. But Hanna is not on the train. She has decided that she belongs at the camp, helping those children who were still alive. Mrs. Murray doesn't tell her about Karel but takes Hanna back to the camp so that she can be there when a new group of children arrive. Steve tells the boy to join the new children. Karel walks by his mother without recognizing her, and his mother almost misses him as well. But suddenly she turns and calls out, "Karel!" He turns, and the two become reunited.

The film doesn't emphasize the Jewishness of the displaced children, although it is mentioned that they are waiting to go to the Land of Israel. Indeed, the lost little boy is presented as Czech, and he is not, or at least not clearly, Jewish. As with the two American films about anti–Semitism, being a displaced Jewish child is indistinguishable from being a Gentile displaced child. The same message applies: underneath we are all the same, and we should treat each other like that.

There are two clearly-defined Jewish characters in the film — Miriam, who discovers that her mother has died when she finds a blouse that is included among clothes belonging to those who have died, and Joel, who hides by becoming a Christian choir boy.

The film ends with the children preparing for their voyage to the Jewish homeland by singing a Hebrew song, "Hine Ma Tov."

The Search, unfairly overlooked and unfailingly warm, approaches dealing with the Holocaust for the first time in a Hollywood film and deserves credit for that. Its additional strength is that it is about how human relationships, a soldier helping a boy, a mother desperate to find a child, have a healing effect. Against the background of what happened in Europe, such a message was needed and vital.

The Diary of Anne Frank (1959) is, of course, based on the world-famous and absolutely incredible real-life diary of the young girl forced with her family to hide in an Amsterdam attic to escape the Nazis. The film's story is universally known, the tragic tale of the hiding out, the keeping of a diary, and of Anne's ultimate capture and death. The sheer yearning, the humanity, of her words in the diary captivated readers everywhere, and while six million Jewish deaths seemed beyond the capacity of the human imagination to grasp, Anne Frank became a symbol for all of them, of the willful murder of innocence and promise for no reason other than her religion.

The film represents a maturing of Hollywood's willingness to deal with the Holocaust. The Jewish characters aren't perfect. They are human. And, although the film shies away from any onscreen brutality (apart from some documentary footage), audiences bring their own knowledge and can fill in what is suggested.

The casting of the film was interesting. Shelley Winters, who was

Jewish, was thirty-six at the time the film was being cast. She wondered if she could somehow play the thirteen-year-old Anne. But instead she was cast as the fifty-year-old Mrs. Van Daan. Winters thought Susan Strasberg, age twenty, should play the part because Strasberg had done so on Broadway to great acclaim. But Strasberg was settled in New York. A trip to Hollywood would, in addition, separate her from Richard Burton, her then-boyfriend. After a nationwide search, director George Stevens hired a virtually unknown seventeen-year old model named Millie Perkins, who bore a striking resemblance to Audrey Hepburn, then a very popular actress. Perkins, a Gentile, relied heavily on Winters for tips on being Jewish. Winters went on to win an Academy Award. She donated it to the Anne Frank House in Amsterdam.

The film tries to deal with unusual emotions, such as how it felt to wear a Jewish star:

> ANNE FRANK [to Peter after he has removed the Star of David badge from his coat]: You took off your star.
> PETER VAN DAAN: That's right.
> ANNE: You can't do that. They arrest you if you go out without your star.
> PETER: Who's going out?
> ANNE: What are you going to do with it?
> PETER: Burn it.
> ANNE: I don't think I could burn mine. I don't know why.
> PETER: You couldn't? Something they made you wear so they could kick you around?
> ANNE: I know, but after all, it is the Star of David, isn't it?

It was Anne Frank's father, Otto, who was the only survivor of the group and who arranged to have his daughter's diary published. Their relationship is therefore particularly poignant, such as when he tries to find some tiny good that can be seen in their situation:

> Being here has certain advantages for you. Now for instance, you remember that battle you had with your mother the other day on the subject of overshoes? You said you would rather die than wear overshoes, remember? And what happened? In the end you had to wear them. Now, you see, for as long as we are here, you won't have to wear overshoes, isn't that great? And the piano. You won't have to practice on the piano. I tell you, this is going to be a fine life for you.

However well intentioned, the film lacks what the diary itself has: Anne's quiet yet commanding voice. We see all through her eyes. The film is ... a film. It makes all in its scope more objective. It creates an unintentional emotional distance between us and Anne.

And the movie deliberately tries to make Anne universal. In her diary, Anne reflects that she and her family were not the only Jews to suffer, that all through history Jews have faced danger and death. But this idea in the film is transformed to "We are not the only people that've had to suffer. There have always been people that've had to—sometimes one race, sometimes another." This is a noble and true idea, but it violates both the message from Anne's diary and the uniqueness of the Holocaust.

Conspiracy of Hearts (1960) is not well-known but is a remarkable, deeply-moving film. It is a British picture that was shown in the United States. That may explain in part why it is not more widely-known and yet should be.

The movie is set in Italy during World War II. More particularly, it takes place mostly in a convent. Lilli Palmer stars as Mother Katharine, the Mother Superior who oversees the nuns' efforts to smuggle Jewish children into the convent from an internment camp near them. There is an Italian army officer who clearly is aware of these efforts but chooses to ignore them. However, when the Nazis take over the camp, the nuns are caught and face the harshest punishment.

Particularly moving is the interplay between the nuns and the children, and the internal moral struggle some of the nuns have about saving Jewish children.

Judgment at Nuremberg (1961) is a courtroom drama about the war crime trial held in Nuremberg after the war. As such, the film's moral focus is on Nazi responsibility. It is worth quoting from the film at length to see its true dramatic tension. There is an attempt to understand ordinary Germans and what the attractions of Nazism were for them. This is in contrast to the American view of what the Nazis did. First, consider the statement by Ernst Janning, one of those accused, as he seeks not so much justification as explanation. He wants Americans to understand what happened:

> There was a fever over the land.... We had a democracy, yes, but it was torn by elements within. Above all, there was fear. Fear of today, fear of tomorrow, fear of our neighbors, and fear of ourselves. Only when you understand that can you understand what Hitler meant to us. Because he said to us: "Lift your heads! Be proud to be German! There are devils among us. Communists, Liberals, Jews, Gypsies! Once these devils will be destroyed, your misery will be destroyed." What about those of us who knew better? Why did we sit silent? Why did we take part? Because

we loved our country! What difference does it make if a few political extremists lose their rights? What difference does it make if a few racial minorities lose their rights? It is only a stage we are going through. It will be discarded sooner or later. Hitler himself will be discarded ... sooner or later. The country is in danger. We will march out of the shadows. We will go forward. Forward is the great password. And history tells how well we succeeded, your honor. We succeeded beyond our wildest dreams. The very elements of hate and power about Hitler that mesmerized Germany, mesmerized the world! We found ourselves with sudden powerful allies. Things that had been denied to us as a democracy were open to us now. The world said, "Go ahead, take it, take it! Take Sudetenland, take the Rhineland—remilitarize it—take all of Austria, take it!" And then one day we looked around and found that we were in an even more terrible danger.... What was going to be a passing phase had become the way of life. Your honor, I was content to sit silent during this trial.... I was even content to let counsel try to save my name, until I realized that in order to save it, he would have to raise the specter again. You have seen him do it—he has done it here in this courtroom. He has suggested that the Third Reich worked for the benefit of people. He has suggested that we sterilized men for the welfare of the country. He has suggested that perhaps the old Jew did sleep with the sixteen-year-old girl after all. Once more it is being done for love of country. It is not easy to tell the truth; but if there is to be any salvation for Germany, we who know our guilt must admit it ... whatever the pain and humiliation.

But in the conflict of the film the American judge Dan Haywood rejects this explanation. He considers the prisoner directly:

Janning, to be sure, is a tragic figure. We believe he loathed the evil he did. But compassion for the present torture of his soul must not beget forgetfulness of the torture and death of millions by the government of which he was a part. Janning's record and his fate illuminate the most shattering truth that has emerged from this trial. If he and the other defendants were all depraved perverts—if the leaders of the Third Reich were sadistic monsters and maniacs—these events would have no more moral significance than an earthquake or other natural catastrophes. But this trial has shown that under the stress of a national crisis, men—even able and extraordinary men—can delude themselves into the commission of crimes and atrocities so vast and heinous as to stagger the imagination. No one who has sat through this trial can ever forget. The sterilization of men because of their political beliefs.... The murder of children.... How easily that can happen! There are those in our country today, too, who speak of the "protection" of the country. Of "survival." The answer to that is: survival as what? A country isn't a rock. And it

Four—The Oldest Hatred

isn't an extension of one's self. It's what it stands for, when standing for something is the most difficult! Before the people of the world—let it now be noted in our decision here that this is what we stand for: justice, truth ... and the value of a single human being!

However strange it sounds, this is more characteristic of the film than a discussion of the Nazi hatred of Jews. Somewhat amazingly, there is less emphasis on anti–Semitism and on what the horror meant for the Jewish community and the Jewish future. Although the film is intelligent, emotionally compelling and well acted by such actors as Montgomery Clift, it can't be called an important Jewish film.

The Pawnbroker (1964) is a painfully difficult film to watch. Like the two previously discussed movies about American anti–Semitism, *The Pawnbroker* is set in the United States. This is crucial, for it allows audiences to develop a point of view about the Holocaust that doesn't allow the emotional distance offered by films set in Europe. Rod Steiger plays an aged Jewish pawnbroker in Spanish Harlem. He alone of his family survived the Holocaust. His horrible memories and the pain of survivor's guilt torment him. He is alive only in a technical sense. Twenty years of survival have not allowed him to re-enter life.

He has an assistant, Jesus Ortiz, who is fascinated by Jewish skills:

> JESUS ORTIZ: Say, how come you people come to business so naturally?
> SOL NAZERMAN: You people? Oh, let's see.... Alright, I'll teach you. First of all you start off with a period of several thousand years, during which you have nothing to sustain you but a great bearded legend.... You're never in one place long enough to have a geography or an army or a land myth. All you have is a little brain. A little brain and a great bearded legend to sustain you and convince you that you are special, even in poverty. But this little brain, that's the real key, you see. With this little brain you go out and you buy a piece of cloth and you cut that cloth in two and you go and sell it for a penny more than you paid for it. Then you run right out and buy another piece of cloth, cut it into three pieces and sell it for three pennies profit.... You must immediately run out and get yourself a still larger piece of cloth, and so you repeat this process over and over and suddenly you discover something. You have no longer any desire, any temptation to dig into the Earth to grow food or to gaze at a limitless land and call it your own, no, no. You just go on and on and on over and over and suddenly you make a grand discovery....You are a merchant. You are known as a usurer, a man with secret resources, a witch, a pawnbroker, a sheenie, a makie and a kike!

JESUS ORTIZ [*long pause*]: You really some teacher, Mr. Nazerman. You really, really 's the greatest.

The character's name, Sol Nazerman, is a crucial indicator of how the filmmakers see him. The name "Nazerman" has a Christian connotation that renders Holocaust victims as the new, crucified Jesus. But Sol is a Jewish victim. Others sin against him. Unlike Jesus, who, according to Christian doctrine, died for others' sins, it was others sins that almost caused Sol to die.

Such an audacious comparison between Sol and Jesus, made explicit by a spindle later in the film (although this Nazerman does not die), is sure to offend many, but it also makes a powerful statement about the Holocaust. But Sol is more than a Jesus figure; he comes to stand as a God figure. It is his assistant, Jesus Ortiz, who is the one who dies. Their father-son relationship casts Sol in this new light. Still, it is startling that such blatant Christian imagery is connected to such a direct story about the Holocaust.

Despite the imagery and symbolism, the main character is a Jew. Nazerman is the story of Jew as victim, of a Wandering Jew now come to America and suffering still. It takes him feeling profound pain himself in order to approach the end of his guilt. As such, the film offers a powerful assertion of a Jewish identity. But because most American Jews did not themselves suffer through the Holocaust or even suffer in any comparable way in the United States, Sol Nazerman cannot serve as a source of American Jewish identity.

The Pawnbroker was the first non-documentary American film to show audiences scenes of a concentration camp. Everywhere Sol goes he is reminded of his experiences. A subway ride suddenly is transformed into his ride on a cattle car. There his son, a young boy, falls to his death. And if Sol is finally able to live with such memories and such pain, that does not mean it is ever erased or that he is ever whole.

Nor does it mean that the film makes a major contribution to Holocaust cinema, although ultimately it does. Still, its power as a document about the genocide of Jews is undermined by setting the picture in Spanish Harlem and implicitly making a moral equivalency between the camps and an American area filled with crime and struggling minority groups. In trying to tie the film to America, the filmmakers distort the uniqueness of the Holocaust without clarifying American life in any significant way. And yet, despite the pain in watching it, Rod Steiger's power as an actor

Four—The Oldest Hatred

is indisputable. He played a Jewish character in several films, and it is easy to see why. He is able to generate enormous sympathy for Sol Nazerman, letting American audiences close the emotional gap between themselves and Holocaust survivors if not victims.

It is not easy to make a film about the Holocaust. A movie needs to make money. But American audiences may not identify with Jewish characters. This is sometimes overcome by drawing a comparison to America, as in *The Pawnbroker*, or by focusing on a Gentile victim of the Holocaust.

This is what was done in *Sophie's Choice* (1982). Sophie has survived the camps and is in love with Nathan, an

Meryl Streep as Sophie and Kevin Kline as her Jewish lover Nathan in *Sophie's Choice* (ITC, 1982) have to deal with the heart-wrenching experience and the fateful decision she makes as a Nazi prisoner.

American Jew who keeps thinking about the Holocaust. Stingo, a young man and would-be writer, joins them, but Sophie's happiness is at risk because of her "choice"—what she had to decide when she was a prisoner of the Nazis. The "choice" is the most dramatic scene in the film, and reveals the center of Sophie's suffering and post-war trauma:

> SS OFFICER [to Sophie]: You're so beautiful. I'd like to get you in bed. Are you a Polack? You! Are you also one of those filthy communists? [The officer walks away.]
> SOPHIE: I am a Pole! I was born in Cracow! I am not a Jew. Neither are my children! They're not Jews. They are racially pure. I am a Christian. I am a devout Christian. [The officer comes back.]

SS OFFICER: You are not a communist? You are a believer?
SOPHIE: Yes sir, I believe in Christ.
SS OFFICER: You believe in Christ the redeemer?
SOPHIE: Yes.
SS OFFICER [looks at Sophie's children]: Did He not say, "Suffer the children, come unto me?" [Sophie remains silent.]
SS OFFICER: You may keep one of your children.
SOPHIE: I beg your pardon?
SS OFFICER: You may keep one of your children. The other must go away.
SOPHIE: You mean, I have to choose?
SS OFFICER: You are a Polack, not a Yid. That gives you a privilege, a choice.
SOPHIE: I can't choose. I can't choose!
SS OFFICER: Be quiet.
SOPHIE: I can't choose!
SS OFFICER: Make a choice. Or I'll send both of them over there. Make a choice.
SOPHIE: Don't make me choose! I can't!
SS OFFICER: Shut up! Enough! I'll send them both over there! I told you to shut up! Make a choice!
SOPHIE: I can't choose! Please! I can't choose!
SS OFFICER [to an officer]: Take BOTH children away! [Sophie clings tightly to her son. The Nazis take her screaming and crying daughter away from her.]
SOPHIE: Take my little girl! Take my baby!

As terrifying and horrible as this scene is, it is an example of what some Jewish observers complained about. In making Sophie so sympathetic, in making the scene so brutal, William Styron, the author of the novel on which the film is based, and the filmmakers made a film about the Nazis, about suffering even, but not about the Holocaust.

And yet it can legitimately be asked how the Holocaust can be understood. Here is one answer: by having double outsiders. The film is about a Polish-Catholic survivor and is narrated by a Gentile struggling to be a writer. And yet Sophie's "choice" is in a crucial sense a Jewish choice. And because her situation was precisely that of a Jewish woman, because the Nazi environment was precisely that faced by Jews, the film (and the novel) are interesting experiments in rendering the Holocaust more comprehensible for Gentile audiences. If there is a risk of making the Holocaust universal, there is also the benefit of rendering Jews more sympathetic. Such an effort is helped tremendously by the casting of Meryl Streep as Sophie.

Four—The Oldest Hatred

Streep had literally begged director Alan J. Pakula for the part (Styron had envisioned the bombshell actress Ursula Andress, and Pakula originally wanted Liv Ullmann).

It might be thought that America didn't need, and audiences didn't want, any more films about anti–Semitism in the United States.

School Ties (1992) is even odder because it goes back to the 1950s to discuss the subject, as though anti–Semitism were no longer a problem. The film is about a Jewish athlete at an elite prep school who witnesses cheating and won't reveal the culprit even when he is about to be punished. Dick Wolf, the producer and co-writer, used his own experiences as the basis for the movie. The film is more powerful than might be expected. Part of that results from the excellent cast that included Brendan Fraser, Matt Damon, Ben Affleck, and Chris O'Donnell.

The film is quiet and covers somewhat familiar ground, but it is underrated and deserves to be more widely remembered than it is. It captures a real moment in American culture very forcefully and forces viewers to confront the anti–Semitism that once infected some of the social class depicted so effectively in this film.

Schindler's List (1993) is perhaps the most famous film about the Holocaust. It returns to the idea of a Gentile as the focus of a Holocaust film. It received much acclaim, including seven Academy Awards. Among them were Best Picture and Best Director (Steven Spielberg). It is somewhat perverse, then, to begin with how the film was attacked.

In his study of "100 Greatest Jewish Films" for the online site *Tablet Magazine*, Liel Leibovitz put *Schindler's List* at the bottom and didn't restrain his dislike of the film:

> It would take a doctoral dissertation to elaborate on just how much is wrong with Steven Spielberg's astoundingly stupid Holocaust melodrama, and, certainly, many dissertations have been written on the director's films. Still, a highlight reel is in order: the baffling scene with the showers that turn out to be nothing more than showers; the soppy final scene in which actors and real-life survivors march together; the excessive use of Christian iconography; and the fact that the movie, really, is about a Christ-like gentile who saves a horde of hapless Jews who have no agency or resolve of their own. This makes *Schindler's List* not just one of the most ham-handed Holocaust films ever made but also, peculiarly, one of the least Jewish in sensibility. And yet, for all of its wretched awfulness, we couldn't help but include the film in our list; its massive visibility helped educate wide swaths of the population pre-

viously only dimly aware of the subject. It also drove Spielberg to invest his considerable resources in an infinitely more valuable kind of Holocaust-related filmmaking, namely the collection of videotaped testimonies by survivors, a singularly important historical enterprise. If the cost of these terrific resources is three hours of kitsch, death, and Liam Neeson, so be it.[10]

Such an indictment, though, does miss the film's power and Spielberg's virtuoso direction.

The film tells the story of Oskar Schindler, hardly a model citizen. He was a member of the Nazi party. He engaged in bribery, swindling, and much else as an industrialist. He gambled. He liked women. He really liked women. He was, in effect, a perfect man for the Nazis. He was seemingly without scruples. He was interested only in his own success. He should have been a willing cog in the Nazi war machine.

But somehow from the despicable person that was Oskar Schindler, a good person, a hero, emerged. He ended up preserving the lives of more

Sir Ben Kingsley (seated) as Itzhak Stern and Liam Neeson as Oskar Schindler in *Schindler's List* (Universal Pictures, 1993), director Steven Spielberg's brilliant Oscar winner for Best Picture about a flawed hero who rescues Jews during the Holocaust.

Four—The Oldest Hatred

than one thousand Polish Jews by employing them as workers in his factory.

The charge that the film takes away from the Holocaust by focusing on a Gentile is at least partially misplaced. What Spielberg has done, beyond bringing the subject to millions of people, is to raise a moral issue about those who let the Jews die. It's a crucial question. After all, if Oskar Schindler was able to see the horrors of Nazism, to see that what was being done was wrong, why didn't ordinary citizens? Schindler is the symbol of indifference. His very weaknesses make him a perfect candidate to be that symbol.

The film does not try to explain Schindler's motivation, only that he had it. Indeed, at one point he feels sorry that he did not save more Jews, even a single additional Jew:

> OSKAR SCHINDLER: I could have got more out. I could have got more. I don't know. If I'd just ... I could have got more.
> ITZHAK STERN: Oskar, there are eleven hundred people who are alive because of you. Look at them.
> SCHINDLER: If I'd made more money ... I threw away so much money. You have no idea. If I'd just...
> STERN: There will be generations because of what you did.
> SCHINDLER: I didn't do enough!
> STERN: You did so much.
> SCHINDLER [looking at his car]: This car. Goeth would have bought this car. Why did I keep the car? Ten people right there. Ten people. Ten more people. [He removes a Nazi pin from his lapel.] This pin. Two people. This is gold. Two more people. He would have given me two for it, at least one. One more person. A person, Stern. For this [He sobs.] I could have gotten one more person ... and I didn't! And I ... I didn't!

Kathryn Bernheimer offers an interesting assortment of potential motives for Schindler. Maybe, she suggests,

> Schindler was simply a weak man with no stomach for suffering. Maybe he enjoyed life so much he couldn't bear to see anyone deprived of the pleasure of living.... An arrogant egotist, he might have resented being told what he could and couldn't do.... Some survivors have even suggested he was trying to save his own skin after the war's inevitable conclusion. Then again, he may have been motivated by common decency or a latent sense of justice.[11]

Because the film focused on Schindler rather than the Jews, it would have improved the picture to have chosen a point of view and provided an explanation of Schindler's actions. Doing so would have put into relief why so many others didn't act. Without the explanation, we are left with admiration and gratitude but without understanding. And without understanding we have no permanent insights about the Holocaust.

But the critics of the film are wrong. Yes, the focus is on Schindler, but his character could not be shaped without the Jews. They are, in fact, the moral center of the movie, the vital element that transforms Schindler. It is the Jews who are the true moral heroes of the movie for they move Schindler. That is why *Schindler's List* is, in fact, a great film about the Holocaust, for it places the Jews in a new role — not simply as victims but as moral teachers, their key role in all of history. Had more of the focus been on how the Jews transformed Schindler, the picture would have been one of the greatest films about the Jewish role in the world above and beyond the movie's enormous educational role and artistic achievement.

Schindler's List comes close then to defining a Jewish identity, and not just a Jewish identity as victim. The identity as moral instructor based on Jewish texts and traditions is a clear, useful, and appropriate identity for American Jews. If only it had been more explicit in the film. If only the film had understood all that it had to offer.

The Pianist (2002) is based on a memoir and shows, in startling images, how the Nazis tried to destroy the Jews of Warsaw. The film is told through the eyes of a brilliant pianist who escapes death. The director, Roman Polanski, used not only the memoir but some of his own experiences as a boy trapped in Poland. During filming, Polanski even came across a man who had helped the Polanski family survive. The movie's technical excellence, the extraordinary acting by Adrien Brody, then the youngest-ever winner of the Academy Award for Best Actor, and the undeniable power of the imagery make *The Pianist* a very good film about the Holocaust.

But it has two faults. First, even with its power it doesn't expand our knowledge of the event. Indeed, there is a danger of Holocaust exhaustion, of having too many books and movies.

But, as Omer Bartov emphasizes, there is another side to the problem as well. The images and the power of the acting are to some extent undermined by a curious emotional detachment. As Bartov writes, "Polanski chooses to detach himself from [his Holocaust experiences] by telling the real story of another person, thereby avoiding any direct autobiographical link and preserving an emotional distance. Moreover ... [the] memoir, on

Four—The Oldest Hatred

which the film is based, is itself distinguished by an emotional aloofness that seems to suit Polanski's style."[12]

There have been various other films about the Holocaust, with many looking for a unique angle, a different story. To some extent they have succeeded, but all without going beyond what had already been said elsewhere. Still, each new story contributes in its own way.

Everything Is Illuminated (2005) has a different attitude to the past than other films about the Holocaust. First of all, it is set in the Ukraine, not Germany or Poland. And, as its very title implies, the film suggests that when we study the past our entire present is illuminated, clarified, and, when seen in this new light, makes sense. Even the suffering and murder discussed in the film, then, have at least some redeeming value in the present. The movie is more than a memorial.

Everything Is Illuminated is about Jonathan Safran Foer (the name of the author of the novel on which the film is based). Jonathan is a young American Jew interested in exploring what happened to his grandfather. All that he has as clues are a photograph and the village's name. To help him, the American hires an old man and his grandson. They are joined by the grandfather's bizarre dog.

Jonathan collects all the artifacts he can find, placing them in small plastic bags which will prompt his memories. Their search for the village, their encounter with an old woman, and the facts they learn about the slaughter in the Ukraine do indeed provide illumination. The two tour guides come to terms with the past, and the film becomes an invitation to audience members to do so as well.

The movie is also funny. It is not the first film that tries to mix humor with horror, specifically the horror of the Holocaust. Indeed, in 1972 Jerry Lewis created a movie titled *The Day the Clown Died*. That film, though, was never finished and has yet to see release. The idea of mixing comedy with the Holocaust somehow seems not only wrong but almost blasphemous. It works reasonably well in *Everything Is Illuminated*, perhaps because the humor is outside the environment of the camps and the time period.

At a certain point the idea of Jews simply as victims proved an insufficient identity for a depiction of Jews during the Holocaust. Two films emerged that saw the Jews as engaging, as they did in real life, in acts of self-defense.

Defiance (2008) was about the Bielskis, Jewish brothers in the forests of Eastern Europe who join the resistance. They try to build a village for self-protection and to protect Polish Jews who are fleeing from the Nazis. In the forest they built a school, a hospital, and a nursery. Twelve hundred survived because of the brothers.

Certainly part of the power of the film is that it is based on a true story, and the images are troubling and emotionally stunning. But even in pushing back at the notion that Jews were passive during the Holocaust, itself an accurate and useful purpose, the film is unable to offer much for American Jews beyond pride and historical knowledge. American Jews don't face any situation comparable to what's described in the film and so there is no part of their identity that can be built apart from seeing themselves as potentially subject to anti-Semitism. This identity is not helpful because it is not realistic and because it takes energy away from building an identity based on the real situation of American Jews.

Unlike *Defiance*, *Inglourious Basterds* (2009) is completely fictional in its efforts to show resistance to the Nazis. The film was written and directed by Quentin Tarantino and describes two plots to murder the entire Nazi leadership, including Hitler. One plot is concocted by a young Jewish woman who escapes the Nazis in the opening scene and becomes a proprietor of a cinema. The other plot involves a group Allied soldiers, all of whom are Jewish, led by a character played by Brad Pitt.

The film's opening scene with Christoph Waltz as the Nazi is mesmerizing and, unlike some of the exaggerated, even cartoonish, elements of the rest of the film, a blood-curdling portrayal of a crafty officer in search of hidden Jews. This scene, and some others, are juxtaposed against other parts of the film that are far removed from reality. This undercuts the movie as a moral one because morality requires a complex set of realities. *Inglourious Basterds* is an interesting film. Tarantino's technical excellence, his brilliant way with a camera, and the good cast make this a picture worth seeing. But it is not a film that makes any moral progress beyond what is available in understanding the Holocaust; it has no pretensions of making a statement about American Jewish identity.

The many films about the Holocaust reflect its place as a moral hinge of history. We can never quite look at humans in the same way again after it. Because of that there is a troubling aspect of making a fictional attempt to grasp it. The very limits of fiction itself are tested by the Holocaust, and perhaps the fictional imagination is not capable of equaling the imagination of evil. Even attempts to tell "true" stories about people who suffered offer too much emotional distance too often.

Four—The Oldest Hatred

The works of Elie Wiesel, starting with his memoir *Night*, provide the best ways to grasp some part of the Holocaust. Maybe it speaks well of us as humans that we can't grasp all of it.

The films of American anti-Semitism are generally good, but the era of overt and debilitating American anti-Semitism at least seems in the past. Swastikas are still painted. Jewish gravestones are overturned. Even explosive devices are sometimes planted near synagogues. Certainly anti-Semitism exists in the world. It is now often disguised using anti-Zionism or anti-Israel rhetoric. And Jews are genuinely in danger in various places around the world.

But in the United States Jews are relatively safe, free, and prospering. Surely their identity includes support for Israel and for Jews in any danger around the world; and, in that sense, films about the Holocaust and anti-Semitism keep American Jews ever alert to dangers.

But anti-Semitism can't provide the foundation of an American Jewish identity. More is needed for that.

CHAPTER FIVE

The Invisible Jews: Films About Assimilation

Every nation confronts the reality of newcomers. Sometimes those new to a country face hostility and suspicion. Sometimes, such as when cheap workers are needed, they are welcomed. Or rather, they are welcomed but with suspicion about how well they will fit in and what will happen when workers are no longer needed. Jews, in particular, had to be adept at moving. Subjected to hunger, persecution, and economic deprivation, they soon found the term "home" elusive. Their Promised Land, the Land of Israel, had been taken by the Romans, and the Jews had been forced to leave, sent into an exile, a dispersion known as the Diaspora. The Jews learned to prize that which was portable—their prayers and religion, their learning, their families—and to discount the material aspects of life which could be removed from them in a tragic moment.

But as the Jews moved, they were only partly accepted. Their skills, especially their financial skills, were needed, especially where Christians were forbidden by their religion to lend money. In all the countries where the Jews wandered, they were rarely left alone for a long time. For example, during the Crusades the rampaging soldiers headed to free Jerusalem from the Moslems wantonly slaughtered Jews along the way. And just as King Ferdinand and Queen Isabella were preparing to fund Columbus on a voyage, the royal pair were preparing an edict to expel unconverted Jews. The Jews were quickly expelled from Portugal as well. Even when they were allowed to stay for an extended period of time, even when they were invited to enter, as in the case of Poland, the Jews were a people apart. They learned the native language for commercial reasons but rarely interacted with the native populations. The Jews kept to themselves, carefully maintaining their religious traditions (as Tevye described them in *Fiddler on the Roof*). That was the Jewish fate. Never did they truly face much of a problem of assimilation in Eastern Europe.

As the Enlightenment spread across Western Europe, the situation for the Jews was different, depending on the country. Ironically, it was in Germany where they were more widely accepted. Still, there were strict limits on the borders of that acceptance. Many German Jews, barred from jobs, from social progress in the society because of their religion, converted to Christianity. The poet Heinrich Heine was among the most famous. And many Jews married a Gentile partner. That is, in Eastern Europe there was almost no assimilation. In Western Europe there was considerable assimilation. Indeed, assimilation came to have a specific meaning in Jewish life. It meant the separation of people from the Jewish community and their loss to the community. Assimilation was a zero sum game. You were either Jewish or you assimilated.

But America is a unique country. It certainly turned out to be very different for the Jews. Its foundation has been built not on an indigenous native population that retained power (its native population was mostly put on reservations; it had no political power whatsoever). Instead, America's political and economic power rested on successive generations of immigrants. Sometimes early immigrants looked down on later ones, and that prejudice found its way to acts of discrimination. Any "American culture" is mixed. But that is not to say there isn't an American ethos or American character.

America, by tradition, is a land in which immigrants were expected to surrender their language, their arcane customs, their ethnic uniqueness. In the last half-century that has changed, but what is pertinent is that from 1880 until 1920—that is, the era when the bulk of Jewish immigrants arrived in the United States—that traditional American view still pertained. It was, ironically, a British Jew named Israel Zangwill who gave prominence to the American view in his 1908 play *The Melting Pot*. The idea was that people from different cultures would come to the United States and their differences would melt so that everyone became simply an American.

The notion of a melting pot was challenged starting as early as the 1920s by the idea of cultural pluralism, an idea later more commonly called multiculturalism. These notions champion the retention of the foreign culture. But they come at the cost of feeling a part of the same culture as other Americans. That is, relatively early, there was a subtle shift in the meaning of assimilation for American Jews. Unlike Western European Jews, few felt any pressure or any compulsion to switch to the majority religion. There was a slow, steady acceptance of intermarriage, and then, starting around the 1960s, a very wide acceleration of such intermarriages. But, surprisingly, even such an act did not automatically mean that the Jewish partner in an intermarriage meant in any way to abandon Judaism. Sometimes they weren't very Jewish. But sometimes they were and they kept their faith. Ironically, there was even a modest increase in the number of Gentiles who converted to Judaism, a very rare event indeed in Europe.

American Jews generally wanted to keep on being Jewish. But they loved America's freedom, its unparalleled willingness to let Jews be judged on their abilities, not their religion. America had an open acceptance of differences that was so attractive. What were American Jews to do? Stay apart? Become American?

It is this struggle between wanting to maintain the tradition and wanting to be accepted that drove American Jewish attitudes as they arrived in the United States. They felt driven to assimilate. The heart of assimilation rested on linguistic, socio-economic, geographic, and romantic integration into the wider culture. And American Jews did all of these. They abandoned Yiddish in favor of English. When and where they were allowed to do so, they gleefully and very successfully entered the American economic system and found their way, very slowly, to the higher strata of society. They increasingly spread out from New York across the country. And in ever increasing numbers they intermarried with willing Gentiles who found the Jews very good marriage partners indeed.

There is a distinction for American Jews between assimilation and acculturation. In assimilation, generally most of the initial cultural markers disappear, and people who assimilate become part of the wider culture without much of their original culture left. Acculturation is a broader concept involving how a new or minority culture reacts to the wider culture. So assimilation is one part of acculturation, the part in which people reject the minority culture from which they came and adopt the cultural norms of the wider, or dominant, culture. For example, Jewish immigrants who assimilated rejected Jewish traditions and thought of themselves not as Jews but as Americans.

Separation is a form of acculturation in which people reject the dominant culture and so preserve their original culture. The idea of separation is sometimes psychological and sometimes literal, in the creation of ethnic

Five—The Invisible Jews

communities. For Jews this occurred on the Lower East Side of New York and later in the Catskills. It continues in some neighborhoods and in some Hasidic enclaves.

Integration, the preferred tactic of most American Jews, involves retaining a Jewish identity while simultaneously adopting American cultural norms. In sociology, this is sometimes termed biculturalism.

And finally, marginalization refers to those people who reject their birth ethnic culture and the dominant culture, and, as the name implies, feel they are on the margins of both. They are without a full identity at all.

For American Jews, assimilation and marginalization transform the identity question. With them, American Jews surrender their Jewish identity. But these identity issues are subtle and complex. Rarely is the choice quick or even conscious. And it has some historical context.

As David Dresser and Lester D. Friedman note:

> The emergence of a large Jewish community in America in the late nineteenth century might ... have looked like yet another example of the Diaspora—the exile from the Jewish homeland in Israel and the dispersion of the Jewish people across the globe that began with the destruction of the Second Temple.... But American Jewry, with a population larger than any in the world and its own rich cultural legacy, faced a new and distinct relationship to some fundamental aspects of traditional Judaism.[1]

Filmmakers have traced this identity option for a long while. Moviemakers have found many ways to get at the question of assimilation, of a dissolving Jewish identity in favor of adopting an American one. Even when such an effort was desired, it was not always so easy to let go of the past. And even when it was desired to keep Jewish traditions, it was not always so easy to ignore the alluring aspects of American culture.

One way to deal with such complex, frustrating and difficult circumstances is to laugh at them. For American Jews, the films of the Marx Brothers were a prime method of describing assimilation while easing its anxieties as a subject through humor.

The Marx Brothers got their start in vaudeville because of their mother Minnie's incredibly vision and drive. Minnie's brother, Al Shean, was a vaudeville comedian and evidently Minnie believed that if her brother could succeed then certainly her sons could. In 1905 she convinced her son Julius (later known as Groucho) to audition for a job as a singer.

While the ad she read noted that the person to be hired had to dance and Julius couldn't do that at all, Minnie ignored this minor flaw and pushed him. He got the job and was promptly abandoned in Denver. When he returned, Minnie made sure he took a job as an actor. Anyone, she assured him, could be an actor. Harpo started as a bellhop and at fourteen began playing piano to accompany silent movies. Soon the boys got together and formed a vaudeville act.

It was probably in Galesburg, Illinois, on May 15, 1914, during a poker game that the boys got their nicknames. Art Fisher, a monologist (the name for what would evolve into a stand-up comic), gave them the names. Fisher had a habit of following the style of "Sherlocko the Monk," a popular comic strip of the day, so a person's characteristic was given an "O" at the end. Harpo was easy — he played the harp. Groucho was named because he was always quarrelsome, though some in the family unconvincingly claimed the name's origin was the "grouch bag," a bag worn around the neck under clothing. Vaudevillians kept their valuables there when they went on stage because those valuables otherwise would disappear. Chico (pronounced "chick-o" not "cheek-o") was given his nickname because of his penchant to run after "chicks" (young, attractive women). Zeppo's nickname came either from the zeppelin or Zeppo, a well-known trained chimpanzee. Gummo's name came from his wearing gumshoes.

Except for Harpo, it is doubtful that the Marx Brothers would have progressed beyond their very successful Broadway career into the movies had sound films not been developed and proved so popular. Their first film, *The Cocoanuts,* was released in 1929. Groucho saw it on a Sunday afternoon and was so disappointed he decided to buy back the rights to the film so that it would no longer be shown. Indeed, movie exhibitors had loudly complained that Groucho had spoken so quickly that audiences were unable to understand what he said. But by the time all this was happening, Groucho learned the film was wildly successful, and the exhibitors saw audiences returning again and again to catch all of those lines they had missed.

But film was still in an experimental stage. A lot of paper was used in the making of props for the movie. All of it was soaked through to prevent a crinkling noise made by the paper that the sound equipment would pick up. There was no soundproofing in the New York City studio where the film was made, so the Marx Brothers had to film in the very early morning hours to prevent loud traffic noises from outside from disrupting the dialogue. Harpo wore his traditional red wig, but it turned out that

Five—The Invisible Jews

on film it looked very dark. Learning from this, in subsequent films Harpo wore a blond wig so that his hair looked lighter in color.

The film had its Jewish linguistic references. In this exchange, Groucho plays the Hammer character:

> HAMMER: All along the river, those are all levees.
> CHICO: That's the Jewish neighborhood?
> HAMMER: Well, we'll pass over that.

The Marx Brothers were not religiously Jewish in any traditional sense. Their identity as Jews depended on a sense of family, of belonging to an ethnic group, of being urban and linguistically fast. They mostly restrained their Jewishness in public. There is, of course, the famous story of Groucho attempting to bring one of his children to a club that didn't admit Jews, Groucho was told, that he couldn't use the swimming pool. His reply was that his child was only half-Jewish, so perhaps the child could walk in the pool up to his knees.

But the characters the brothers created were distinct and, at least to Jewish audiences, recognizably Jewish. Groucho was a cynical trickster, an irreverent wit who, without shame, sought wealth by seducing rich widows. He was a con man to the core. He made fun of all that was around him, especially romantic rivals or the powerful. He insulted people in rapid-fire quips. He uttered two more insults while his victims were trying to understand the first one. His glasses, cigar, and mustache were a disguise and made him funny in appearance. He was a sight gag, so that all he had to do was walk onscreen to get a laugh.

Harpo and Chico wore disguises as well. They were poor immigrants struggling to make sense of American life. They all feared their real selves would be exposed. They were outsiders trying to get in, and this feeling showed up in all their films. Zeppo, who didn't wear a disguise, soon enough left the act. The disguises spoke clearly to immigrant Jews who felt they had to hide their real selves, which they simultaneously feared might be discovered at any moment. The masks let audiences laugh at themselves and relieve their anxieties.

In a justly famous scene from *Horse Feathers*, Groucho, as a college president, is trying to get into a speakeasy, but Chico at the door needs a password:

> BARAVELL: [through speakeasy's door]: Who are you?
> PROFESSOR WAGSTAFF: I'm fine, thanks, who are you?

BARAVELL: I'm fine too, but you can't come in unless you give the password.
WAGSTAFF: Well, what is the password?
BARAVELL: Aw, no. You gotta tell me. Hey, I tell what I do. I give you three guesses. It's the name of a fish.
WAGSTAFF: Is it Mary?
BARAVELL: Ha-ha. That's-a no fish.
WAGSTAFF: She isn't? Well, she drinks like one. Let me see: Is it sturgeon?
BARAVELL: Hey, you crazy. Sturgeon, he's a doctor cuts you open when-a you sick. Now I give you one more chance.
WAGSTAFF: I got it. Haddock.
BARAVELL: That's-a funny. I gotta haddock, too.
WAGSTAFF: What do you take for a haddock?
BARAVELL: Well-a, sometimes I take-a aspirin, sometimes I take-a Calamel.
WAGSTAFF: Say, I'd walk a mile for a Calamel.
BARAVELL: You mean chocolate calamel. I like that too, but you no guess it. Hey, what's-a matter, you no understand English? You can't come in here unless you say, "swordfish." Now I'll give you one more guess.
WAGSTAFF: ...swordfish, swordfish ... I think I got it. Is it "swordfish"?

So seemingly imbued are the Marx Brothers with a Jewish sensibility — with a mocking attitude toward authority, with an anarchic approach to social conventions, with a humor ever at the ready as a weapon against the world's indifference and injustice — that it is startling to consider just how very few actual references to Jews there are in the Marx Brothers films. This is so, in part, because they often played immigrants struggling for money. In the films they were hungry for laughs and hungry for food. They wanted class, but those with it wanted to keep them as outsiders. They played music, but it wasn't the music that high culture wanted. They had little respect for anyone or any belief system. They were urban and streetsmart. They were filled with the energy of the frustrated, ambitious outsider.

But the real rebelliousness of the Marx Brothers came from something they never intended and audiences didn't quite grasp. Most of the Jewish comedians — George Burns, Jack Benny, and Ed Wynn, for example — wanted to and did pass in the wider society. Most of their audiences didn't know they were Jewish. Their material had no Jewish content or sensibility. They were the models for the fervent Jewish desire for assimilation then very common in the Jewish community.

But the Marx Brothers were counter-assimilationists. They didn't fit in. They weren't trying to change themselves to fit in with the wider society,

Five—The Invisible Jews

the very definition of assimilation. Instead they wanted the wider society to understand them as they were, complete with a Jewish sensibility, even if one that was not explicitly announced as Jewish.

To enhance their Jewish sensibility, the Marx Brothers reversed what the assimilationist comedians did. Jack Benny talked slowly, carefully. Groucho talked so rapidly audiences had trouble keeping up with him. Burns and Benny were clean-shaven. Groucho had a prominent greasepaint mustache, glasses, cigar, and dancing eyebrows. That is, he seemed to wear a mask to cover his real self. Burns and Benny had no mask nor need of one. The Benny character (as opposed to the real Jack Benny) was cheap. The Groucho character had no money to be cheap with.

> The Marx Brothers ... mirrored Jewish life. They were outsiders who didn't feel comfortable or fit into the wider society or, more commonly in Jewish history, weren't let into the society. Their assault on the kinds of political and social institutions that had been historically hostile to Jews was so fervent because the desire to attack them had been repressed for so long. Jewish audiences, then, could emotionally identify profoundly with the various assaults of the Marx Brothers. In ways they perhaps didn't understand, mass film audiences were beginning to absorb and appreciate a Jewish sensibility and see that its concerns were their own. The emotions unleashed by Jewish comedians strangely met the needs of American audiences. Those American depression audiences could suddenly understand the Jewish experience with poverty and feelings of powerlessness.[2]

This last point is important. It may seem odd for poor immigrant Jews to speak to the White Anglo-Saxon Protestants in the audiences for film (and vaudeville and radio). It makes some sense that Italian, Irish and other immigrant groups found a commonality with the recent Jewish arrivals, but the more settled American identification with Jews is more difficult to grasp.

Part of the problem rests on the definition of "immigrant." When we think of an immigrant, we picture someone arriving from overseas struggling to learn a new language and adapt to the culture, including the economic culture. But, more broadly, the age of immigrants in America was also the very same age of urban growth. Untold numbers of ordinary Americans left their farms and headed for work in America's cities. Metaphorically at least, they were immigrants as well. They struggled for jobs. They had to learn a new "language." With these combined groups of immigrants looking for an explanation, the question can be asked: What group in history learned to pick up, move to new lands, and adapt quickly, relying on themselves, their families, their hard work, and, perhaps most especially, their wits? To ask the question is to answer it. Oddly enough, the Jews fit the need for exactly what Americans wanted. As practiced immigrants they had many lessons to teach all Americans, and they did it with great humor.

Similarly during the Great Depression, all Americans had to learn how to accept poverty and survive. And what people had done that in history? Again, Jewish historical experience met specifically American needs. The Jews, oddly enough, spoke for all Americans.

Duck Soup (1933) is, by most accounts, among the very best of the Marx Brothers films. Its anti-government, anti-war sensibilities fit the Marx Brothers' attitude well, and reflected perfectly the feelings of most Americans as the Great Depression wore on. People were unhappy with how the federal government had handled the economy. Franklin Roosevelt had just taken office. (His inauguration was on March 4, 1933, and the film was released on November 17.) Most people didn't yet have faith that he could help them. And post–World War I feelings that America should not be involved in a European war stayed strong. Ironically, Adolf Hitler had come to power in Germany on January 30, 1933, but most Americans were not paying attention and simply didn't care what happened overseas. They wanted escape from their desperate poverty, from the guilt they felt at not being able to help their families. In some cases, families told older children to leave home. The young hobo became a common figure.

Jews interpreted *Duck Soup* in the same way, but with an addition. As did later audiences, especially young people in the 1960s, Jewish audiences could see in the film a social message, a belief that desperate times called for political action. It is unusual that for so politically conscious a people, so few explicitly Jewish movies are about political action. There were films like *Street Scene*, which attempted to lay bare desperate social circumstances with the intention to seek redress, but most movies of social drama were not explicitly Jewish. Perhaps filmmakers were reluctant to have Jews be identified with left-wing political movements. Such an identification, indeed, proved very trying for Jews during the McCarthy era and especially regarding the Rosenberg spy case of the 1950s.

But *Duck Soup* presented these social concerns in a humorous manner. The Marx Brothers were able to take Jewish interests and find ways to present them without incurring any political or social backlash. Poor

Five—The Invisible Jews

Margaret Dumont always played the wealthy, matronly, put-upon widow who was part of the American upper class and suffered incessantly from Groucho's insults, as in this exchange:

> DUMONT: I've sponsored your appointment because I feel you are the most able statesman in all Freedonia.
> GROUCHO: Well, that covers a lot of ground. Say, you cover a lot of ground yourself. You'd better beat it. I hear they're going to tear you down and put up an office building where you're standing. You can leave in a taxi. If you can't leave in a taxi you can leave in a huff. If that's too soon, you can leave in a minute and a huff. You know you haven't stopped talking since I came here? You must have been vaccinated with a phonograph needle.

In this film Dumont plays Mrs. Teasdale who has loaned the country of Freedonia a large enough amount of money that she can demand that Groucho (playing Rufus T. Firefly) replace the current president. Freedonia's enemy state seeks advantages and does so by sending two spies (Harpo and Chico). That is probably not a good spy plan, but it does result in a lot of laughs.

All of the Marx Brothers films in one way or another deal with assimilation, including what is probably their very best film. *A Night at the Opera* (1935) has the Marx Brothers as stowaways on a ship bound for America. It is the first movie in which Harpo is struck. The brothers bring two lovers together and mock the high culture of the opera world.

The film is filled with famous sequences, such as when everyone eventually falls out in features of a crowded stateroom. And is one of the most famous Marx Brothers dialogue exchanges, in which they mercilessly, mock lawyers. As Otis P. Driftwood, Groucho negotiates with Chico as Fiorello; Driftwood takes out contracts and hands a copy to Fiorello:

> DRIFTWOOD: Now here are the contracts. You just put his name at the top and you sign at the bottom. [Fiorello carefully looks at the contract.] There's no need of reading that because these are duplicates.
> FIORELLO: What does it say?
> DRIFTWOOD: Now pay particular attention to this first section because it's most important. It says, "The party of the first part shall be known in this contract as the party of the first part." How do you like that? That's pretty neat, eh?
> FIORELLO: No. It's no good.
> DRIFTWOOD: What's the matter with it?
> FIORELLO: I don't know, let's hear it again.

DRIFTWOOD: Says, "The party of the first part shall be known in this contract as the party of the first part."
FIORELLO: Sounds a little better this time.... Hey wait, wait! What does this say here? This thing here?
DRIFTWOOD: Oh that. Oh that's the usual clause ... that's in every contract. That just says ... eh ... it says ... eh.... "If any of the parties participating in this contract are shown not to be in their right mind, the entire agreement is automatically nullified."
FIORELLO: Well, I don't know...
DRIFTWOOD: "It's alright, that's in every contract! That's what they call a "sanity clause."
FIORELLO: Ha ha ha ha ha ha ha ha ... you can't fool me. There ain't no sanity clause!

It was dialogic exchanges like this that kept audiences returning to the theater to see a Marx Brothers film over and over.

But, alas, for Jewish audiences there was humor and release from anxiety, but there was no identity they could absorb. In a way, then, the Marx Brothers, with their lack of Jewish material and their release of anxieties that let Jewish audiences feel more comfortable in America, presented, a more subtle means of facilitating assimilation than the simple assumptions made by Benny and Burns that audiences could just decide to be American. The Marx Brothers were more psychologically subtle, more attuned to the depths of their audience's roiling minds. But, in the end, despite the Jewish sensibilities, despite the masks, the Marx Brothers were way stations for assimilation. The rebellion against America could be experienced and left in the theater. Jewish audiences didn't have to be anarchic. The Marx Brothers did it for them. That left the Jewish audiences free to be more like Burns and Benny.

If comedy did not work to aid assimilation, there were also dramas.

Body and Soul (1947) is about a Jewish boxer who faces difficult ethical choices about throwing a fight. This is certainly the first important film about boxing (in part because the sequences in the ring are so realistic). And it's certainly another great bit of acting by John Garfield. Exactly how much of a Jewish movie it is becomes another question. We barely know that the main character is Jewish. It is explicit and not just hinted at, but Charlie Davis' Jewishness is not focused upon.

Kathryn Bernheimer has an interesting interpretation of the film:

> With the Holocaust fresh in the American public's mind, *Body and Soul* sent out a message of Jewish resilience and integrity. The film expressed

faith in the future of the savaged Jewish people, represented by the fictional boxer. Davis has taken a beating, but he will not be defeated. He has allowed himself to be a victim, but he will end his career a victor. His body has been punished, but he will save his soul.[3]

This is an insightful viewpoint, for it assumes interpretive acumen on the part of the audience. That seems like quite a stretch, but it is significant because it illustrates a strategy American Jews have used to interpret not just films but American culture itself. It is a divided–self strategy. Jewish audiences see not just what's there, but a secondary interpretation not always obvious or even present to Gentile audiences. This strategy is sometimes misleading as in the case of *Body and Soul.* But it is useful in the case of the Marx Brothers, who had those masks, who did operate on multiple levels. American Jews have a complex ethnic identity. They don't just have to absorb an American identity but have to, separately, understand themselves as American Jews. Films that help them consider that, like *A Night at the Opera*, are worthy of deep interpretation. But films that seem to but really don't, like *Body and Soul*, should be appreciated on their own terms.

It is possible that the subject of assimilation is so painful that comedy is the best way to handle it and for Jewish audiences to deal with it. *The Producers* (1968) was Mel Brooks' first feature. The premise of the film is that two crooked producers struggle mightily to create a flop so they don't have to pay back their investors, all of whom have been promised a high percentage of the profits. This premise had been around Hollywood for decades; it was originally considered for a Marx Brothers film. Mel Brooks may not be the Marx Brothers, but his outrageous satirical style is perfectly suited to this film.

Mel Brooks was Woody Allen's rival for the title of great contemporary Jewish comedic filmmaker. He had worked for Sid Caesar, but eventually his career stalled. He considered a story he had written titled "Springtime for Hitler" and pondered transforming it into a novel which might then become the basis of a film. But as he considered the story, he noted that there was so much dialogue and so many quick scenes, that it seemed more appropriate for a film than a book. The story that would become *The Producers* was about an immoral theatrical producer who sold many times the 100 percent of shares in a play, and so as not to be caught he had to put on a play guaranteed to fail. The answer is obvious when he comes across a play about Hitler. But the producer doesn't grasp how low the

The Producers (Embassy Pictures, 1968) stars, left to right, Gene Wilder as Leo Bloom, Kenneth Mars as the mad Franz Liebkind, and Zero Mostel as Max Bialystock. Wilder and Mostel played the title producers who took money from too many investors. They have to create a flop, and they think for sure they have one in a musical titled *Springtime for Hitler*. Where did they go right?

culture has become. Patrons cannot distinguish between a horrific story and a clever parody, and the show becomes a huge hit. As Max Bialystock, the producer, asks, "Where did I go right?"

Brooks always liked to shock his audiences. But this was also a clever script, a parable about Jews who had suffered a series of failures until coming to America and achieving surprise success. Brooks liked what he had written and so took the script, still called *Springtime for Hitler*, to all the studios. They did not find dancing Nazis as funny as Brooks did. No one would listen to Brooks until he met the producer Sidney Glazier, who laughed as Brooks described what he wanted to do. Glazier convinced Brooks to direct, and the film was made.

Brooks has an interesting strategy in the film, one he will employ in many of his later pictures. He mocks anti-Semitism and traditional Jewish identities by making fun of them himself without waiting for others to do it for him. The characters in *The Producers* are Jewish stereotypes that, in anti–Semitic hands, would be seen as cruel and mocking. The manipulative Jew. The crass Jew. The flashy Jew. The Jew who lives off others' talents. But the characters are funny and likeable. This is due in part to the incredible acting skills of Zero Mostel and Gene Wilder. They are appropriately punished, but it's all in fun.

Perhaps most importantly, and perhaps what gets Brooks angry (not as angry as at the Nazis, but angry enough), is the fact that the manipulators are nicer than the manipulated. One of the truly horrific notions in the film is that the flop becomes a hit. The title of the intended Broadway flop was the same as the script's original title, *Springtime for Hitler.* The studio found this so offensive that they almost shelved the picture. The actor Peter Sellers stepped in because he loved it so much, but the title had to be changed. But audiences in the movie made *Springtime for Hitler* successful. American audiences, it might be concluded, have some underlying strain that found Nazism attractive. It is this propensity in humans that infuriates Brooks. He wants to fight it by pointing it out and holding it up to ridicule.

Underneath it, though, Brooks, perhaps unintentionally, is making a statement about American Jewish identity. He isn't willing to have Jews hide behind masks, to be quiet, to avoid making trouble. He wants to call out those who hate Jews, to make fun of them. Observers can legitimately disagree about Brooks' in-your-face approach. It does make some in the audience cringe. But even granting it success on its own terms, there are identity limits. Most Jews simply don't have Brooks' talent or chutzpah. The approach taken in the film is good for entertainment and for provoking discussions. It cannot, however, serve as a model for an American Jewish identity because most Jews don't want to or can't behave like this.

Brooks finds redemption in the film not from the audience but from the brotherhood of the two principal Jewish characters, the producers. This friendship is what is stable in the world. It remains a wall against the madness. And here Brooks is making an important statement about Jewish identity. Jews, he implies, need to bond, need to become a united family to stay strong because the world outside them is crazy and, actually or potentially, homicidal.

The two men can be seen in other ways as well. As Brooks himself suggested, "Maybe in having the male characters in my movies find each other, I'm expressing the longing I feel to find my father and be close to him."[4] Brooks' father had died when Brooks was two-and-a-half years old.

And there's still another way to interpret the male relationships in his films:

> The two males can be seen as parts of the same person struggling to find a way to live together. In the case of Bialystock and Bloom, both are Jewish, though one is the assertive insider and the other the passive outsider.... The assertive side "wins" in trying to trick the public, but both sides are eventually punished.[5]

But not every portrayal of Jews was intended to be kind, not every humorous look was intended to be warm. *Goodbye, Columbus* (1969) is as satirical as *The Producers*, but its wit regarding Jews is biting. Its tone directs anger toward the Jews not the Gentiles. It is a well-written film that lapses into stereotype the more it strays from Philip Roth's novella, on which it is based. Roth shared the same sensibilities as the movie, but his novella's short length did not allow for the fuller and even less pleasant portrayal of Jews that were seen in the film version.

The movie is about the clash of two Jewish worlds, one nouveau riche and the other still poor. A generous interpretation of *Goodbye, Columbus* concludes that Roth and the filmmakers were horrified at the moral and spiritual costs of assimilation even while they simultaneously found that they didn't fit into the traditional Jewish life their parents or grandparents had lived.

Still, the film is unusual in its uninhibited look at American Jewish life. There are no Jewish sensibilities hiding behind a Gentile character. The film deserves a lot of credit for its direct, if sometimes cringe-worthy, portrait of an upwardly mobile suburban Jewish family. But the courage it took to make the movie is the same courage Roth needed to make the Jews unpleasant.

This was a painful mirror for some Jews to see, and some observers accused both the novella and the film of reinforcing anti–Semitic stereotypes. Additionally, while Roth paints an unforgiving portrait of those American Jews who have surrendered their spirituality for money and status, his viewpoint isn't wholly clear. He has no answers because he is not in favor of returning to the old ways, and the new way of money is unsatisfying. We are left with a simple story mostly (though not exclusively) of stereotyped characters. The power of the story lies precisely here, though. Roth refuses answers that don't satisfy. He raises uncomfortable questions others simply ignore or, worse, pretend are not really questions. There is no identity answer in *Goodbye, Columbus*, but there are many questions.

Mel Brooks returned to his satirical self with *Blazing Saddles* (1974). In spoofing the Western, an archetypical American form, Brooks is using the classic technique of having minority groups mock the majority. He does this also by making fun of the town's racism after a black sheriff is appointed. It's no accident that Brooks himself plays a Native American in a scene, and, to make his point about minority groups, has the character speak Yiddish (wear a headband emblazoned with the Hebrew words meaning "Kosher for Passover"—except that Brooks, ever the trickster, has reversed the letters of what in English are the "K" and the "P"). It is this unifying of the outsiders in society that is the message of *Blazing Saddles*. The result is not so much a melting pot of America but a melting pot of minority groups within America who become one in order to protect themselves and fight for joint causes: the eradication of prejudice and discrimination, equality of opportunity, and so on. The message is that together, using their brains, united minority groups can overcome the power of the majority. Such an approach of blending minorities is a subspecies of assimilation and as such doesn't provide a unique American Jewish identity.

Blazing Saddles was Brooks' breakthrough film. He accomplished this by shifting forms. *The Producers* was a satire. It poked fun at various social conventions, but there was a serious message under the fun. *Blazing Saddles* was a spoof. It also poked fun at those conventions but without an accompanying serious message. A spoof also is different from a parody, its close relative, by not closely following what was the original product. In spoofing the Western, Brooks didn't so much seek to attack anyone, though clearly racism is attacked in the film. Brooks was after pure humor, letting audiences laugh as a way of releasing the anxieties they had brought with them to the theater from everyday life. Brooks didn't offer Woody Allen's therapy. His was a simpler way to approach anxiety.

In finding the spoof form in *Blazing Saddles*, Brooks had also found a perfect way for him to present his view of integrating an American and a Jewish identity. As a comedic form, the spoof connects two subjects that are related, the object that is being spoofed and the spoof itself. If America is considered the object being spoofed and Jews those who do the spoofing, then Jews can be seen as mocking the wider society but with no revolutionary intent, no desire to change it. Additionally, spoofing provides Jews with an aesthetic distance from America, the object being spoofed, so as not to be absorbed by the country. In Brooks' conception, then, an American Jewish identity makes Jews permanently partial insiders and simultaneously permanently partial outsiders. This identity allows Jews a connection to the country without disappearing in it, though the tenuous nature of the dual identity is never explored in Brooks' films.

Brooks' humor in this and other movie was different from Woody Allen's humor. For Allen, anxiety in life was always present. No matter what his characters did, especially in regard to romantic relationships, they could not genuinely enter society. Brooks had another message entirely. Brooks attracted the same alienated audience as Allen did, the same people who felt like outsiders. But Brooks produced a message of good humor and tolerance, of welcoming. In Brooks' films you could overcome your anxiety and enter society. Brooks also differed from Allen's humor in the use of sometimes crude vulgarity, as in the most famous scene in *Blazing Saddles*—the symphony of cowboy flatulence around a campfire. The scene made audiences laugh, but critics didn't like it. Of course, this, to some extent, was a matter of class. Brooks was dealing with blue collar humor, while Allen (and the critics) preferred more intellectual comedy.

Identity meshing is not quite the same as identity confusion, but assimilation produces both. The confusion is seen in a fascinating if lesser-known film, *The Man in the Glass Booth* (1975). Clearly inspired by the capture of the Nazi war criminal Adolf Eichmann, the writer and actor Robert Shaw wrote the play on which the film was based. The movie is about Arthur Goldman, who is a Jewish survivor of a Nazi death camp. Goldman is now living in New York and is wealthy. Suddenly, Israeli agents take him to Israel, accusing him of being a Nazi war criminal. Much of the movie is set in the courtroom where Goldman's trial takes place and in which he sits protected in a glass booth. The ending is a surprise; Goldman's genuine identity causes him profound tension when it is revealed in the courtroom.

The problem with the film is a moral one. With a survivor's guilt (which serves as a partial exculpation and explanation of Goldman's behavior), Goldman illustrates a complexity in human motivation. It appears, in the film's world, that guilt and innocence are not as easily understood or assigned as most people believe. And yet such a claim undermines a bright line between victim and executioner, as though there is a little of both in each. Such a claim provides a moral escape hatch for Nazis. Surely, it is possible to recognize that humans have a violent side without confusing those who act violently with those against whom they commit violence. The lesson for Jewish identity is to allow some complexity without erasing the boundaries between the two parts.

Not all films were as concerned with moral complexities. *The Front* (1976) is about a cashier named Howard Prince (wonderfully played by Woody Allen) who fronts as a television writer for several blacklisted friends. This is a movie with a clear moral divide between good (those victims of the blacklist) and bad (those who did the blacklisting or went along with it).

There is a certain poignancy to the film because some of those involved in its production were themselves blacklisted. They include the writer Walter Bernstein, the director Martin Ritt, and the actors Zero Mostel (who once again is absolutely stunning in his portrayal of the doomed comedian Hecky Brown), Hershel Bernardi (who bravely took the role of a television executive willing to go along to survive), Lloyd Gough, and Joshua Shelley.

Furthermore, some of the incidents of the film were taken from real life. The most moving involved Hecky Green going to a hotel room. This incident is based on what happened to one of Mostel's real-life friends, the actor Philip Loeb, who had been blacklisted and subsequently resigned from the popular television show *The Goldbergs*. Loeb became deeply depressed, in part because he provided sole support for his son, who was mentally disturbed. In 1955, Loeb committed suicide in the Taft Hotel in New York City. Unlike the Hecky character, Loeb swallowed an overdose of sleeping pills. He did not leave a suicide note.

One interesting aspect of the movie, beyond Prince's unexpected heroism, is that despite the fact that it dealt with a serious subject and was strongly felt, it had many comic moments, most of them unsurprisingly supplied by Woody Allen's perfect delivery of some very good lines. Oddly, there are very few direct political statements. This isn't meant to be a semi-documentary but an entertaining movie. As such, the humor might be said to undermine the seriousness, although more precisely it serves to make the subject more understandable and the characters more sympathetic.

And yet the film doesn't play up the obvious Jewishness of virtually all the characters (and, in many cases, the actors). For these characters, their identity wasn't as a Jew, it was as a blacklisted actor.

As in some other films, some of the lines border on, or cross the line into, anti–Semitic stereotyping, such as when Prince meets a woman he likes who works for a television show:

> HOWARD PRINCE: Where are you from?
> FLORENCE BARRETT: Connecticut.
> PRINCE: That's very ritzy.
> BARRETT: It's very proper anyway. I was very well bred—the kind of family where the biggest sin was to raise your voice.
> PRINCE: Oh yeah? In my family the biggest sin was to pay retail.

As such, *The Front* had no unique contribution to make to a study of American Jewish identity.

The Front also showcase an unusual species of assimilation. Many American Jews tie their identity to a commitment to social justice and equality. This sounds very much like political liberalism, and, indeed, for many American Jews there is little differentiation between liberalism and Judaism. These Jews have come to see Judaism identified with social progress as they understand it. This interpretation of Judaism is understandable since there is so much emphasis, especially among the prophets in the Bible, on feeding the hungry, taking care of the stranger, visiting the sick, and so on. Being kind, char-

Gene Wilder as Rabbi Avram Belinski makes a point in *The Frisco Kid* (Warner Brothers, 1979). The film is an underappreciated gem about a Polish rabbi headed to San Francisco who becomes best friends with an outlaw, played by Harrison Ford. The clash and ultimate connection between Jewish and American values is told with heart and humor.

Five—The Invisible Jews

itable, socially conscious, and attuned to the need for freedom in the fullest sense of the word are certainly genuine Jewish concerns. But they are not the sole identity of Judaism, and the confusion of social liberalism with Judaism is an inadequate Jewish identity and an inaccurate one. But it is crucial to note that such an identity is, in fact, the Jewish identity of many American Jews.

All Jewish identity starts with a sensibility. In *Blazing Saddles*, Mel Brooks tried to marry a Jewish sensibility and an American movie genre. The result was a comic success but without substantive comments on a Jewish identity. But *The Frisco Kid* (1979) was an incredibly interesting and entertaining example of how to blend Jewish and American values. At the end, though, the Jewish protagonist relents on his religious values in the face of American realities.

The Frisco Kid is a buddy film, a comedy with great acting from Gene Wilder as Rabbi Avram Belinski and Harrison Ford as Tommy, a bank robber and generally tough Western hombre. Poor Rabbi Belinski isn't in America long on his way to a new pulpit in San Francisco when he gets robbed. He then meets Tommy, and together the two make the journey west.

The pivotal moral moment comes when Rabbi Belinski, whose life has been saved by Tommy, has a sudden self-realization. He declares: "When those men were shooting at you, I ran and saved the Torah.... I care more about a book than I do for my best friend." And there, in that declaration, is the movie's theme: a lifetime of dedication to religious objects is meaningless and wrong when compared to helping a friend. It's a warm human message and an interesting illustration of how Orthodoxy became Americanized.

Patricia Erens has correctly located the film's importance: "*The Frisco Kid* is one of the few films to seriously question the difference between Jewish and American values, finding neither inherently superior. In the end, Avram has come to terms with a composite system which takes into account both traditions."[6]

The best example of this comes at the end of the movie when the Rabbi experiences an internal struggle. He has arrived in San Francisco. He finds a beautiful bride to marry. But he feels he cannot truly take on the duties of a rabbi because he has killed someone. The last of the outlaws who stole from him appears, and it looks as though there will be, in true Western tradition, a gunfight to settle the dispute. That is an American value. But Avram draws on Jewish tradition, specifically from Solomon's wisdom. He makes a deal with the outlaw: the rabbi will keep San Francisco, and the outlaw has control of the rest of America. The outlaw accepts. Jewish wisdom has triumphed.

It's a good ending. But throughout the film Avram has been trying, in a comic but sincere way, to explain what Judaism's beliefs are. Here is his exchange with a Native American:

> CHIEF GRAY CLOUD [in reference to Avram's god]: What does he do?
> AVRAM: He ... He can do anything!
> CHIEF GRAY CLOUD: Then why can't he make rain?
> AVRAM: Because he doesn't make rain. He gives us strength when we're suffering. He gives us compassion when all that we feel is hatred. He gives us courage when we're searching around blindly like little mice in the darkness ... but He does not make rain!
> [Thunder and lightning begin, followed by a downpour]
> AVRAM: Of course ... sometimes, just like that, he'll change His mind.

Avram seems unable to avoid teaching. He even tries this with a chicken:

> Chicken, chicken, chicken! Chickie-chickie-chickie-chicken! Come here,
> [*sing-songs*] I don't want to hurt you, I just want to eat you.
> [*He repeats in Yiddish, and 'chicken' flies away.*] Come here, wait! I don't want to hurt you! I just want to make you kosher!

In a subtle, comedic way, the film is very important. It refuses to blend American and Jewish values. It refuses simply to submerge Jewish values, to have them melt into a pot. But it doesn't exactly keep Jewish values unvarnished either. The negotiation between an American and Jewish identity in the film is complex, and in a way it is too simple to serve as a model for Jewish life.

But it's a start. With the film, audiences can grapple with how to mix the identity, what a unified identity would look like, and, ultimately, to question whether such a mix should be made in the first place.

Whereas *The Frisco Kid* looked back into American history to search for questions of identity, *Private Benjamin* (1980) was very contemporary, looking directly at the question of how Jewish women should be treated. Goldie Hawn plays Judy Benjamin, a spoiled and sheltered Jewish woman whose husband dies on their wedding night. Overcome with grief, Judy joins the army. Judy comes from a *Goodbye, Columbus* Jewish world and grows as she enters the tough reality of American life. The Jewish life she led kept her from growing up, but the American life forces her to do so. The film is a tribute to assimilation. To drive home the point, Judy meets a French-Jewish doctor who cheats on her. That is, the Jewish values that harm her are not just American. The Jewish-American Princess disappears; the Jewish Prince stays the spoiled, self-indulgent, hormone-driven adolescent.

The film can be seen as a feminist film, so that Judy's maturity is not so much from a Jewish world as from an American world that keeps women subjugated as girls unless they go through a rigorous test, as provided by the army. If it is a feminist argument, it is watered down by having Judy be Jewish. Her Jewishness inevitably makes the character stereotypical.

The film's argument becomes that Jews are spoiled by their culture and need to go through the rigors of America to grow up. That is not a message most American Jews want to hear or even need to hear, though it is doubtful many heard it because the movie is a successful comedy and Goldie Hawn is, as always, charming.

It should be noted that many films about assimilation are disguised so they appear to be about other subjects. One example of this is Steven Spielberg's *E.T.: The Extra-Terrestrial* (1982). The film is, of course, about a boy who meets a small lost alien. It is a charming film, but one about Jewish identity? Re-consider it this way: Suppose the film were described in an alternate manner as one about an immigrant who arrives in America and is lost, friendless, unable to speak the language and wants desperately to go back home to a place that is recognizable and safe. Authorities don't trust the immigrant, who remains hidden as he discovers friendship and learns the ways of the new land. Now this little fantasy has new meaning. That's what makes writing about Jewish films so elusive and difficult. Many movies can be interpreted through the lens of assimilation, and in this case because the film was made by Steven Spielberg through the lens of a Jewish sensibility. That is not to say the movie is a Jewish picture, but its alternate interpretation does make the borderlines of what constitutes a Jewish film more confusing.

Zelig (1983), on the other hand, is a Jewish film of crucial importance. Indeed, it is perhaps the most astonishing film ever made about Jewish assimilation. It took a long time for Woody Allen to get there, although he had taken some major steps along the way, such as *Annie Hall,* which will be discussed later.

Allen started his career as a stand-up comedian and developed a cul-

Woody Allen holds some pumpkins as the title character in *Zelig* (Orion Pictures, 1983). The film has some of the most ingenious cinematography in movie history as it tells the story of a man who blends into his surroundings, literally transforming himself to look like those he's with.

tural stance in which urban, alienated, left-wing Jews were the stand-ins for all decent humanity. It was a simplistic view, but one many of his early viewers found congenial. Allen figured out a way to represent the various identity crises felt by his generation of American Jews. His parents' generation felt anti–Semitism in a way he didn't. That earlier generation eagerly wanted to assimilate. Allen's generation wasn't so sure it was worth it. They were aliens, but not in a land of a foreign tongue. They were aliens in a land of strange gadgets and mysterious foreign (that is, long-time American) women.

American Jews faced an enormous strain on their identities, although many didn't know it. As inheritors of the Jewish heritage, they were part of the chosen people. This wasn't a designation of superiority, but one of mission and obligation. They were, as part of that people, of supreme historical importance, playing a pivotal role in the redemption of humanity. As Americans they were newcomers, statistically laughably small. In a Jew-

Five—The Invisible Jews

ish world they read shared texts, attached themselves to a people and felt their own fate was contingent on the fate of that people, and looked back at a shared history, along with, to some extent at least, a shared consciousness. As Americans, they had mostly a very limited shared history. For most American Jews of Allen's youth, that history stretched back less than a century. They didn't share the many experiences of the Christian year, the Christmas trees, the Easter ham, the Sunday service in church. They didn't have a shared consciousness. Therefore even Jews who had left Jewish life, much less Jews trying to conjoin a Jewish and American identity, felt caught between two worlds, and those worlds were often in conflict.

Allen's generation of American Jews was the first generation truly free to become all they could be. They had the opportunities American society was famous for extolling. Furthermore, in the 1960s, as Allen's fame emerged, American Jews were not only accepted but also widely admired. They were considered sober, industrious, intelligent, neighborly, funny, and faithful. They were, that is, considered to be highly suitable marriage partners.

This freedom and acceptance, so long sought and so long denied, was unexpectedly accompanied by guilt at leaving their Jewish life. Their living parents or grandparents were sometimes painful reminders of what they were giving up, as well as how far they had traveled in American culture.

It is this sense of being unfaithful that captures their feelings. Woody Allen reflected it most often in stories of romantic relationships involving desire for others or outright adultery. This subject matter made his films more popular than they might have been had he stuck to sociological themes of Jewish assimilation, but the unfaithfulness, the difficulty with forming a stable relationship, reflected the Jewish relationship with America. The Jewish partner's faithlessness reflected an abandonment of the Jewish heritage.

Jews may have completed their assimilation very thoroughly in the 1960s. After all, large numbers had abandoned the traditions of their parents or grandparents. They were comfortable in the rhythms of American life, not Jewish life. They wanted and were wanted by Gentile romantic partners.

But the culture pulled a surprise. Just when religion had walked offstage for many, ethnic identity arose. This began, by most accounts, with African Americans re-discovering what it meant to be proud of being black. Armed with a newfound pride in themselves, blacks joined with others who wished to help them obtain civil rights. It was their pride that allowed their justifiable anger to be channeled into political activity that succeeded. That ethnic pride soon became infectious. Jews were among the groups that developed an ethnic pride. Some Jews understood that blacks had uncovered a truth they had abandoned: that their heritage was not to be casually dismissed. Jews began to find a pride in being Jewish to replace the shame that some of them had felt at being apart from other Americans.

Many American Jews went through this process of ethnic identification without being fully aware of what was happening to them. Like Woody Allen himself, they went for regular therapy when they needed ethnotherapy. They didn't fully grasp how being raised as Jewish had affected and shaped them, how deeply their heritage was involved in defining their selves, how crucial it was to reconcile with their Jewish selves for their full personalities to function in the society. They thought that because they didn't go to synagogue or keep the Sabbath or keep kosher that they weren't Jewish. But they were — in ways apart from practices, which were really institutionalized methods of preserving an identity. They confused the institutions with the identity itself. Like almost all of the characters Woody Allen portrayed, they needed to understand that identity, embrace it, and "talk" to it as they integrated it into a wider personal identity. They accepted what the majority had said about them. Woody Allen, unsurprisingly, was sometimes accused of self-hatred because he didn't embrace being Jewish. He has often claimed his self-hatred existed, but that it wasn't because he was Jewish. In that, he was completely correct, but the missing part is that it perhaps might also have existed because he didn't adequately explore what being Jewish meant to him.

That is why Allen's characters fail. They are independent, funny, artistic, and even (in a word not often applied to Allen's characters but nonetheless accurate) brave. That is, they thought of themselves as able to ignore their own social identities and the forces of society that saw them as Jewish. In this dismissal they were wrong. Allen's characters simply do not grasp that their anxieties could be reduced by a deeper grasp of the effects of a Jewish identity on their lives and an appreciation for that identity.

Of course, it is unfair and oversimplifying to suggest that Allen's characters are defined by their inability to select a stable identity or carefully examine the nature of their Jewish identity. Allen's very strengths rest on his ability to allow audiences to identify with the character in a

Five—The Invisible Jews

variety of ways. The characters are prisms through which audience members can see the reality of their lives, distorted as in a funhouse, to be sure, but nonetheless humorously and sometimes painfully recognizable. Despite this, seeing all the identity tensions as central to Allen's films gives them a thematic unity and a clarified way of interpreting them. The fight between identities, for example, sheds a new spotlight on Allen's struggle between making the comedies his audiences want (and that reflexive part of his personality) and the more serious films that he desperately wants to make as an artist (and the inherent limitations of his abilities to make a film as good as, say, Fellini's).

Allen's inclusion of identity issues can be seen even in very early Allen films. *Take the Money and Run* (1969) is a loosely-connected series of comic bits. The mock documentary approach tells the story of Virgil Starkwell, surely the country's most incompetent criminal. Allen is interesting here. He taps into a Jewish identity not often discussed in a comic way: the American Jew as criminal (this book offers a chapter on this subject). But it should be noted that Allen's vision of the Jew as the alienated outsider is already visible in this film. Virgil, at least in his own way, also struggles with assimilation and acceptance. The film's narrator notes about him: "He wants nothing more than to belong, if only to a street gang." There are some fleeting Jewish references, the most interestingly visual one of which occurs after Virgil agrees to undergo an experiment so that his prison term can be reduced. The result is that he becomes a rabbi for a few hours. This leads to a shot of Virgil in full Hasidic garb. Virgil is beyond being a criminal, he is also a prisoner. It's a perfect Woody Allen metaphor for life. He's trapped but desperately wants to escape from metaphorical prisons—from his own self, from parents who don't approve of him, from a world in which he doesn't quite fit, from an identity he doesn't feel is a real part of him. He thinks all of this can be overcome through the redemptive act of romantic love, but, as most Allen heroes will eventually learn, love is not a strong enough force. In the original ending planned for the film, Virgil and his love are killed.

These themes occurred in many Allen movies and led up to *Zelig*, the most important of his films about Jewish identity In *Zelig*, Allen has made a faux documentary about an extraordinary man, Leonard Zelig, whom can take on the appearance of those with who he comes into contact, and mix in to any surroundings. Supposedly in the film Zelig was a human chameleon who became a phenomenon in the '20s and '30s.

Allen got the idea from some specials Time-Life was making for HBO. For the shows, Dick Cavett, a friend of Allen's, served as host, and as part of the filming it appeared as though Cavett truly appeared in the historical footage that was shown. This is the photographic basis for much of *Zelig*.

Of course, Leonard Zelig is Jewish, but beyond the literal identity, he is a perfect metaphor for the Jew undergoing assimilation. Zelig's identity disorder is exactly that of Jews struggling in a Gentile society. And why does Zelig blend in? "I want to be liked," he says. He wants to be like others. He doesn't want to stand out. This is the cry from the heart of someone on his way to assimilation. With Woody Allen's comic exaggerations, the effort becomes simultaneously hilarious and horrifying.

It is not that Jewish life is presented as wonderful and the assimilationist pressures unfair. In the film Leonard tells this story: "I'm twelve years old. I run into a synagogue and ask the rabbi the meaning of life. But he tells it to me in Hebrew. I don't understand Hebrew. He wants to charge me $600 for Hebrew lessons."

To make all this explicit, Allen has the writer and critic Irving Howe deliver an interpretation of Leonard Zelig: "His story reflected a lot of the Jewish experience in America, the great urge to push in and to find one's place and to assimilate into the culture. I mean he wanted to assimilate like crazy."

Leonard is "cured" only by the dedicated love of a (Gentile) woman. It is a reconciliation with assimilation that stops his internal struggle. He wanted to assimilate, and he succeeded.

Woody Allen has not been characterized as a champion of Jewish life. But there is a way to read this film to see it as extraordinarily sympathetic to Jewish fears of the wider society and the psychological pain American Jews have to go through. It is also a film about self-hatred, about disliking oneself so much that you desperately want to be anyone else. The movie takes it to an extreme to make its point; Zelig becomes a member of the Nazi party and is seen behind Hitler during a speech.

Read this way, and sifting out the mockery of American Jewish life such as the money-grubbing rabbi portrayed for comedic purposes), this is a profoundly serious and excellent film. In some ways it is one of the most important American Jewish films ever made.

Biloxi Blues (1988) is the second part of a trilogy of films based on Neil Simon's plays. Simon generally employs the strategy of creating Jewish characters but giving them neutral names and making no explicitly Jewish references to their lives. *Biloxi Blues*, like *Private Benjamin*, is about a Jewish character in the army who finds the experience has a way of providing maturity. There is intolerance in the army near the end of the Second World War, as seen in the film. Eugene Jerome's experiences at a Mississippi boot camp are not enjoyable. But if Eugene is a Jew with one foot in Jewish life and the other in American life, Simon interestingly creates a character named Arnold Epstein who is not the timid Jew, not the Jew ready and willing to hide behind a punch line. He is not, that is, the typical Neil Simon sort of Jew. "The army has its logic. I have mine," Arnold says. The unusual conundrum for Simon is how his alter ego Eugene will deal with a proud Jew, one who won't hide, one who is Jewish before he's anyone else.

Epstein is Eugene's mentor and even his writing coach:

> EUGENE: Why is it that we come from the same place but I can't understand you?
> ARNOLD: You're a witness. You're always standing around watching what's happening, scribbling in your book what other people do. You have to get in the middle of it. You have to take sides. Make a contribution to the fight.
> EUGENE: What fight?
> ARNOLD: Any fight. One you believe in. Until you do you'll never be a writer, Eugene.

The interplay can be read psychologically, as though Simon the writer can't achieve a breakthrough until he finds his Jewish self. And that's an interesting message for Jewish identity — that all attempts at assimilation result in Jews just being witnesses to their own lives and to existence itself. It is only when they take a stand as a Jew will they ever lead a full life. This is an unusually assertive statement by Simon, one he doesn't carry through in later pictures, but it's an important step in understanding the importance of keeping a Jewish identity in America.

In contrast to Arnold Epstein, Daisy Werthan in *Driving Miss Daisy* (1989) is tied not to a Jewish identity but to a southern one. That doesn't mean that her neighbors don't think of her as Jewish, but she doesn't use her Jewishness to define herself. The movie is a warm tale of the relationship between Miss Daisy and her African American chauffeur. (Both Jessica Tandy and Morgan Freeman, acting as the pair, add immeasurably to the film's appeal.)

There are interesting moments in the film when Daisy's Jewish radar makes viewers acutely aware that she knows the world around her very well. Here is one bit of dialogue in which she is talking with Hoke, the chauffeur, about her daughter-in-law Florene. Like many Southern Jews, Florene and her husband Boolie have a tree at Christmas and celebrate the holiday with a party. Note also the use of a Jewish stereotype. As they're driving, Miss Daisy sees houses with extravagant displays of Christmas lights:

> DAISY: Everybody's wishing the Georgia Power Company a Merry Christmas.
> HOKE: I bet Miss Florene got 'em all beat with the new house.
> DAISY: If I had a nose like Florene's, I wouldn't go around wishing anybody a Merry Christmas!
> HOKE [laughs]: Yes'm ... but, I tell ya, I do enjoy a Christmas at their house.
> DAISY: Of course, you're the only Christian in the place!
> HOKE: Well, they got that new cook.
> DAISY [sighs]: Florene never could keep help. Of course, it's none of my affair. Too much running around, if you ask me.
> [Hoke agrees.]
> DAISY: The Garden Club this, the Junior League that ... as if any of them would give her the time of day! But, she'd die before she'd fix a glass of iced tea for the Temple Sisterhood! I just hope she doesn't get it into her head to *sing* this year!
> HOKE [as they are arrive at Boolie and Florene's house and see an ostentatious show of lights]: Oh, Lord, look what Miss Florene done done!
> DAISY: If her grandfather, Old Man Freitag, could see this ... what is it you always say?... he'd jump up out of his grave and snatch her bald-headed!

There is a complex set of feelings about being Jewish here, more complex than what's found in most of the film. Miss Daisy is proud of being Jewish and wants her daughter-in-law to be more Jewish, but Miss Daisy herself finds her friendship with Hoke, not a Jewish man. As in other movies, the Jewish identity is tied directly to the Jewish connection to justice, in this case racial tolerance in the South.

The film won the Best Picture and Best Actress Academy Awards because it told an American story.

Driving Miss Daisy is not a complex film filled with symbolism. Nor is it, over time, particularly thought provoking. It is certainly moving, and its message of racial harmony is obviously important, but as a work of art it is not a dense film.

Five — The Invisible Jews

Woody Allen may not be Federico Fellini, but a surprising number of his pictures do provide extraordinarily provocative characters, moral dilemmas, and portraits of Jews that invite analysis and discussion. It is, of course, true that Allen's Jewish characters can be cartoonish, unpalatable stereotypes.

But in movies like *Zelig* and *Crimes and Misdemeanors* (1989), Allen gets at moral questions better than almost any other filmmaker. This film is about an ophthalmologist with a mistress who threatens his marital relationship, a rabbi going blind, and a married filmmaker who is in love with another woman. Judah, the ophthalmologist, has a criminal brother who offers Judah a way out of his problem: have the mistress killed. Clifford, the filmmaker (played by Woody Allen), falls in love with Hallie, the producer of a show by Clifford's annoyingly successful brother-in-law. There are two misdemeanors: Clifford's inappropriate attraction to Hallie (despite his loveless marriage), and Hallie's ultimate decision to make the wrong choice in love. The story is interesting and complex enough to warrant a more complete plot synopsis.

Judah Rosenthal is a highly successful ophthalmologist. Cliff Stern is a not very successful filmmaker. These are the two characters at the center of the story. Judah, although seemingly devoted to his family, is in fact having an extramarital affair with Dolores Paley, a flight attendant. She is needy and clingy, expecting Judah to end his marriage and stay with her. He, however, has no intention of doing so. As she begins to realize his true intentions, feeling hurt and feeling scorned, she vows to Judah that she will reveal all to his wife. But Judah discovers her letter to his wife and destroys it. Dolores, though, won't give up. She continues to tell Judah that she will tell his wife all about them, that she will ruin his marriage unless he takes her as his partner. And she has additional ammunition. Judah has been involved in some shady financial doings, and Dolores threatens to reveal them as well.

Distraught, Judah decides to tell his problems to one of his patients, a Rabbi named Ben. The Rabbi is going blind but seems serene. He cautions Judah to tell his wife the truth. Judah, however, is afraid that by doing so he will imperil his marriage and indeed the stability of his entire life. He is not about to do that.

Increasingly anxious, Judah goes to Jack, his brother, who advises him that there is only one alternative: Dolores must be killed. Reluctant at first to accept such a morally outrageous act, Judah delays, but finally he accepts what Jack has told him. Jack goes ahead and hires a hit man. She is killed. Judah goes to her apartment to get letters he wrote her and other items, so his name will not be mentioned when there is an investigation of her death.

Overwhelmed with guilt, Judah recalls his family and the Jewish religious heritage he had neglected. Judah realizes that he believes that God watches and sees all he does, and will pass judgment on his actions.

Cliff's sister is married to Lester, a self-important television producer. Lester hires Cliff to make a documentary about how great Lester and his work are. Cliff hates Lester's pomposity, his self-importance. Lester has an associate producer named Halley Reed, and Cliff falls in love with her. Cliff's marriage to Wendy, Lester's sister, is coming apart. Cliff tries to tell Halley that he wants to make an important film, one about Professor Louis Levi, a significant philosopher, but is doing the film about Lester just for the money. Cliff is unable to hide his contempt for Lester as the film first screens. Cliff has juxtaposed images of Lester with images of the Italian dictator Benito Mussolini. Lester is also seen screaming at his employees and chatting up a pretty young woman who is in one of his shows.

Cliff's life is falling apart. His life, like Judah's, really is at the edge of a cliff. Cliff learns that Professor Levi has killed himself. His suicide note read: "I've gone out the window." Halley arrives to provide some solace to Cliff, and he tries to get romantic. She tells him she is not looking for romance. Halley goes to London because Lester has offered her a job producing. She returns several months later, and Cliff is astonished to learn that she and Lester have become engaged.

Judah and Cliff meet at the wedding of the Rabbi's daughter. Judah has reconciled himself to his actions, justified them. He is clear because the murder was assumed to have been done by a mysterious drifter who cannot be located. Judah tells Cliff that time will be a cure for any immediate crisis. But Cliff is not convinced. He says we all bear the burden forever for any crime or misdemeanor we have committed.

This film is a profound moral investigation into the nature of attraction, of guilt, even of God. Cliff is making a documentary about Professor Levy (based on the late Holocaust survivor and author Primo Levi). In Cliff's film, Levy says:

> You will notice that what we are aiming at when we fall in love is a very strange paradox. The paradox consists of the fact that, when we fall in

Five—The Invisible Jews

love, we are seeking to re-find all or some of the people to whom we were attached as children. On the other hand, we ask our beloved to correct all of the wrongs that these early parents or siblings inflicted upon us. So that love contains in it the contradiction: The attempt to return to the past and the attempt to undo the past.

All the characters have to come to terms with their past and then their futures. The blind rabbi happily dances with his daughter at the end of the film. He has insights that those who can see are unable to find. People who make wrong choices aren't punished directly in the film, but it is clear that their futures will haunt them. As Judah Rosenthal, the ophthalmologist, notes, standing outside himself:

> And after the awful deed is done, he finds that he's plagued by deep-rooted guilt. Little sparks of his religious background which he'd rejected are suddenly stirred up. He hears his father's voice. He imagines that God is watching his every move. Suddenly, it's not an empty universe at all, but a just and moral one, and he's violated it. Now, he's panic-stricken. He's on the verge of a mental collapse—an inch away from confessing the whole thing to the police. And then one morning, he awakens. The sun is shining, his family is around him and, mysteriously, the crisis has lifted. He takes his family on a vacation to Europe and as the months pass, he finds he's not punished. In fact, he prospers. The killing gets attributed to another person—a drifter who has a number of other murders to his credit. So, I mean, what the hell? One more doesn't even matter. Now he's scott-free. His life is completely back to normal. Back to his protected world of wealth and privilege.

But Judah is wrong. The conscience will return and will eventually punish him. Crimes and misdemeanors have moral consequences in this film's spiritual world.

The movie has a good deal to say about Jewish identity as well. For Allen, Jewish identity focuses on moral choices and honesty with oneself. He is at odds with traditional Jewish morality in the matter of marriage, for in the film he seems to justify leaving one's wife for "true" love. In one way this message is part of the murder story as well Judah cannot be honest with his wife, and that is (in his mind at least) what leads to the logical conclusion that he must agree to murder to protect the hypocritical relationship he has with her. Allen's focus on love's honesty relies too much on personal emotion, on the fleeting aspects of feelings, to make a genuine contribution to Jewish identity. But he doggedly attempts to search out whether or not God exists, what God sees, what God wants, and how we should react to tragedy (e.g., the rabbi's acceptance of his blindness). Allen wants us to wrestle with God. Indeed, the word "Israel" means not someone who believes in God but someone who, like Jacob in the Bible, literally wrestles. For Jews, spiritual life and identity requires constant searching. In this interpretation, doubt is not the opposite of belief, but its useful companion. Allen does not seem to grasp this, seeing belief as at odds with struggle.

He has Professor Levy say:

> We are all faced throughout our lives with agonizing decisions. Moral choices. Some are on a grand scale. Most of these choices are on lesser points. But we define ourselves by the choices we have made. We are, in fact, the sum total of our choices. Events unfold so unpredictably, so unfairly, human happiness does not seem to have been included in the design of creation. It is only we, with our capacity to love, that give meaning to the indifferent universe. And yet, most human beings seem to have the ability to keep trying, and even to find joy from simple things like their family, their work, and from the hope that future generations might understand more.

For Allen, human beings are alone. God is absent or silent. Using the professor's voice, Allen asserts that it is only our ability to choose that makes us human and gives us a chance to find meaning in life. For Jews unable to believe in a supernatural deity, Allen, in this respect, has a very interesting and useful identity.

Not all films, though, were able to provide this kind of insight. Avalon is an island prominently mentioned in the legends of King Arthur. It is associated with mystical occurrences and people. *Avalon* (1990) is also the film directed by Barry Levinson about Jewish immigrants who come to Baltimore and make a home there. It is the third of Levinson's "Baltimore Films" after *Diner* and *Tin Men*.

Tellingly, the words "Jew" and "Jewish" are not spoken in *Avalon*. The United States is the mystical land, the place where dreams come true, but they don't come true for people seen as Jews. They come true as the family becomes more and more American. The film, that is, is a loving, insightful portrayal of assimilation in action.

As film critic Warren Rosenberg puts it:

> In *Avalon* Levinson clearly intends to create a universal immigrant story that would be recognizable to any group tracing its lineage to Europe. In fact, he seems to be consciously imitating Coppola's *Godfather* films in the nostalgic music, evocative cinematography, and fre-

quent flashbacks. Yet while Coppola's immigrants are obviously Italian, and he makes heavy use of Catholic imagery and ritual, albeit often ironically, Levinson's immigrants almost never speak Yiddish, nor do any of them practice Judaism in any form. The effect of these omissions, in my view, is to make *Avalon* a less richly textured film than it might have been. This is frustrating since in so many ways it is a richly textured portrayal of Jewish immigrant lives; however, only Jewish viewers would fully appreciate the representation because we can individually and collectively fill in the gaps based on our own experiences.[7]

David Desser and Lester D. Friedman agree with this assessment. They think the film represents "the most disturbing example of [Levinson's] ethnic whitewashing":

> Focusing on several generations of Jews, he squanders a golden opportunity to investigate the evolution of Jewish life, from the ghetto to the country club.... The immigrant Krichinskys plod through five decades with few distinctly Jewish experiences. There is no tug between Old Country values and the new land's promises, no run-ins with anti–Semitism, no mention of religious ceremonies or holidays, and no discussions of intermarriage.[8]

Avalon is a good film — enjoyable, warm, and decent. But it is not a good Jewish film in the sense that it suggests the way for American Jews to live is to abandon Jewish memories and practices and to make no spiritual or moral choices that emanate from their Jewishness. Rather, it is suggested, assimilation provides economic and social success, and that's what happiness should mean for Jews. This is, in that limited sense, a film about the end of Jewish identity.

Almost as if to make up for this neglect, Levinson's fourth Baltimore drama, *Liberty Heights* (1999), jumps into a wide variety of Jewish issues, particularly anti–Semitism, black–Jewish relations, and interfaith (and interracial) romances. It also covers crime involving Jews (Levinson had also previously directed *Bugsy* about the Jewish gangster Ben "Bugsy" Siegel).

One difference between Levinson's films can be seen immediately. The words "Jew" and "Jewish" appear ten times in the first minute of *Liberty Heights*. This seems to be an announcement that the movie is not going to be ethnically abstract to appeal to a wider audience but is finally going to make a unique statement about American Jews. Indeed, three minutes into the film the setting shifts to a Rosh Hashanah service in synagogue. The story, taking place from fall of 1954 to fall of 1955, is about

American Jewish Films

Ben Kurtzman, a sixteen-year-old boy growing up in Liberty Heights, a Baltimore neighborhood. Ben has an older brother, Van, and the two deal with Gentiles in their own way. Ben becomes friends with a black classmate, and Van tries to attract a beautiful non–Jewish young woman. The racial and religious boundaries the brothers cross is an example of how Levinson sees assimilation as a goal of his characters. The film's crossing works both ways, however, for an interesting plot element occurs when Ben and two friends enter a pool where Jews are not allowed. They, too, cross boundaries, and though this scene offers a welcome attack on anti-Semitism, there is an undercurrent as well of the worth of attempting to assimilate.

But despite the outward trappings of a potentially significant Jewish film, Levinson pulls back. As Warren Rosenberg notes:

> Yet beyond the word "Jewish," relentlessly intoned, the film has as little actual Jewish content as any of the previous Levinson films. We remain in the synagogue only a moment, as the camera follows Ben's father Nate (Joe Mantegna) down the aisle and to a Cadillac dealership so he can purchase the first new model of the year. (This is apparently what the Jewish New Year traditionally means to him, and one wonders if Levinson, in reinforcing this particular stereotype, is canceling out some of the more positive cultural messages of the film.) The entire dramatic trajectory of the film is structured around Jewish men exposing their Jewish identity to the "other kind" and then waiting, with fists raised, for the hostile or violent reaction. Samson becomes the relevant biblical reference, as Ben cutely asks his mother Ada (Bebe Neuwirth) and his thickly accented grandmother, where the jawbone of the ass is.[9]

Liberty Heights is an entertaining, interesting film. Levinson is, after all, a highly-gifted filmmaker. But the Jewish references mask a specific assimilationist attitude. This can be seen in one of the dramatic, even shocking, episodes of the film. Ben plans to attend a Halloween party. Then we see his costume. He is dressed as Adolf Hitler. His outraged father tells him he can't go in that costume and offers him a clear choice: Ben can either pick a more suitable subject or remain in the house. Ben, the defiant young man that he is, stays, unwilling to bend to his father's will. Ben is ready to be assertive, defiant. It is not that he is a self-hating Jew. Quite the opposite. He is ready to be a pugnacious Jew. But this is another species of assimilation, this tough Jew he wants to be, for it ultimately does not represent the spiritual, moral core of Judaism any more than does playing the victim, an identity he associates with the older generation and which he flatly rejects. His approach leads to violence, or at least a view of the criminal as hero, hardly a suitable Jewish model, and hardly a model to which Jews should aspire.

Ben is more ready than his mother to accept integration. In one scene, Ben tells Ada about the African American young woman he thinks is pretty:

> ADA: How are the coloreds doing at school?
> BEN: Okay, they're doing okay. They're getting better grades than I am. The girl's pretty attractive.
> ADA: What?
> BEN: She's attractive.
> ADA [angrily]: Oh, just kill me now! Just kill me now!
> BEN: What are you talking about?
> ADA: What do you mean "she's attractive?"
> BEN: Pretty.
> ADA: Oh my God.
> BEN: Mom, I said she was attractive, that doesn't necessarily mean I'm attracted to her!

There is a Manichean world view at work here. The old Jewish attitudes, the sense of separateness, is racist. The new Jewish attitudes are inclusive, tolerant, American. This is the heart of assimilation, the disbelief that somehow a traditional Judaism can live with American values. Such a point of view leads a Jewish identity to speed through the stop signs of American life headed toward the sweet, happy land of acceptance. As such, assimilation is seen as not only worthwhile but also noble.

CHAPTER SIX

Assimilation with a Heart: Romance in American Jewish Films

Assimilation as the accursed enemy, the counter to a positive Jewish identity, has in it the ring of some dangerous, unwholesome enterprise. But assimilation did not come about by accident. It is not a nasty devil offering flavorful but deadly treats to innocent immigrant children. America was the land of lures for very grown-up adults. It was the beckoning land where there was freedom from religious obligation, the chance to partake in forbidden foods and romantic partners, to explore new definitions of sensibilities (such as a tough masculinity in the area of crime — also available in Zionism for American Jews), or to seek out exciting jobs (such as a singer, actor, or comedian) and enter professions forbidden in many parts of Europe. Assimilation seemed friendly. It meant you could blend in. You might have to change your name. You might even want to change your appearance. But Jews were as white (or were eventually thought of as being as white) as Protestants. They could blend if they only wanted to do so.

America's open arms ultimately provided the same freedom to Jews that it offered to other white ethnic groups. That freedom didn't come immediately, however. At first, American hotels were sometimes restrictive. Elite American colleges sometimes limited the number of Jewish students. Neighborhoods kept out Jewish families, as did country clubs. But all of that disappeared over time so that in contemporary America there are almost no obvious restrictions on Jewish freedom.

This freedom has been wonderful. It has given Jews unparalled opportunities. Apart from their own country, this chance to develop themselves was as unique as it was sweet. But the success has come at a huge cost. Jews have acquired money and status but often lost their heritage.

The acceptance and assimilation they found in America had its most personal and concrete exemplification in the search for romantic partners. At first, very few Jews interdated, much less intermarried. Over time, however, interfaith romances became commonplace and much more widely accepted. From their beginnings, American films charted interfaith romance, looking at it mostly favorably.

An examination of films about romance often reveals the attraction of Jewish males for Gentile women. This attraction often carried with it a harsh accompanying attitude toward Jewish women, and it is worthwhile to begin a discussion of attraction with an analysis of feelings about Jewish women.

As was seen most poignantly in films (and also illustrated in much of Jewish culture, such as in the Yiddish theater), the Jewish mother was commonly portrayed as a model of warmth and kindness, someone who put her children's lives above her own, someone who in some ways lived just for her children. In a society marked by sexism, Jewish women, often barred from entering professions and entertainment themselves, put their energies and hopes especially into their sons. Milton Berle's mother did this. Perhaps most famously, so did Minnie Marx, whose sons revolutionized American comedy.

But this image of the Jewish mother changed, as did the image of Jewish women. As women became more independent in the culture, as they gained access to jobs that had been closed to them, as they grew more confident, their emergence proved threatening to some men. For male Jewish comedians this threat proved double-edged. Jewish women comedians became direct rivals for jobs. Worse yet, for some Jewish comedians (like Henny Youngman), their entire routine depended on a particular perception of Jewish women by the audience. If women changed, and the audience perception of women in general and Jewish women in particular changed, then some male Jewish comedians would have no routine left.

In a sense, no one in power likes to lose any of it. That's what happened to males. For Jewish males, nurtured by the Yiddishe mamas who protected them, a sense of control was suddenly shattered. Inevitably, the emergence of women led to tensions. Divorce rates went up. Marriage rates went down. And relationships between men and women suffered. The arc of the story of those relationships can be seen in Jewish films.

American Jewish Films

The film *Abie's Irish Rose* (1928) has survived only in parts. The third through seventh reel, and the ninth through twelfth, exist in the Library of Congress. The rest is gone. That, of course, is too bad, especially because the film is such an early predictor of the how Jews would intermarry and assimilate in large numbers.

The story is about Abie Levy, a soldier who has been wounded in World War I. Levy falls in love with an actress, Rosemary Murphy. Both the Jewish and Catholic fathers are unhappy when the two get married (they eventually marry *three* times). Only grandchildren—Patrick and Rebecca—can reconcile the Jewish father with his son. The film is an explicit endorsement of intermarriage,

Abie's Irish Rose was filled with ethnic stereotypes, such as Jews hungry for money. There are thick Yiddish accents. There's a scene in which the Jewish mother tries to bake a ham. The film is filled with ethnic stereotypes. The humor is of the era and has lost much for modern audiences, although the humor is warm and loving rather than unkind. But if the film is no longer entertaining, it is of historical importance.

Marjorie Morningstar (1958) was, like *Private Benjamin*, the story of a spoiled, well-off young Jewish woman, the sort of woman who would acquire the terrible and mocking nickname of Jewish American Princess. Marjorie, however, is not quite like Judy Benjamin. She's sincere. She wants to work hard. She doesn't need a non–Jewish environment like the army to find herself. Marjorie instead looks to a Jewish summer camp. But Marjorie is not grown-up either. Noel Airman is the man Marjorie loves. Noel finds success only with the summer camp's adoring young women and not in the real world. He notes of Marjorie that she is a "Shirley." Then he explains what he means. "It's a trade name for a respectable middle-class girl who likes to play at being worldly." Noel is aware of their differences. He tells her, with precise foreknowledge, "You're on a course charted by 5,000 years of Moses and the Ten Commandments. I'm a renegade."

The film, not a successful artistic project, nevertheless is important for several reasons. It focuses on the internal dynamics of a Jewish family, something rarely done in the movies. (But its casting is bizarre. Natalie Wood and Gene Kelly are both Gentiles. They both have talent, but not in pretending to be attracted to each other, which is the film's central point.) The film re-defines Jewish roles. The Jewish father in most films is a stern and unbending figure, a patriarch fiercely holding on to the Jew-

Six—Assimilation with a Heart

Marjorie Morningstar (Beachwold Productions, 1958) is the story of a young Jewish woman struggling with love and identity and the extent to which she wants to follow her family's traditions. Here Ed Wynn as Uncle Samson advises Natalie Wood as Marjorie.

ish heritage and unquestionably in charge of the household. But Marjorie's father is weak, kind but powerless. The patriarchal figure, still crucial, is played by Ed Wynn as Uncle Samson. It is a powerful statement about such a role in modern life that Uncle Samson dies in the film. Marjorie's mother is the one in charge. She is not unquestioningly supportive. She probes. She disapproves of Noel. She wants her children to do well, but only because it will make it seem that *she* has succeeded. She is the opposite of the romantic, as evidenced by this exchange:

> MARJORIE MORGENSTERN: Were you in love with Papa when you married him?
> ROSE MORGENSTERN: When I met your father I was in love with Rudolph Valentino.

This role reversal—the supportive father and the unbending mother—makes *Marjorie Morningstar* a sociological document.

It is also interesting as a film about romance. Marjorie is not involved in an interfaith relationship with Noel. He's Jewish, but he's a non–Jewish Jew. He will spend his life running away from Judaism. This is an interesting aspect of American Jewish identity. Jews not only have to struggle to find romantic partners who are Jewish, but within Judaism there are potential romantic partners who have no attachment to Jewish tradition. The film demonstrates a subtle internal Jewish struggle between remaining within Jewish traditions and going outside them to assimilate.

At the end, Marjorie rebels against rebellion. She reconciles herself to traditional notions of success and to an upper middle-class life. She will marry Wally, a successful playwright, and settle down. She is no longer the Jew without a home, the Jew alienated from society, like Noel. Marjorie represents American Jews who, having been tempted to be true to themselves, surrender to the rules of society. In this sense, *Marjorie Morningstar* becomes a film about the American domestication of the Jews. In Lester Friedman's view, "Like the fictional Marjorie Morningstar, the American Jew of the fifties, both on and off screen, looked, spoke, and acted far more like his Gentile neighbors than his immigrant ancestors."[1]

However this transformation of Jews is characterized, for Jewish identity it is not a pretty sight. Even loving other Jews can lead to assimilation.

The Hollywood tradition of being on the side of interfaith relationships and against any old-world opposition to them is grounded in the liberal notion of tolerance. That plea for tolerance can be seen in almost all romantic movies about interfaith or other sorts of relationships that cross once-forbidden romantic lines. *A Majority of One* (1961) is one of the films that makes the case for tolerance gently and with the best of intentions. (The title is taken from a Yiddish proverb from the era when "man" stood for all people: "Any man more right than his neighbors constitutes a majority of one.") The film is about a Jewish widow named Bertha Jacoby whose son was killed by the Japanese. She meets Mr. Asano, a wealthy Japanese widower who can help her son-in-law's business career.

Mr. Asano is played by Alec Guinness, who is, of course, one of the great actors of his time. Still, even with such a great actor, it is important to ask why an actor of Japanese ancestry was not chosen for the part. For that matter, the Jewish widow is played by Rosalind Russell, an Irish-American Catholic. Like with *Marjorie Morningstar* and *Gentleman's Agreement*, this film softens its Jewish content by its choice of actors. They can speak the words, but they don't have a lifetime of experience playing the part.

But Bertha Jacoby is an interesting character, a throwback to the warm Jewish mother. As Kathryn Bernheimer notes:

> Bertha is a kind, caring, loving, understanding, unpretentious, and sensible woman.... She adapts quickly and is open to the strange Japanese customs she encounters.... Unlike numerous Jewish movie mothers, she does not interfere, meddle, dominate, or lay guilt on her children. Rather, she is nurturing and supportive, although no pushover. She is revealed to be less bigoted than her children, who pay lip service to egalitarian ideals but balk at the idea of intermarriage.[2]

This last part is important. The film reverses the modern notion of the Jewish mother in two ways. The first is by making her traditional, but the second is by making her very modern. That is, the character was inconsistent, artificially structured to make her fit the film's ideal. As such, she seems to be presented as a Jewish ideal, but it is an ideal that includes not just tolerance for people of other cultures or tolerance (eventually) for someone whose country was responsible for her son's death. Mr. Asano makes that possible because he, too, has lost a son in the war. And he notes their commonality: "All we wished for was a happy and peaceful existence with the flowers and the moon and the sunshine. Is that so different from what you wished for, Mrs. Jacoby?"

All this tolerance might fit in to a particular Jewish point of view. But it is the extension of that tolerance to include an interfaith romance that makes the film inadequate as a model for an American Jewish identity. And yet, at the end of the movie the two do not get married. This, however, is only because Mrs. Jacoby realizes Mr. Asano's romantic overtures are grounded in his loneliness for his departed wife. They will remain friends, and that friendship becomes much more of a basis for Jewish identity.

Funny Girl (1968) is the biographical musical based on the life of the great entertainer Fanny Brice and starring the great theatrical entertainer Barbra Streisand. People who have seen Streisand live say her magnetic personality and powerful presence can't quite translate to the screen. This is true of many performers (the Marx Brothers are one prominent example). And once again there was a casting question. Omar Sharif, a very good actor who was Egyptian, plays Nicky Arnstein, Fanny's lover and then husband. Beyond the question of having another non–Jewish actor playing a Jewish character, the casting was questioned even more because the Six-Day War in the Middle East, a war that included fighting between Israel and Egypt, had recently taken place. The idea of an onscreen romance between a high profile Egyptian actor and Jewish actress didn't sit well with some viewers.

Streisand's singing is so good and her underrated acting skills are so developed that it is possible to miss her crucial historical contribution. The critic Stanley Kauffmann wrote of this directly by discussing "the social importance of her face":

> What is the theme of the show other than a homely girl's problems and triumphs? Why else was Miss Streisand, a relative unknown at the time, cast in the Broadway show originally? And she is *Jewish* homely. To disregard both these elements is to disregard the importance of Miss Streisand's emergence.[3]

Indeed, the movie intends to tell the story of Fanny Brice, but, as Streisand's fame bloomed in the role, the film, inadvertently or not, becomes Streisand's story and (if Kaufmann is correct), the story of unattractive women who, without changing their appearance, succeed in society. It is a story of triumph. And the triumph includes a touch of self-mockery and pride. Barbra Streisand's first words in the film emerge when Fanny stands in front of the mirror. She takes a look and says, "Hello, gorgeous."

Jewishness is another part of that triumph. Fanny (and, in subtext, Barbra) can attribute her drive, at least in part, to her heritage. She is resilient, like Jews who faced hardships. She is filled with an excitement about life. She feels overlooked by the world but perfectly capable of performing well if given a fair chance. In a way, Fanny Brice's story is the story of American Jews.

Funny Girl isn't a film about an interfaith romance. Once again, as in *Marjorie Morningstar*, it is a film about an inter-Jewish romance that doesn't work because one of the partners is more assimilated than the other. Nicky is a gambler. He has no Jewish values. Fanny knows she is Jewish, acts Jewish, wants to be Jewish. Her Jewish identity informs the rest of her identity. This theme is never explicitly examined in either film, but it is an important one. Assimilation doesn't just affect the Jewish identity of those Jews who do the assimilating but of all Jews because the assimilated Jews form romantic relationships with unassimilated Jews who believe they have found true love within Judaism. Their realization, like when one partner suddenly becomes religiously devout, is an interesting comment about what it takes for two partners to succeed in a marriage. American Jews have enough problems finding partners, what with the stereotypes about Jewish women and Jewish men they have adopted from the wider culture, and the demographic lack of suitable partners. Beyond these problems is the more subtle difficulty of uniting two Jews with very different American Jewish lives. It would be interesting if some film were able to discuss this issue or to chart some of these differences, although it is difficult to imagine that such a movie could find a very wide American audience.

No Way to Treat a Lady (1968) features Rod Steiger in a wide variety of disguises and using a seemingly endless repertoire of accents to play a serial killer. He is tracked down by a Jewish detective (played by George Segal) who has a far more typical Jewish screen mother than Mrs. Jacoby in *A Majority of One*. Segal's character, Morris Brummel, is harried and seeks to escape the notion of women as exemplified by his mother through a relationship with a potential victim of the killer, Kate Palmer, who is most definitely not Jewish. Eileen Heckart plays Mrs. Brummel. She's not calculating, like Marjorie Morningstar's mother. She has the warmth and caring spirit of a Mrs. Jacoby. But she's not in any way restrained in her feelings toward her son. She's controlling and interfering. She is an interesting character in this respect, for she is halfway between the kind Jewish mother and the harridan.

But she still wants to break up her son's relationship with a non–Jewish woman. She is, in fact, horrified by it:

> MRS. BRUMMEL: So, what do you, what do you do with her, go to mass?
> MORRIS BRUMMEL: No, we just ... we walk and we talk.
> MRS. BRUMMEL: Oh, please, please. I don't want to hear another word. Already I won't sleep another wink tonight. Please, don't say another word.
> [pause]
> MRS. BRUMMEL: Morris...
> MORRIS BRUMMEL: I thought you didn't want to hear any more.
> MRS. BRUMMEL: Aw, you think I want to? You think I want ... I'm in agony. I ... I ... It's my duty. Go on, go on.
> MORRIS BRUMMEL: Well, she ... her, her name is Katherine. Katherine. Katherine Palmer.
> MRS. BRUMMEL: Short, blonde, beautiful?
> MORRIS BRUMMEL: No, she's, er, she's, she's tall and er, she's only got one eye right in the middle of her forehead.
> MRS. BRUMMEL: Of course. Of course. She'll break your heart!

What is unusual about the film is that the killer, Christopher Gill, has profound feelings about his own mother. He feels love, but he also feels hatred. Indeed, even before the credits have rolled, Gill strangles a woman, and, as she is dying, he utters, "Now, mother, rest in peace."

The two men, the killer and the cop, are thematically related. As Patricia Erens notes, after Gill is finally dead, Morris is leaving the building and "walks past a picture of Gill's mother in the role of Cleopatra with a snake headdress."

> The message is transparent: certain women, especially mothers, are actually poisonous vipers. Gill has evolved into a murderer because of such a woman. Morris was a potential candidate, but has been saved by this cathartic experience.... Morris is another manifestation of the Jewish Man-Child, unduly tied to mother's apron strings.[4]

The message is clear. Even a Jewish mother not as cold as Marjorie Morningstar's mother is still dangerous. The way to escape this trap for Morris is to marry a Gentile woman. The film, though, goes beyond skewering Jewish mothers. All mothers, all women, are considered potentially dangerous.

The Heartbreak Kid (1972) is in some ways the archetypical movie about the Jewish male attraction to Gentile females. To tighten the emotional setting, Neil Simon (who wrote the screenplay, based on a story by Bruce Jay Friedman) has the protagonist, Lenny Cantrow, on his honeymoon with Lila, a nice, if stereotypically Jewish, young woman when he meets a blonde Gentile goddess, Kelly Corcoran, played by Cybill Shepherd. The honeymoon is revelatory for Lenny. He has followed tradition. He has met and married a "nice" Jewish woman. But he finds her incredibly annoying. At one point he screams at her, "It's not a question of not appreciating you. It's that I don't like one ... thing about you." Suffering from sunburn, Lila must stay in her hotel room, and so Lenny goes alone to the beach, where he meets Kelly, who opens up her conversation with him by saying, "You're in my spot." Lenny, though, doesn't mind her controlling him. He lies to his wife in order to meet Kelly. Lenny decides to dump his wife and pursue the goddess. It's not the case that he loves her. He has adopted perfectly the White Anglo-Saxon (or, in her case, wealthy Irish) attitudes that a Jay Gatsby in *The Great Gatsby* did. He is overwhelmed by wealth, power, status. He thinks others will perceive him differently if he is married to Kelly. He dislikes Lila so much because she reminds him of what he thinks of as his cramped Jewish life. Kelly opens up the world for him. Kelly may not have a Jewish mother, but she does have a father who is, to put it mildly, unhappy with his daughter's romantic choice.

Lenny and Kelly do eventually marry, but the story is more complicated than it seems. This isn't a case like *No Way to Treat a Lady* in which the Gentile woman saves the Jewish man. Indeed, part of the heartbreak for the "Kid" Lenny is that, beyond breaking Lila's heart, he has also unknowingly broken his own. In finding American success, marrying a tall, beautiful blonde Gentile, he has become empty. He has given up his soul for some external possessions and for appearances that will eventually decay. Seen in this way, *The Heartbreak Kid* is an argument against romantic assimilation. Lenny would have done better to have understood Lila and remained true to his self, a self that would have given him meaning.

It should be noted, though, that the film was not seen very often in this way. Mostly, its surface story of a young Jewish man divorcing his Jewish wife to marry a Gentile was seen as an abandonment of Judaism, a betrayal. Simon wanted to cast the attractive Diane Keaton in the role of Lila to make it clear that the story wasn't about looks but about Lenny's vapid nature. Some also saw the film as an exemplification of Jewish self-hatred, the same charge sometimes leveled at Woody Allen and Philip Roth.

But both of them are like the makers of this film in a way. The romantic notion that love can conquer every problem, that love is a cure for whatever disease ails the protagonist, is not present in this film (or in films by Allen or any based on Roth's work). The stories are much more complicated, more conflicted. As Lester Friedman notes, "Kelly represents the romanticized American dream made flesh. To capture this dream, Len gives up his family, friends, and heritage, a poor bargain in the eyes of [director Elaine] May and Simon."[5]

Not every film was about a Jewish male who finds what he thinks of as dream attainment in the form of a Gentile woman. Sometimes it is the Jewish woman who is attracted to the handsome WASP prince. Perhaps the most famous of those movies was *The Way We Were* (1973).

> KATIE MOROSKY GARDNER: I don't have the right style for you, do I?
> HUBBELL GARDNER: No, you don't have the right style.
> KATIE: I'll change.
> HUBBELL: No, don't change. You're your own girl, you have your own style.
> KATIE: But then I won't have you. Why can't I have you?

HUBBELL: Because you push too hard, every damn minute. There's no time to ever relax and enjoy living. Everything's too serious to be so serious.

KATIE: If I push too hard it's because I want things to be better, I want us to be better, I want you to be better. Sure I make waves. You have ... I mean you have to. And I'll keep making them till you're everything you should be and will be. You'll never find anyone as good for you as I am, to believe in you as much as I do or to love you as much.

HUBBELL: I know that.

KATIE: Well then why?

HUBBELL: Do you think if I come back it's going to be okay by magic? What's going to change? What's going to be different? We'll both be wrong, we'll both lose.

KATIE: Couldn't we both win?

The Way We Were (Columbia Pictures, 1973) stars Robert Redford as the handsome writer Hubbell Gardiner, a Gentile. Here he stares across the table at Barbra Streisand as the Jewish social radical Katie Morosky in this story of the bumpy road of romantic assimilation.

Six—Assimilation with a Heart

Katie is played by Barbra Streisand and Hubbell by Robert Redford. Again, the Jewish woman is not presented as beautiful, but the Gentile is presented as physically ideal.

The film is almost always understood as a romantic drama, and that it is. But in terms of identity, interfaith relationships are commonplace in American films, although usually such relationships end in happiness and rarely do they involve a Jewish woman. Interestingly, Streisand did this as well as Fanny Brice.

What is different about *The Way We Were* in terms of American Jewish identity is that the film depicts Jews as having social concerns. For dramatic effect, and in partial adherence to history, Katie is interested in radical politics. But the broader Jewish involvement in social issues to improve the lives, for example, of the poor and the forgotten are insufficiently covered in American films and yet form a consistently large part, rightly or wrongly, of how American Jews see themselves.

Patricia Erens captures this idea well, noting the movie

> also serves as one of the few Hollywood films to portray Jewish social commitment (the socialist movement of the thirties and the protests during the 1950s). Although the movie remains a romance, not a political tract, the inclusion of this material is significant. More importantly, the film deals with the cultural differences that separate the Jewish community from the larger Gentile world.[6]

At one point Hubbell notices this, pointing out that he likes to deal with people. He's a writer and is interested in close observation of individuals, their way of talking, their pattern of thinking, the way they deal with others. But Katie, he notes, is much more interested in causes. This is an interesting shorthand for the difference between her as a Jew and him as a Gentile, and it is this difference, not the difference in religions, that makes them ultimately incompatible. That is, *The Way We Were* uniquely goes beyond romance to find a more crucial identity difference between American Jews and Gentiles than religion.

There is another way of looking at this difference, though. Although the film does not in any way imply this, and it would be a misinterpretation to claim that it does, *The Way We Were* can be understood to say that having social causes as the core of an American Jewish identity is inadequate. It impedes love in terms of this film, but, more importantly, it may block access to deeper, more meaningful aspects of a Jewish identity than having particular political positions or even more generally being in favor of social justice. Those deeper aspects are needed to explain the sensitivity to injustice and the urgent desire to repair a broken social system.

The film's other strength is that, amazingly, in the end, it opposes assimilation through interfaith marriage, arguing that the social commitment inherent in an American Jewish identity cannot be given up so easily, even in the cause of love. In the case of this movie, Katie tries. She marries Hubbell, moves to Hollywood, and makes a valiant effort no deny the person that she is, the Jew as the film understands what it means to be Jewish. But when the House Committee on Un-American Activities comes along and Hubbell doesn't want to get involved, she can no longer wear a WASP mask.

While the film is against romantic assimilation, and its argument coheres well with American Jewish identity, it fails to grasp that the social commitment will eventually lead to assimilation as well, only the assimilation will not be solely along romantic lines.

It is worthwhile to remember that not all Jewish-Gentile relationships in films last. In Woody Allen's movies, it's hard for any relationship of any kind to last. In perhaps Allen's most famous example of a Jewish-Gentile relationship movie, *Annie Hall* (1977), charmingly starring Diane Keaton (whose real name was Diane, or Annie, Hall), the title character, along with Allen, tries to understand such a relationship.

The film was a departure of sorts for Allen, who had, up until this picture, made a series of films that were joke machines. In *Annie Hall*, however, Allen sought to create a serious love story, grounded though it was in humor. And, ultimately, the movie makes the same point as *The Way We Were*—that cultural differences inevitably complicate romantic relationships between Jews and Gentiles, that love is not the melting pot into which those differences are poured and disappear.

To make his point, Alvy, Allen's character in the film, goes up to a couple on the street:

> ALVY SINGER: Here, you look like a very happy couple, um, are you?
> FEMALE STREET STRANGER: Yeah.
> ALVY SINGER: Yeah? So, so, how do you account for it?
> FEMALE STREET STRANGER: Uh, I'm very shallow and empty, and I have no ideas and nothing interesting to say.
> MALE STREET STRANGER: And I'm exactly the same way.
> ALVY SINGER: I see. Wow. That's very interesting. So you've managed to work out something?

Six—Assimilation with a Heart

Diane Keaton as the offbeat, stylish title character with Woody Allen as Alvy Singer in *Annie Hall* (Rollins-Joffe Productions, 1977). The winner of the Academy Award for Best Picture, *Annie Hall* became a symbol of its age, especially of the comic tensions of modern romance.

It's a funny exchange, but heartbreaking as well. For Allen, the only relationships that work are the ones in which each member of the couple has stopped thinking. And it's a very revealing exchange because it allows for a different interpretation of the film — that this is not so much about Jewish and Gentile differences alone, but about the differences between those people who think and feel and those people who don't. That's the big distinction for Allen. He gets his laughs from the cultural differences that result in character differences in perceptions, but the real differences to him are, he thinks, more significant than culture. The premise of such a view is that Judaism is purely cultural to him, not at all religious.

Allen mocks religion, such as in this exchange in which the Hall family and the Singer family talk to each other on split screens:

> MOM HALL: How do you plan to spend the holidays, Mrs. Singer?
> ALVY'S MOM: We fast.
> DAD HALL: Fast?
> ALVY'S DAD: No food. You know, to atone for our sins.
> MOM HALL: What sins? I don't understand.
> ALVY'S DAD: To tell you the truth, neither do we.

Because Judaism is just cultural, the differences may still be there but they aren't deep or important like thinking is. Had Allen had a different perception of Judaism — one, for example, in which spirituality was the foundation of a Jewish identity — then even differences in thinking would be less important differences in worldview.

Allen's worldview about love is grounded in comedy. He talks about it in terms of jokes:

> ALVY SINGER [addressing the camera]: There's an old joke — um ... two elderly women are at a Catskill mountain resort, and one of 'em says, "Boy, the food at this place is really terrible." The other one says, "Yeah, I know; and such small portions." Well, that's essentially how I feel about life — full of loneliness, and misery, and suffering, and unhappiness, and it's all over much too quickly. The ... the other important joke, for me, is one that's usually attributed to Groucho Marx; but, I think it appears originally in Freud's *Wit and Its Relation to the Unconscious*, and it goes like this — I'm paraphrasing — um, "I would never want to belong to any club that would have someone like me for a member." That's the key joke of my adult life, in terms of my relationships with women.

His wider worldview comes also from desire. Anhedonia, the inability to experience pleasure, was to be used as the original title of the film. This,

Six—Assimilation with a Heart

too, for Allen, is part of the Jewish cultural baggage. The depression and anxiety, though, provide for him an access to a comic point of view as a defense mechanism. His comedy depends on his being dissatisfied. Therefore he can never really find happiness with anyone like Annie Hall, any Gentile goddess, for such happiness leads to the annihilation of his soul. Unhappiness is the key to his work and his being. In a perverse way, only by being unhappy can he be happy.

Alvy and Annie are the opposite of the couple that get along so well. Alvy is anxious. He has never in his life lived up to his promise. He is short and thin and not conventionally attractive. He is an intellectual. He belongs in cities. He is politically liberal. He is not socially adept but very self-conscious. He wants to control people. He sees dread around every corner. He is in analysis and believes in its efficacy. He is, to sum it up, what Woody Allen believes to be the entire psychological profile of the American Jewish male. Annie is the American model Gentile woman. She is from the Midwest. She has none of Alvy's sophistication. She is unsure of her own ideas and shy about offering them. She is a bit odd. She is what Woody Allen thinks of as a prototypical Gentile woman in America. Their romance is the heart of the plot.

Alvy Singer is a comedian who is struggling to explain to himself why his romance with Annie Hall deteriorated a year earlier. Alvy recalls that he was curious as a child, pestering his mother, telling her that there was no meaning to existence. He was also sexually precocious as a child.

Alvy takes Annie to see an Ingmar Bergman film, but afterwards she is uninterested in becoming intimate with him. Alvy tells her about his marriages, both unsatisfying for him. Annie seems to be different. She is not self-assured. She is not a New York intellectual. Alvy and Annie met on a tennis court, and, after some small talk, she offered him a ride. Annie auditions as a singer, and then the pair go on their first date. Alvy suggests they kiss so the awkwardness of a first kiss will be taken care of immediately. Annie slowly falls in love with him. He becomes a teacher of sorts, buying her books, especially about his favorite subject, death.

They go to visit her family in Chippewa Falls, Wisconsin, for Easter. This is a key scene and it involves the contrast of their families. At the Hall household for Easter, everyone looks healthy (though, as exemplified by Annie's brother, there is a craziness under the appearance of normality) and quiet as they eat Granny Hall's ham. Alvy is so self-conscious that he imagines that as they look at this New York Jew they see a Hasid in full garb, with his beard and black hat especially prominent. The Singer family, in contrast, are noisy. They complain about their jobs and what ails them. They are eating brisket. As Alvy sits there, he and the audience both see that there is more to love than just a physical attraction. Alvy and Annie come from separate cultures, and their backgrounds are incompatible.

Alvy sees Annie walking arm in arm with one of her professors. He realizes that their relationship is over. Alvy begins to date again, but no one else seems satisfying when compared to Annie. She suddenly calls him over, but it is only to have him kill a spider. This, though, leads them to get back together. Still, as made evident when they discuss their feelings with separate therapists, they see the world differently.

They plan to go to Los Angeles so Alvy can present an award on a television show, and it is on the plane ride back that they realize their relationship is truly over. Alvy soon notes that Annie has fallen for a record producer. Desperate, he asks her to marry him, but their relationship is doomed. They do meet again, but they both have found a new partner. The seeming perfect love could not be.

Many Jewish audiences see *Annie Hall* as the great Jewish-Gentile romantic comedy. But it is much more than that. Its disquieting undergrowth doesn't quite tackle the fundamental question of Jewish identity, as Allen himself later did in *Zelig*, but it is a revealing film on its own terms.

There are many other Jewish movies about the joys and hazards of romantic relationships. *Kramer vs. Kramer* is about the disastrous break-up of a marriage. *Enemies: A Love Story* is about multiple romantic entanglements. These are two modern variations of the disintegration of the standard love-marriage-children tale. But old-fashioned romantic movies are still being made, as in the case of *The Wedding Singer*. There were always tensions in love stories; without the tension there would be no story. But the tensions were usually resolved. Unresolved tensions are less satisfying as stories. But, ironically, stories where the tension is romantically resolved, as in *The Wedding Singer*, seem old-fashioned and simple, even as they are pleasing.

Perhaps because American culture is still in the middle of its marriage examination, having started in the late 1960s with the beginnings of the rapid rate of divorce, it would be surprising if there were realistic, happy resolutions in films.

CHAPTER SEVEN

The Borscht Belt Shtetl: Films About Jewish Resorts in the Catskills

American Jews developed various strategies to fight against anti–Semitism generally, and being excluded from places, such as resorts or hotels, specifically. One significant tactic was to build alternatives where Jews could go, a place where they didn't constantly have to be on guard, where they didn't have to make false presentations of their selves, where they didn't have to pretend to be people they were not. They needed places where they could throw in some Yiddish slang, tell jokes that everyone understood, order the food that they liked, and not have to worry about some boorish anti–Semite confronting them. They wanted to be accepted, but they wanted to be accepted without changing. And if they couldn't move into some neighborhoods, they would build their own neighborhoods. They would even build their own universities. They would also build their own resorts.

For example, the Hillcrest Country Club served Jews in the Los Angeles area. There, many well-known people could play golf, eat some lunch, play cards, and mingle like the wealthy Gentiles who had excluded them. The Hillcrest was especially known for its famous table of comedians, such as Groucho and Harpo Marx, George Burns, George Jessel, and many others. The comedians didn't always get along, but they could trade barbs and gossip. They could get tips on their shows that needed help or learn of new entertainment opportunities.

The East Coast had a different answer. Jews in New York had already had the experience of living in a small, tight community, a re-creation of a Jewish village, a shtetl, from Eastern Europe. That experience was the

American Jewish Films

Lower East Side in New York. But Jews didn't want to go back to the smelly, crowded, disease-ridden ghetto. They wanted fresh air, space, sunshine, and food, lots of very delicious food. They also wanted entertainment, especially comedians to provide laughs. They wanted to bring their families. And the young people wanted an opportunity to meet, mingle, date, and marry other young people. They wanted their own separate world.

And they wanted to forget the anti–Semitism. They wanted to forget Father Charles L. Coughlin, a Detroit priest who used radio to attack the Jews through sermons on his weekly CBS show. He eventually had ten million listeners. It was the 1930s, and in the period immediately after the Great Depression began, people began to search for answers. They wanted easy explanations, and "the Jews are the cause of your problems" became one of those easy explanations.

Anti-Semitism in America grew exponentially after the rise of Hitler. William Dudley Pelley founded the Silver Shirts (or, more formally, the Silver Legion) in 1933. This was one of the more famous of the approximately one hundred anti–Semitic groups that emerged between 1933, the year Hitler rose to power, and 1941, the year the United States entered World War II. These and other efforts had a profound effect on Americans. In a public opinion poll taken in 1938, for example, 45 percent of Americans said Jews were not as honest as Gentiles in business, and fully 35 percent said that the Jews in Europe were mostly responsible for the oppression visited upon them. In a question filled with historical resonance, Americans were asked if a significant number of Jewish exiles from Germany should be allowed to enter and live in the United States. Seventy-seven percent of the respondents answered in the negative.

Charles Lindbergh, the famous aviator and American hero, blamed Jews for trying to get America to enter a war with Germany. The America First Committee, founded in July 1940, did its best to prevent America from intervening in the war in Europe. Its members included future president Gerald Ford, writers Sinclair Lewis and E.E. Cummings, Walt Disney, and many others.

American Jews were understandably shocked by all this, but they had their own resources, their own means of escape.

One of the principal resources was a strip of land about ten by twenty-five miles in the Catskill Mountains, northwest of New York City. The Catskills, which were first sighted by Henry Hudson, got their name from the Dutch language. A *kat* is a wall of earth and a *kill* is a creek. Jews first came to the region as farmers trying to escape the urban jungle. Eventually Sullivan and Ulster counties became the home of a thousand hotels and bungalow colonies. Jews flocked there to avoid the city's heat and to escape the emotional tensions of trying to be accepted in America. In the Catskills they could be accepted for themselves. They could eat. They could laugh.

But for Jews, the Catskills represented a change of thinking as well. At the beginning they simply didn't grasp the notion of a vacation. When they had a vacation it was for the Sabbath, from sundown on Friday to sundown on Saturday, or one of the Jewish holidays. The idea of leaving one's home and stopping work certainly sounded attractive. But Jews couldn't quite get the notion of leaving for the purpose of pleasure. Their culture had made them feel guilty when they did some activity without any purpose other than enjoyment. They were used to using their time to work or learn a moral or religious lesson, or try to do some good in the world. Their task in life was to study Torah, to take care of their families and community. With the Catskills they were being asked not to take time off for God but to take time off for themselves. However alluring such an idea might me, it was a foreign notion for the Jews. American Jews were not hedonists, and they mistrusted those feelings. But now they had the money. And American assimilationist impulses were strong. As with so much else, Jews learned to adopt American attitudes, including attitudes about enjoying themselves. They turned out to be very adept at the new American ways. For most of them, the idea of having fun (as opposed to the idea, say, of being good) very quickly became an attractive goal. They had transformed from Jews to American Jews.

And so they made their way to the Catskill resorts. Originally, resorts were country escapes. Visitors picked berries, played some games, heard traditional music, and jumped into the pools to go swimming. They were rural escapes, purposefully letting Jews feel an alternative to urban life. But they were not yet centers of fun.

It was a combination of assimilation and anger at Gentile society for not admitting them that drove Jews to eventually want American entertainments. They wanted singers and comedians, golf and tennis, big swimming pools. There was to be no more berry picking. They weren't in Europe's countryside. They were in America's playland.

The hotels became famous for their food. No guest needed to recall Old World concerns about where the next meal would be coming from. Borscht, a soup made from beets, was served either cold or hot, and was often topped with sour cream or a small potato or cucumber slices. The dish's popularity provided the area with a nickname: the Borscht Belt. It was alternatively known as the Sour Cream Sierras, the Jewish Alps, or the Derma Road. Being hungry was a sin in the Borscht Belt. The helpings of food were a profound emotional reminder that they weren't in Minsk anymore. They were in the lush paradise of America, and they were going to celebrate that by never going hungry again. They discarded any diets on the road up to the Catskills. They littered the roadside with their inhibitions and their worries. They were going to a place where there were no restraints on their eating or their desire for pleasure. The food was almost carnal in its satisfaction.

The Borscht Belt filled an immense need. The food was familiar. People were with their families and friends, or at the least other Jews. They felt secure in a way they didn't feel in the world outside. They had, with lavish alterations, recreated the shtetl.

In the very act of providing that security, the Catskill resorts allowed American Jews to rehearse their Americanism. Ironically, the comfort they felt allowed them to be more American. The resorts mirrored this in their names. They weren't Little Warsaw. No, the resort names were filled with the poetry of peace: the Avon Lodge, the Concord, Harmony, Ideal House, and others. These were American, not particularly Jewish, names.

The Borscht Belt was an incubator for Jewish comedians. Here is an incomplete list of some of the people who entertained there: Milton Berle, Fanny Brice, Mel Brooks, Lenny Bruce, George Burns, Sid Caesar, Myron Cohen, Jack Gilford, Buddy Hackett, Moss Hart, George Jessel, Danny Kaye Alan King, Jack E. Leonard, Sam Levenson, Jerry Lewis, Jackie Mason, Carl Reiner, Joan Rivers, Neil Simon (and his brother Danny, who was the model of the sloppy Oscar Madison in *The Odd Couple*), and Henny Youngman. Red Buttons earned a dollar and a half a week as a bellboy and waiter, though he supplemented his income by filling a fountain pen with sweet cream and selling a shot of it to guests, at a quarter a squirt, for their coffee. Cream was strictly forbidden when meat meals were served at these kosher hotels.

The resorts began a slow decline after the Second World War. The horrified reaction to the war led to a decline in anti–Semitism and a slow acceptance of Jews in all areas of society, including hotels and resorts. There was no longer a need for the Catskills, and while attendance brought forth warm memories, and still does, the area also smacked of a particular historical era that had passed. Additionally, air-conditioning made it unnecessary to flee the city, and television provide the entertainers right in the comfort of one's home at a much-reduced price.

The first movie about the Catskills was based on a play by Herman Yablokoff, a star of Yiddish radio. The play, *Papirosn* (meaning cigarette), was filmed at the Parkside Hotel in 1935. It was silent and starred the future director Sidney Lumet (who would grow up to direct *The Pawnbroker*, among many other films). Lumet was an eleven-year-old cigarette seller who was a careful observer of the fate of the many summer romances that took place.

By 1938 Hollywood was ready for the Catskills. *Having a Wonderful Time* satirized the resorts, but the play's Jewish content was virtually expunged. But that didn't mean Hollywood was done with the Borscht Belt.

Woody Allen was one filmmaker who used the area in a movie. Allen's name keeps popping up, and that fact is worth examining. Certainly, he's a very talented comedian and gifted filmmaker. What is surprising is how much he focuses on Jewish matters—not always, to be sure, in the most flattering ways. "I have frequently been accused of being a self-hating Jew," Allen once wrote, "and while it's true I am Jewish and I don't like myself very much, it's not because of my persuasion."[1]

Allen gave a similar line to the character he played in *Deconstructing Harry*. Allen always seems alienated. His characters see being Jewish as being part of a religious group when they aren't themselves religious, or see being Jewish as being part of a specific ethnic group when they feel apart from other members of the group, nearly always starting with their own family. Allen's Jewish characters feel Jewish not because of religion or ethnicity but by their consciousness and temperament, which they comprehend as being particularly Jewish. Their pattern of thinking, their emotional geography, and their psychological strains all stem from being, inescapably, part of a minority group, part of the Jewish people.

In a way, then, the Jewish people stand as a symbol for all alienated people. They are the heroes of such a disorganized group. These new Jews, so different from their parents and grandparents who struggled to be accepted as Americans, are psychologically wounded as they wrestle a world of gadgets that are openly hostile to them and women who are strange, unreachable, or unfaithful. It's not easy being Jewish in Woody Allen's world.

But that world was a pioneering psychological analysis of what it meant to be an American Jew. Jews generally, in the past and in Israel, had a shared history and a shared fate. Their cultural references were similar. Their consciousness was mutually recognizable when they met another Jew. But in America, Jews had a much more limited shared history; they frequently had cultural references that were drawn from the Christian world. They lacked a shared consciousness. American Jews, even (maybe especially) those who succeeded, were caught between two worlds, the American and the Jewish.

Allen is particularly interesting precisely because he was successful. Finally, after much struggle, American Jews became accepted. The Catskill resorts were the way station, the halfway house, the spot halfway between being Jewish and being American. But when Jews symbolically left the Catskills in increasing numbers after World War II, when they finally became accepted, their entry into American life was not an unalloyed triumph.

> This success, though, inevitably triggered guilt, for their acceptance of the rhythms of a secular calendar robbed them of the sense of living in Jewish time. Their parents or grandparents who had struggled so hard, whose sense of *Yiddishkeit* [a Jewish way of life] was undiminished by the opulence of the Golden Land, were reminders of the emotional world they were leaving. They were, in a vital sense, abandoning their heritage even as America embraced them.[2]

One of the ways this theme of betrayal played out in Woody Allen's films was in the frequency of adultery. Ironically, though, just as Jews, however guilty, abandoned their Jewish past, America was embracing ethnicity. This phenomenon in American life was led by African Americans in the Civil Rights movement. They looked at their own culture and found strength with which to confront racism and discrimination. They were newly proud, and that pride proved infectious. Suddenly members of a variety of ethnic groups were seeking their roots.

Allen tried, and tried, psychotherapy to solve his problems. He might have been better off with ethnotherapy, because he, like many American Jews, didn't confront fully how their ethnic heritage affected them. They rejected the theology and incorrectly believed that in doing so they had abandoned Judaism. They too often accepted majority views of themselves. This could lead to what Allen was often accused of having: Jewish self-hatred.

But Allen's characters are more interesting than if they just suffered from self-loathing. They admire courage, being independent, being an artist. They look at individual acts as being capable of overcoming group membership and therefore of overcoming anxiety. But whatever the level of individual achievement, such efforts finally are weak in the face of social forces. Without seeing themselves as part of the Jewish people, Allen's characters are fundamentally unable to work through their anxieties.

Allen sometimes gives his characters names that reflect their being in two worlds. Fielding Mellish in *Bananas*, for instance, has a WASP first name and a Jewish surname, as does Cliff Stern in *Crimes and Misdemeanors*. Even Broadway Danny Rose has a distinctive American nickname combined with a Jewish real name. Their identity conflicts never leave them because the core of their identity, their names, reflects their identity tensions.

Ironically, one of Allen's most significant statements about Jewish identity is almost buried away as part of a film trilogy called *New York Stories* (1989). Allen's is the third of the three films. His contribution is titled *Oedipus Wrecks*, and, as the punning title suggests, the film is about a man's relationship with his mother. Allen, who wrote and directed the film, plays Sheldon, a New York lawyer. His mother, played by the incomparably-voiced Mae Questel, is always criticizing him, always unhappy with his fiancée (played by Mia Farrow). As Sheldon says in his opening line, "I'm 50 years old. I'm a partner in a big law firm. You know I'm very successful, and I still haven't resolved my relationship with my mother."

She constantly embarrasses him, filling him with perpetual torment. Sheldon goes to his therapist (this is a Woody Allen film, after all) and gives voice to his deepest desire. He wants his mother to disappear. At one point Sheldon, his mother, his fiancée and her children by a previous marriage go to a magic show. The mother is invited onto the stage by the magician, who puts her into a box where he will seem to stab her with swords. Anyone who doubts Woody Allen's acting abilities needs only to see the immensely satisfied look on Sheldon's face as he pictures his mother in that box when the magician plunges the blades into the sides of the box and presumably into his mother. But the trick goes awry. The mother disappears, but the magician somehow cannot bring her back. He has lost her. Deeply upset at first, Sheldon quickly realizes that fate has lent him a hand. He is able to relax without his mother's constant nagging, and he feels better about life. But his mother suddenly reappears, not as a regular mother but as a giant facial projection over the New York City sky. She talks to the entire city, telling strangers intimate details about Sheldon's life. Unable to bear the pressure, his fiancée leaves him. Sheldon, although highly skeptical at first, goes to see a Jewish psychic, Treva, who is played by Julie Kavner. Treva is completely inadequate at her task of removing the mother from the sky and making her part of ordinary life. But in the attempts, Sheldon sees how good a person Treva is and falls in love with her. This is so, in part, because unconsciously she reminds him of his mother. He introduces the psychic to his mother in the sky. She approves the new match and returns to Earth.

Talk about a bigger than life Jewish mother. Woody Allen's Freudian comic nightmare is revealing of the deep love-hate relationship he has with Judaism. It is a film well worth viewing and is too rarely discussed among Woody Allen's movies.

Of course, it's unfair to Allen to limit an understanding of his films to their content about Jewish identity or even to see them exclusively through such a prism. They appealed to intellectual, urban Gentile audiences because of their intelligence and the alienation those Gentile viewers felt. Intellectuals, after all, are a minority group just like the Jews and are resented, though not attacked or killed for that group membership. But they do have identity tensions comparable to Jews, and that's what many viewers saw in Allen's films.

Broadway Danny Rose (1984) stars Woody Allen as the title character, an artist manager with a lot of clients who leave him as soon as they become successful. He's always on the verge of failing, but he's always optimistic and, perhaps more importantly, always a fierce advocate for his clients. And he encourages the lowliest of acts. As he tells one act, "If you take my advice, you'll become one of the great balloon-folding acts of all time! Really, 'cause I don't just see you folding balloons in joints. You listen to me, you're gonna fold balloons at universities and colleges." He calls everybody "darling" and likes to say "My hand to God." Danny is a sweet, sincere, deeply sympathetic character.

Danny Rose's client Lou Canova, a singer trying to make a comeback, wants Danny's help. Lou's mistress is named Tina (played with surprising perfection by Mia Farrow). Lou loves Tina and desperately wants her to attend all his concerts. Her presence gives him the emotional strength to sing. Lou's problem is that he's married. But Lou comes up with a solution: Danny will pretend Tina is his girlfriend and bring her to the concerts.

Seven—The Borscht Belt Shtetl

That doesn't work out so well for Danny when two thugs come in search of Tina's lover because he stole Tina from their brother and broke his heart.

Danny talks to Tina about life. At one point he discusses God:

> DANNY: My rabbi, Rabbi Perlstein, used to say we're all guilty in the eyes of God.
> TINA: Do you believe in God?
> DANNY: No, no. But I'm guilty over it.

This take on God makes Danny Rose sound like a typical alienated Allen character. But this film is different in a way. Because many of Danny's acts perform in the Catskills, the Allen character is taken out of his neurotic urban environment. Danny isn't a cynic. He isn't isolated. Instead, he is a part of a warm spiritual community, one in which people get along with each other. This warm Jewish community of the Catskills resorts is far from the cold, isolated, empty landscape of Allen's usual films.

In this movie, even when the setting isn't the Catskills, the region's memory is evoked. The film opens with seven people sitting at a table in the Carnegie Delicatessen. Six of those men are former Catskill comedians: Sandy Baron, Jackie Gale, Corbett Monica, Howie Storm, Will Jordan, and Morty Gunty. Jack Rollins is the seventh man; he is Woody Allen's producer. As the men talk, they begin to discuss Broadway Danny Rose and his own career in the Borscht Belt. "He did all the old jokes and stole from everybody." This is a reference to Milton Berle, who was famous for stealing other comedians' material.

And, as we see Danny, it turns out many of the acts he manages are comically exaggerated examples of the kinds of acts that did in fact play the Catskills. Danny managed a parrot with the ability to sing "I Gotta Be Me," a penguin who is dressed like a rabbi as he skates around the stage, the husband and wife balloon-folding team mentioned above, a stuttering ventriloquist, a one-legged tap dancer, and a blind xylophone player.

As he tells a gangster girlfriend, he has shaped all the acts:

> TINA: I like it when he takes the microphone off the stand and sort of throws the microphone from hand to hand.
> DANNY: That's my gesture. I gave him that.
> TINA: Years ago he took the microphone off the stand.
> DANNY: But he didn't throw it from hand to hand. I used to do that in nightclub acts.
> TINA: So you taught him to throw the microphone from hand to hand...
> DANNY: I taught him everything he knows.

Danny doesn't quite get her past.

> DANNY: [asks about her ex-husband] What'd you do, you divorced him, or got a separation, or what?
> TINA: Nah, some guy shot him in the eyes.
> DANNY: Really? He's blind?
> TINA: Dead.
> DANNY: Dead. Of course, 'cause the bullets go right through.

Danny Rose is so interesting a Jewish character precisely because he insists on being moral, even though he consistently gets into trouble for acting decently. This is an interesting interpretation of Jewish identity and goes far beyond the normal Allen connection to being Jewish just through a consciousness of alienation. In Danny Rose, Jewish identity is defined as being moral. What is unique about such an identity is that the morality is not connected to a belief in God. Unfortunately, Allen doesn't explore the source of the morality apart from the belief in the divine, but, nonetheless, there is an advancement in the notion of Jewish identity in specifically tying it to moral behavior. In a way, *Broadway Danny Rose* is an ethical treatise, a study of moral behavior in action despite facing violence, defeat, and failure.

It's a stretch, but in a way the character of Broadway Danny Rose is a modern-day Job who has given up on God but not on morality. Less grandly, the film can also be seen psychologically, as Allen examining himself using counter-history, imagining his life had he not been a successful comedian but a small-time act constantly struggling.

But not every film about the Catskills was about the acts. Some of those movies were about the guests, the people who came for a week or a weekend, or about the workers, the waiters and the others.

Dirty Dancing (1987) is perhaps the most famous of those movies. A romance between a guest, Frances "Baby" Houseman, played by Jennifer Grey, and Johnny Castle, played by Patrick Swayze, is at the heart of the story. The film is set in the Catskills in the 1960s. Indeed, the movie opens to make the setting clear:

> BRUCE MORROW [a radio disc jockey on the radio]: Hi, everybody, this is your Cousin Brucie. Whoa! Our summer romances are in full bloom, and everybody, but everybody's in love. So cousins, here's a great song from the Four Seasons.
> BABY [voiceover]: That was the summer of 1963 — when everybody called me Baby, and it didn't occur to me to mind. That was before

Seven—The Borscht Belt Shtetl

> President Kennedy was shot, before the Beatles came, when I couldn't wait to join the Peace Corps, and I thought I'd never find a guy as great as my dad. That was the summer we went to Kellerman's.

Baby and her well-to-do family head for Kellerman's, a Catskill resort. Baby is very close to her father, a physician, and her family expects that one day she will grow up to marry a doctor as well. But Baby has her own desires, quite apart from those of her family. She falls for Johnny, the dance instructor. Johnny doesn't come from a privileged background like Baby does. So not only does the romance cross religious lines, it also crosses class lines. This is made clear in a conversation between Baby and Johnny:

> BABY: Have you had many women?
> JOHNNY: What?
> BABY: Have you "had" many women?
> JOHNNY: Baby, come on.
> BABY: Tell me. I wanna know.
> JOHNNY: No, no. Look, you've gotta understand what it's like, Baby. You come from the streets and suddenly you're up here, and these women, they are throwing themselves at ya, and they smell so good, and they really take care of themselves. I mean, I never knew women could be like that, you know? And they're so rich, they're so goddamn rich, you think they must know about everything. And they're slipping their room keys in my hands, two and three times a day, different women. So, here I think I'm scoring big, right? And for a while, you think, hey, they wouldn't be doing this if they didn't care about me, right?
> BABY: That—that's alright, I understand. You were just using them, that's all.
> JOHNNY: No, no that's not it. That's the thing, Baby, see it wasn't like that. They were using me.

Johnny has insights about the guests that Baby hasn't yet learned because her pampered background has prevented her from growing up.

Johnny's dancing partner becomes pregnant, and Baby gets the money for an abortion by lying to her father. But the friend becomes sick after the abortion, and Baby must summon her father for help. The father saves the woman's life and discovers the truth.

Dirty Dancing is not *Goodbye, Columbus* in its unflattering portrait of upwardly mobile Jews, although it is Johnny who is the moral guide in this Jewish world. The community has its immoral characters, but the Catskills warmth is still present.

Sweet Lorraine (1987) is far less well-known than *Dirty Dancing*, but it captures the sweetness and the nostalgia of the Catskill Resorts in a more authentic way. The film is about the impending fate of the Lorraine Hotel. This isn't a period piece; the film is not about a Borscht Belt resort in its prime but in its old age. Lillian Garber, the owner, is struggling with a problem about whether she should seek to fix up the Lorraine and continue its great but rapidly decaying tradition or sell the hotel to developers for some much-needed money. Against that background, the film portrays the summer season's revealing portrait of the guests, the workers, and the owners. The Lorraine is about the Catskills, but in a very gentle manner it transcends the location to become a metaphor for what humans should do with their own pasts. What happens when sweet memories confront a harsher present, when long-time working relationships and friendships may disappear, when we have to say good-bye to our own past and accept the inevitable flow of time?

That flow of time is not always kind, especially to comedians. Not everyone liked *Mr. Saturday Night* (1992), but the underappreciated film, which stars Billy Crystal, offers a brilliant portrayal of a comedic career, one filled with great insights. Crystal wrote, produced, directed and starred in it. Audiences that had problems with it may not have appreciated the wincing pain brought about by Buddy Young, Jr., the Jewish comedian created by Crystal. Much like the equally brilliant 2002 documentary *Comedian*, which followed Jerry Seinfeld and another comedian, *Mr. Saturday Night* goes behind the humor to the backstage truths, which are not funny and not always nice to look at. Many audience members just want to laugh, but Crystal bravely forged a real portrait of a comedian who played the Catskills and had a hit television show and then went into decline. The film isn't obviously based on any one Jewish comedian, but there are parts of many. Buddy starts out lip-synching songs, just as Jerry Lewis did. Buddy performed in a variety show like Milton Berle, Sid Caesar, and Red Buttons. They had the same pressures to perform and succeed that Buddy did. Buddy gets into trouble with the great impresario Ed Sullivan, just like Jackie Mason did.

Part of the emotional power of the film comes from the relationship between Buddy and his brother, Stan (well-acted by David Paymer). Stan doesn't want to be a performer. Buddy just uses him. At one point Stan wants to change some of the dialogue that isn't working on Buddy's television show. But Buddy won't have it. He says, "Stanley, let's each do what we do best. I'll tell the jokes, you'll get me a soda when I'm through." When Stan likes a woman at the Catskills hotel where Buddy is performing, Buddy makes him introduce the young woman to Buddy instead.

As the brothers talk at one point, the dialogue is poignant:

> BUDDY YOUNG, JR.: I didn't take your life, Stan. I gave you one.
> STAN: Yeah, but you coulda been nicer.

Buddy isn't nice. He's a self-centered user. He's a man who is perpetually cruel to those who are the very ones who are close to him, including, besides his brother, his wife and daughter. He can't accept what Fate has done to him, and he takes it out on everyone. He is a nasty man, but a funny one. He is offensive in his humor and aggressive in his life. He always had ambition. As he says late in the film, "I wanted to be the guy who, when he walked into the Friars, everybody turned around and said, 'Why him...?' I wanted to be that guy. I still do." It's a revealing statement about Buddy and maybe about other comedians as well. He lived for the approval of others. He couldn't accept a reality in which he wasn't seen as the best.

Buddy started as a youngster performing in front of his family, making lighthearted fun of them. For him, an audience was a large number of moms and dads, aunts, uncles, and cousins shouting their approval of him. He needed to be loved. And his statement had an aggressive bit of competition, that it didn't matter if he were better than the other comedians. The goal was to be seen as better. The truth didn't matter.

Why wasn't so excellent a film better received or more warmly recalled? "Buddy Young, Jr. had no struggles with which [audiences] could identity. If Albert Brooks had taken the Jewish side out of the identity struggle between being Jewish and being American, Crystal had taken the American side out. Buddy certainly wants success in America. But behind the scenes he is close to his mother and marries a Jewish woman. There is a professional struggle with which audiences might identify, but no personal identity struggle with which they could."[3]

The film is about the career of a Jewish comedian, but seen against the background of the Catskills it unintentionally also traces the career of the Catskills in the arc of the comedian's career.

Films about the Catskills seemed to disappear for a time, but they returned. There was *A Walk on the Moon* in 1999 and the off-beat comedy *Taking Woodstock* (2009) about a young man working in the Catskills who orchestrates what would become the world's most famous music festival. In the latter movie the decline in the area is nicely captured in a scene in which members of the Chamber of Commerce consider ideas for luring tourists to the mountains:

> FRANK: Well, okay. We got a lot of dairy farms around here, right? And a fair number of bulls. Okay, you've all heard of the running of the bulls in that town in Spain, Pampoona.
> ELLIOT TIBER: Pamplona.
> FRANK: Well, no one's doing one in the Catskills. Seems to be a big draw over there.
> ANNIE: It would be very amusing to see all those Jews from Levitsky's summer colony, you know, the ones with the black top hats and the curls, running for their lives chased by our local livestock. Wouldn't that be a wonderful sight!

The mass exodus of Jews from the Lower East Side and the decline of the Catskill resorts has meant, apart from some Hasidic communities, Jews don't live in one place. There are, of course, Jewish neighborhoods in cities and suburbs, but the closed world of the Lower East Side or the Borscht Belt is rare now.

An American Jewish identity has to be forged apart from a closed community. This makes Jewish identity formation more difficult and accounts in part for the wide American Jewish acceptance of full assimilation into the culture. The retention of a Jewish identity cannot rely simply on geographical proximity, and so the search continues.

CHAPTER EIGHT

Zion on the Screen: Films About Israel

Any search for an identity begins with the familiar. That might be family, a romance, the community, even the society. For Jews and others whose ancestors immigrated, there is also an unfamiliar element — the land from which they came. This unfamiliarity is complicated by a large factor for Jews because they didn't always identify as citizens of the nations where they lived, the nations didn't want them to do so and because they felt separated. This was especially true of Eastern Europe.

If Jews had a single ancestral country, that country is Israel, although the connection to it might go back for several thousand years for most American Jews. There are various ways in which such an ancestral identity for Israel is exemplified. The identification might take the form of a visit, political activity, economic support, or even, in relatively rare cases, making aliyah (moving to Israel). Sometimes such support simply involves the emotions, reading and listening to news stories about Israel, and feeling fiercely protective.

One way to understand this is through analogy. In this case, the American Jew is a sports fan and Israel is the team the fan roots for. The fan can never play but can visit the stadium. The fan follows the team, reads about it, knows its stars and duds, and roots for the team against its accursed opponents. Maybe the sports fan wears a team hat or jacket and feels his or her fate is tied intimately with that of the team. When the team is not doing well, the fan wants a new manager.

But American Jews are more than fans of Israel, and it is here that the analogy falls apart. Israel is truly in perpetual danger. Its support by American Jews is vitally needed. Israel is not just a game. Therefore, any American Jewish identity that includes support of Israel is not just emotional but genuinely useful and needed.

The problem for filmmakers (and, for that matter, for American Jews) is that no society is perfect. But criticism of Israel can potentially endanger it and foster anti–Semitism. Additionally, it is difficult to create compelling dramatic stories that work as art if there is a simultaneous concern to provide support. Because of these delicacies, Hollywood has been relatively reluctant to create films about Israel.

The real story of Israel is very dramatic and too large to be captured in a single film. The Jewish nation, then called Judea, was destroyed in stages, with the Second Temple falling in the year 70 of the Common Era. There were rebellions, and it took another century before the Romans completely controlled the land. The Israelites spread over the world, wandering without a homeland and subject to intense persecution stemming from their weakness.

The modern Zionist movement, the political effort to give a re-birth to a Jewish state in the same land where they had lived, began in the mid–1890s with the Viennese journalist Theodor Herzl writing a pamphlet titled *Der Judenstaat*, often politely translated as *The Jewish State* but more accurately as *The Jews' State*. (Herzl was using a term those who hated the Jewish people used — "Juden" — and saying these people were capable of re-forming their own nation.) Herzl and others convened the First Zionist Congress in August 1897 and began organizing their efforts. Meanwhile, Jews began to move back to the land which was then controlled by the Ottoman Empire and was not considered a separate nation. Jews, especially religious Jews, had lived in an unbroken line since they had been dispersed but not in large numbers and without political organization.

Herzl died in 1904 at the age of 44 without fulfilling his goal of re-establishing a Jewish nation. But others carried on the effort, both in the Land of Israel and outside it. The Holocaust, the systematic planned murder that resulted in the death of six million Jews (of which two million were children), lasted until 1945 and added a significant reason to the other reasons why Jews needed a homeland to provide safety for them.

Finally, after the vote of the United Nations, David Ben-Gurion, the man who would become Israel's first prime minister, declared Israel as an independent nation on May 14, 1948. Harry Truman, the U.S. president, provided recognition of the new nation a few minutes later. Israel immediately faced war, and many people were concerned that the fragile new nation would not survive against trained enemy armies. But Israel did survive, and because of the odds against it, many regarded its existence as a miracle.

Eight—Zion on the Screen

Sword in the Desert (1949) was the first American film about Israel. The movie is set in late 1947 — that is, before Israel became a nation. At the time, the land was controlled by the British, who had seized it from the Ottoman Empire during the First World War. In the movie there is a tramp freighter captain named Mike Dillon, played by Dana Andrews, who cynically smuggles Jewish refugees past the British, who are desperately trying to stop the effort. Dillon wants money and is doing this illegal effort solely for the cash. But then one day the British catch him with the refugees. The Jewish underground, the Haganah, frees Dillon and the other newcomers to the land. Dillon receives a Zionist education and becomes committed to the effort to help the Jewish people.

The story is simple and melodramatic. The British are portrayed in the film as unalloyed bad controllers of the land, and that depiction led to the movie's poor reception in England.

Perhaps because the film didn't win a large audience, or perhaps because Israel was itself controversial, Hollywood stayed away from the topic for some years, despite the fact that Israel was very much in the news.

But the films were to return, culminating in a blockbuster.

Before that, though, came another movie, this one starring Kirk Douglas. *The Juggler* (1953) makes a direct emotional connection between Israel and the Holocaust. The film was directed by Edward Dmytryk, who also had made *Crossfire*, the interesting study of anti–Semitism, and *The Young Lions*, which also featured some Jewish content. In *The Juggler* Douglas plays Hans Muller, a German Jewish refugee who has come to Israel after the horrors in his home country. Despite being physically present in Israel, though, Muller is unable to come to emotional terms with his past. He becomes a fugitive after attacking a police officer and travels with a boy who helps him. It is Muller's rescue at the end, the beginning of his healing, that provides the arc of the story. The story itself is interesting and bears well its novelistic origins.

As the film opens in feels, Hans Muller leaves his ship at Haifa. Hans suffers from a common ailment. He is guilty that he has survived while other people, other people, have perished in the most gruesome and cruel ways possible. He has lost touch with reality, as made evident in the scene when he sees a woman with her children and believes they are his own family. But his real family is not there. They were murdered by the Nazis.

Hans cannot stand to be locked up any longer and makes a break from the refugee camp, headed for Haifa. It is when he enters the city that the incident with the police officer occurs. Hans sees the police officer as a hostile authority figure and runs. The officer chases him and begins to ask him questions. It is then that Hans attacks the police officer until the man is unconscious and lying in the street. He does eventually recover and goes after Hans.

Hans runs to the countryside where a teenage orphan named Yehoshua (or "Josh") finds him. Josh is a sabra, a native-born Israeli who has not suffered through the Holocaust but nevertheless suffered his own family losses. Hans tricks Josh by claiming to be a strange American man on a visit to see the Jewish homeland. Josh is taken with the oddity of his behavior and offers to serve as his guide. As they travel, Hans reveals that at one point he was a professional juggler. Excited, Josh wants to learn how to juggle. Juggling is an original and interesting metaphor in the film for a Jewish identity. The Jew must keep a lot of objects flying around simultaneously and not drop any. It is a difficult identity to maintain because it is so complex, filled with so many constantly moving parts that can collapse at any second. Hans was once an expert juggler, but his skills faded, as did all of European Jewry when the Nazis arrived.

Josh is hurt in a minefield and is rushed to a kibbutz hospital where it is discovered that he has only suffered a broken leg. As Josh heals, Hans gets to know a woman there who wants him to remain on the kibbutz. He begins to open up to her, revealing some of his guilt. He had, he thought, ignored the many warnings his friends had offered about the rise of the Nazis. Like so many others he thought his contributions to society would be enough to keep him and his family safe.

The police officer finally tracks Hans to the kibbutz and attempts to arrest him. Hans, though, barricades himself inside the woman's room. There is a rifle there that he holds to defend himself.

The film ends as the officer and the woman make him realize that he desperately needs help. He surrenders in a metaphoric statement that the new nation of Israel can heal the deeply-wounded Jewish soul.

The Juggler is historic in the sense that it was the first American film made completely on location in Israel. It also is important because, as an early movie about the Jewish state, it established character archetypes in the minds of moviegoers. In the case of Hans Muller, the type was an outsider, but in dealing with other Israelis in the film, a variety of character types were developed, building on *Sword in the Desert*. These included sabras, native-born Israelis. The term "sabra" comes from a desert plant which is tough on the outside but soft on the inside.

Eight—Zion on the Screen

Many new Israelis were, like Hans Muller, refugees. He's not, for example, pleased to be there. As he notes, "A home is a place you lose." This is hardly an enthusiastic embrace of his new homeland. But Israel was a place where outsiders and survivors came. They had to become part of the country, to engage in a form of assimilation. *The Juggler* provides audiences with the symbolic journey of many Israelis who had to learn what it meant to be in a new country, learn a new language, and, most difficultly and most importantly, absorb a brand new Jewish identity.

Indeed, what is interesting about Israeli films is not the alienated newcomer but the model of that new identity, the fighting Israeli, the warrior. Here is a type not widely noted in recent Jewish history because Jews were deprived of their ancient land. But with the revival of Israel, and the accompanying need to fight to keep it, Jews had to, by necessity, become fighters. The American Jewish identity was one of cultured intellectuals, political and social activists, and hard working entrepreneurs. It was not at all associated with military prowess. That explains, in part, why the identity is comparable to a sports fan's.

But the American Jewish attachment to Israel had far subtler effects. In identifying with the fighting Israeli, those American Jews who looked to Israel for part of their Jewish identity underwent psychological changes as well. They came to view the political world through a more Israeli perspective, to see that the Israelis were living in a tough neighborhood. For however many American Jews it affected, this fact made them more sensitive to national security matters, more willing to accept fighting as an unwelcome but necessary part of existence. While such a changing perspective didn't affect the majority of American Jews, it did affect a significant and vocal minority who journeyed further toward the center or right on the American political spectrum. Other American Jews stayed where they had been — on the left. Some of them grew increasingly concerned about Israeli policies, and others reconciled their politics and Israel's without experiencing cognitive dissonance.

Similar to the notion of Israeli military prowess, there was another change. That can be seen in *The Juggler*. The character Yael in the film is a beautiful Sabra. The Jewish woman, running around in khaki shorts, flashing her stereotype-busting blonde hair, bravely and competently toting a gun, has come a long way from the Yiddishe mamas on the Lower East Side or the spoiled brats from the suburbs. Yael is the new Jewish woman.

American Jewish Films

Yael can be compared to the transformation of Goldie Hawn in *Private Benjamin*, another blonde who becomes competent with a weapon. Patricia Erens interprets all this from a feminist perspective:

> Though both are consonant with realities of Israeli life, the frequency with which they [blonde hair and rifles] recur in American films indicates that the image represents an obsessive sexual fantasy, the attraction for blond [sic] women, especially among Jewish males, reinforced by the erotic connotation of the gun. Pertaining to the latter icon, here the freedom and equality of the Israeli woman is co-opted and transformed into a symbol of sexual freedom (*cum* promiscuity).[1]

However accurate this observation may be, it bypasses what is important about the strong female in terms of an overall American Jewish identity.

But *The Juggler* was a small film, even with Douglas' terrific performance. It did not have a major impact on how American audiences perceived Israel or on American Jews. That was to come with another film.

Exodus (1960) was and remains the major American film about Israel. This movie entered the consciousness of Americans, making Israel a land of heroes and handsome fighters. The film, based on Leon Uris' groundbreaking novel, included many real events. While the title might echo the Biblical book with the same name, it also refers to the name of a ship carrying "illegal" Jewish refugees trying, as also depicted in *Sword in the Desert*, to get past the British blockade and enter the Land of Israel. The character of Akiva Ben Canaan (played by the great actor David Opatoshu), who in the movie was the commander of the Irgun, was based on Menachem Begin, the controversial underground Jewish leader at odds with the main Jewish political leaders in the country and sought as a criminal by the British. Begin, of course, later became Prime Minister of the country. Appropriately enough, Opatoshu again portrayed Begin in another film, *Raid on Entebbe.*

Exodus was epic. It was 208 minutes long and covered a lot of material. Its length engendered a comment that became a Hollywood legend. When the film was being premiered, by the time the third hour began, the then very popular satirist and political comedian Mort Sahl stood up in the theater and shouted at Otto Preminger, the film's producer, "Otto, let my people go."

The film intends to debunk stereotypes. In one famous scene, for example, Paul Newman, who plays Ari Ben Canaan, the story's hero, is

Eight—Zion on the Screen

talking to a British officer. Ben Canaan is pretending that he, too, is a British Gentile:

> MAJ. CALDWELL [about Jews]: They look funny, too. I can spot one a mile away.
> ARI BEN CANAAN [pointing at his eye]: Would you mind looking into my eye, sir? It feels like a cinder.
> MAJ. CALDWELL: Yes, certainly.
> [Caldwell looks into Ben Canaan's eye.]
> MAJ. CALDWELL: You know, a lot of them try to hide under gentile names, but one look at their face, you just know.
> ARI BEN CANAAN: With a little experience, you can even smell them out.
> MAJ. CALDWELL: I'm sorry Bowen, I can't find a thing.

The films about Israel all did this in one way or another. The Jews weren't victims; they were brave military heroes. The Jews weren't physically deformed; they were physically attractive. The Jews weren't cowards; they were fighters. One by one every stereotype about Jews was exploded in films about Israel. It's easy to see why these Israeli Jews became popular figures among some American Jews.

Some have criticized Paul Newman's performance as being bereft of emotion, but even if that is true, it fits with the tough character he's playing. And his good looks and confident demeanor were major contributions to the image of Israelis that American audiences took from the film.

Ari Ben Canaan is no utopian. He knows exactly what he's doing. As he tells Kitty, the Gentile American woman who comes over to the Zionist cause, the ship they are on to break the blockade is not some foolish errand. "Each person on board this ship is a soldier," he tells Kitty, "and the only weapon we have to fight with is our willingness to die."

It is an uncompromising, tough stand, but for the Jews there is not a death wish, only a dry-eyed understanding that they have no place else to go. "Ein breira" was a popular Hebrew expression of the time. Translated, it means "There is no alternative," and indeed they had none.

Kitty has a question of her own about those who have chosen to stay on the ship and risk starvation. "But for what purpose?" she asks Ari.

His response is direct: "Call it publicity, a stunt to attract attention." He is partially avoiding the real intention — to make a stand, to refuse to give in to authority. But his answer is that of Thoreau and Ghandi, as it would eventually be of Martin Luther King, Jr. Without a weapon, facing force, those in the moral right had only themselves to offer. And if they risked physical harm, so be it, because they knew they were in the right.

Exodus (Carlyle Productions, 1960) tells the incredible birth story of the nation of Israel. Here Paul Newman as the heroic Israeli freedom fighter Ari Ben Canaan prepares for one more battle.

Eight—Zion on the Screen

And Ari Ben Canaan is a good guide to the land and its power, its lure for the Jews returning to re-claim their ancient homeland.

At one point he and Kitty are journeying from Jerusalem to his home in the north of Israel. Ari pulls the car to the side of the road and stops. And then he speaks to Kitty.

> ARI: Every time I come home I stop here and just look for a minute. Do you want to look with me?
> KITTY: Sure.
> [The two get out of the car and walk up to the top of the hill. They go by three cyprus trees and then go down a bit. The view is spectacular, one of many in Israel, as visitors are stunned to learn].
> ARI: The Valley of Jezreel. If you dug straight down far enough, then you'd find the ruins of Megiddo. You'd find the very same paving stones that Joshua walked on when he conquered it. [Ari points.] That's Abu Yesha. It's an Arab village. To the left is Gan Dafna. Do you know your Bible?
> KITTY: In a Presbyterian sort of way.
> ARI: That's Mt. Tabor.
> KITTY: I remember. When Deborah gathered her armies....
> ARI: I just wanted you to know I'm a Jew. This is *my* country.
> KITTY: I do know. I understand.
> ARI: Sometimes it's not that easy.
> KITTY: ...All these differences between people are made up. People are the same no matter what they're called.
> ARI: Don't ever believe it. People are different. They have a right to be different. They *like* to be different. It's no good pretending that differences don't exist. They do. They have to be recognized and respected.

The film started with Dore Schary, who was the head of Metro-Goldwyn-Mayer, and who had made *Crossfire*. Schary wanted to make a movie about Israel, but he needed material. He turned to Leon Uris, then well-known for his World War II novel *Battle Cry*. Schary paid for Uris to spend two years in Israel collecting facts and finding out how to assemble real history into a dramatic story.

Ingo Preminger was a literary agent and saw an early copy of the book. He knew MGM planned to make a film of the book and told his brother, the film producer Otto Preminger. Otto read the book and, like its millions of fans would be, was immediately swept up in the grandeur of the narrative and the sheer power of the story.

Preminger went to MGM and met with its president, Joseph Vogel. Preminger had an argument. MGM had had considerable experience during the 1930s and 1940s with its films being banned in Europe generally and Germany specifically. There had been a lot of money lost. Preminger made the case that if MGM went ahead and filmed *Exodus* then Arab countries would ban all MGM films and close the MGM theaters in the countries. MGM, Preminger suggested, would suffer lasting negative consequences from an Arab boycott. And Preminger wasn't finished. Preminger, after all, was an independent producer. He had no theaters in Arab countries. He made few films. He told Vogel there were few serious consequences if he, Preminger, went ahead with the film.

Vogel at first refused to sell the rights to what many believed would be an important film. Other MGM executives were less emotionally attached to Israel and more to their ledgers. They saw the power of Preminger's argument.

Preminger eventually received the rights. By most accounts Otto Preminger was not the easiest man to work with. He must not have thought much of Leon Uris as a movie writer, mistrusting the author's ability to create crackling dialogue. In this case Preminger was as brave as he was in making the film. He hired Dalton Trumbo, a highly talented screenwriter but one who had been blacklisted during the McCarthy era. And Preminger didn't get along very well with Paul Newman. The star had a lot of directorial suggestions for Preminger, who didn't take kindly to those suggestions.

Lester Friedman has a theory about how Preminger worked in presenting an Israeli story to an American audience. He thinks the Israel in the movie

> functions as a kind of mini–America, the Jewish struggle for a homeland becoming suspiciously like our own western history. Ari and his compatriots are the explorers and settlers of a new land, the Arabs represent the heathens who refuse to share their land with the newcomers, and Kitty symbolizes the typical "Easterner" who comes West to civilize the wilderness. It's a Hollywood Western played out in the desert instead of on a prairie, a tale of brave men overcoming the dangers of a wild frontier to bring law, order, and civilization to a new land.[2]

There may be an analogy to be made, but the American Western, quite popular on television at the time the movie was produced, doesn't have the scope of the film and has limited themes compared to *Exodus*. Whatever Preminger's intent, the result was not universally accepted.

As has been mentioned, where the Middle East is concerned, everyone

Eight—Zion on the Screen

becomes interested in the result, and so the British were more than a bit displeased that they were portrayed so harshly in the film. *Exodus* was deeply sympathetic to the Zionist cause, and so it might be assumed that the Israeli government would find no fault at all with the film. But Israeli politics were more complex than audiences realized. There had been the rivalry between Begin and Ben-Gurion, between the underground, more militant movements and the regular provisional Jewish government. The Israeli government believed the film had portrayed the underground movements too sympathetically.

Preminger seemed to please no government completely, but he did please millions of moviegoers who shaped their vision of Israel according to this film. The movie drove even more people to the book, which had a life of its own. Indeed, the novel *Exodus* was passed around by Jews in the former Soviet Union and was an inspiration to them as they sought freedom to travel to Israel.

And, as Patricia Erens rightly notes:

> Preminger created an image of Israel that survives to this day, despite the changing realities. Although Preminger did not invent the Israeli character types, he expanded them, fixed them firmly on the screen — ten times bigger than life. Furthermore, he lent a sense of grandeur to the Israeli cause and gave the victimized Jews a sense of dignity in their ability to fight bravely.[3]

It is surprising in a way that the film does not emphasize the difference between Arabs and Jews. In a way the movie is a depiction of an internal Jewish family struggle, of different ways of interpreting Jewish nationalism. That simplifies the film, but the familial dispute makes it more dramatic, more intimate for audiences, and less political.

That image fit the emotional needs of American Jews. They didn't want a political fight to witness. They wanted a symbolic homeland (though not a real one because they didn't want to move to Israel), and they wanted heroic projections of themselves. They wanted to think of themselves as great fighters. *Exodus* was, in this sense, a sort of fantasy film for the American Jewish self-image.

But a fantasy is an inadequate foundation on which to build an identity. At least in part.

Exodus is the perfect case study to consider how film affects Jewish identity because it had one of the most profound effects on Jewish identity of any film. There are many documentary films about Israel and even more non-fiction works. And yet it is the overpowering emotions that come from a fictional account, either in the Uris novel or the movie, that have the most profound effect, that work the best in shaping our beliefs and attitudes. In this film we can talk directly about attitudes toward Israel, but the point is a wider one about how movies (and novels and television shows and daydreams and fairy tales and all the other examples of fiction in our lives) shape our identity. So while the discussion here is about films, those pictures stand as a working metaphor for all kinds of fictional endeavors. And why are films so effective? Unlike a documentary, fictional films do not try to assemble evidence or cobble together an argument. When we watch a documentary, we do so with wariness. Our critical antennae are up, listening for arguments that don't make sense. Our skeptical selves doubt the claims. Our critical selves see all the flaws, the wandering lines of argument that go in the wrong direction.

However, when we watch a fictional film we flow down a narrative river, letting it carry us along. Our critical selves and our skeptical selves have abandoned us. We give ourselves over to the story itself. Put simply, the fictional film is not proceeding by argument. It is not trying to persuade us through logic. It is trying to move us emotionally. And the more we are absorbed by it, the more moved we are by the emotions it creates, the more it affects us.

What *Exodus* does is brilliant. It grounds its emotions in history that has already moved us emotionally. Viewers stunned by the Holocaust, stirred by the redemption inherent in the rebirth of Israel, already at the edge of letting go because of the Phoenix-like near death and revival of the Jewish people, is prepared for the emotions of the story. And the filmmakers don't disappoint. They take the already primed emotions that audiences have and ratchet them up with a love story, a rescue story, a story of heroism and war, filled with enemies, both external and internal. *Exodus* found a perfect storytelling recipe. And those of us in the audience are willing, even eager, to be shaped by the film's emotions.

That makes the movie (and every work of fiction) sound manipulative. Of course, in some sense it is. It deliberately and purposefully sets out to make us think and feel a certain way through the creation of a specific story. But here a judgment can be made. If the film changes us, it changes us for the better. We have more empathy for the Israelis, more understanding of their plight. The film makes us concerned about the right. It brilliantly casts Kitty as a Christian, not a Jew, so that the moral

Eight—Zion on the Screen

message is not seen as ethnocentric or tribal. The redemption from near annihilation, the film's intimate connection between the Holocaust and Israel, is moving and moral for all people, not just Jews, not just political progressives or political conservatives.

Beyond a charge of being manipulative, films like this one, again like any fictional creation, can be accused, quite accurately, of deliberately telling untruths. They do not purport to portray reality. They do not pretend they are transmitting accurate facts. They openly, even gleefully, admit they are lying. And audiences have to, in Coleridge's famous phrase, suspend their disbelief and accept the work of fiction as having some useful and interesting message.

Calling films lies sounds forbidding. They become insidious, subtly affecting our beliefs. But an examination of *Exodus* specifically, and movies (and fiction) generally, tells a different tale. This film and others make us understand other people. Movies make huge deposits in our internal empathy banks. The films contribute to our moral development. They can therefore make us kinder human beings. Films make us choose between the hero and the villain, between, put simply, the right and the wrong. Yes, they can oversimplify, but the point is that we choose. We become active moral agents, and the movies become a rehearsal for our real lives when we have to make complex moral choices. Films are generally on the side of the good and the righteous. Generally the bad people are punished eventually; however interesting they are on the journey, that journey's end is not a happy one. The lesson for audiences of all films is that it pays to be good.

That powerful moral message in this movie that Jews suffered but were eventually saved, that overwhelming odds can't stop a triumphant redemption, is not just aimed at individuals. We in the audience are separated but we are also together. The in-fighting among the Jews in *Exodus* doesn't prevent them from seeing themselves and their "enemies" as part of the same community, as glued together socially by a belief in Israel and its values. So, too, films and fiction about any subject bind the audience together in common consent that the values portrayed are good for all. Such an overwhelming realization promotes social harmony and creates an invisible force linking humans one to another.

It seems plausible that in the wake of the success of *Exodus* that other movies about Israel would be made. But its controversies proved too daunting for Hollywood. They certainly wanted to make money, but they didn't want controversy. Hollywood is about taking only certain kinds of chances. And so Israel languished as a subject, in a way to be replaced by the Holocaust. It was far easier to portray Jews as victims than as fighters. There was no disagreement about the Holocaust, no threats of boycotts, no national anger from any country. Everyone, including the Germans, agreed the Holocaust had been a paradigm of moral evil. Its very ugliness, murder, and horror made it a dramatic subject. Its emergence in the culture made it well-known. And so Jews were the subjects of films, but not films about Israel.

There were some exceptions, of course, but not many. *Judith* (1966) was a film about a woman (played beautifully, but not always convincingly, by Sophia Loren) who was a concentration camp survivor betrayed by her Nazi husband. She ends up on a kibbutz where she recovers her emotional well-being. This material had been covered already in *The Juggler*, so there was no thematic breakthrough.

Cast a Giant Shadow (1966) was a more interesting movie, bigger in scope, and again put Kirk Douglas, himself Jewish, in Israel, this time as Colonel David "Mickey" Marcus, a real-life American soldier who helped the Israelis with their struggle for independence and died just as the war was ending. But the filmmakers had learned a lesson or two from the marketing of *Exodus*. In the case of *Cast a Giant Shadow*, the words "Israel" or "Jewish" didn't appear in the marketing materials. Instead, the film was pitched to audiences simply as an adventure in the exotic desert.

Unlike Ari Ben Canaan, Mickey Marcus doesn't start out being a good and proud Jew:

> COLONEL DAVID "MICKEY" MARCUS: Would you give up everything you love to fight an insane war for a little country that's gonna get its brains blown out in a couple of weeks?
> MAJOR SAFIR: If it were my country.
> MARCUS: Maybe it's yours, but ... it isn't mine.
> SAFIR: But you are a Jew.
> MARCUS: I'm an American, Major. That's my religion. The last time I was in Temple I was 13 years old. I made a speech and got 42 fountain pens. I don't have to go again. I've got enough fountain pens.

But Israel transforms him. Israel becomes the catalyst for developing a Jewish identity. This is the value of the film apart from *Exodus*. Unlike the protagonists of *The Juggler* or *Judith*, Mickey Marcus isn't confused or emotionally wounded. He loves his wife in his own way. He certainly loves

Eight—Zion on the Screen

the United States. He has, though, no connection to being Jewish. He is just secular. It is Israel that gives him that Jewish identity as he figures out a way to build a road to Jerusalem.

At one point Mickey and the Israelis have failed in their attempt to capture a fort at Latrun. Mickey is talking to an Israeli military leader named Asher Gonen (played by Yul Brynner). It is a turning point in Mickey's life. Suddenly he is no longer just an American soldier who is helping the Jews recover their state. He has found an identity:

> MICKEY MARCUS: We're all worn out, but we'll do it. We made it across the Red Sea, didn't we?
> ASHER: Mickey, it's the first time I ever heard you say "we."
> MICKEY: Yeah ... you people. Pipsqueak nation ... Tin-can army that fights with seltzer bottles. "We." All my life I've been looking for where I belong. Turns out it's here. The Catskill Mountains with Arabs. I've been so angry at the world ever since I was circumcised without my permission. All of a sudden I find out that I'm not so special after all. Everybody here is in the same boat and nobody's bellyaching. Okay. "Stand up and be counted," the man said. "Grow up," is more like it. I'm not fighting anymore because I'm ashamed of being a Jew. I'm fighting because I'm stiff-necked and proud of it. Next week, Asher. Next week in Jerusalem.

This interesting identity development is hidden in the film. Instead, the filmmakers focus on Mickey's relationship with an Israeli woman and with his wife. At the end of the film he declares to the Israeli that he is going back home. Making Mickey's story romantic certainly plays to the sentimentality of the audience but misses a significant opportunity to make a major statement about Jewish identity.

And, it should be noted, Mickey in the film backtracks on his new identity. He is ready to return to his middle-class life in America rather than forge a new life in his new land.

And so the Israeli identity shines brightly and is extinguished. It is a case of, as in the title of Saul Bellow's book, *To Jerusalem and Back*. American Jews will visit Israel sometimes, will root for it sometimes. But they won't move there, won't finally and fully transform their identity.

So absorbed were American Jewish filmmakers and audiences with the Holocaust and other forms of understanding what it meant to be Jewish that films about Zionism and Israel disappeared. There were some Israeli films based on the rescue of hostages at Entebbe airport, but by and large Israel was ignored in feature films, if not in the news.

In 1972 Israeli athletes were killed at the Olympic games in Munich. This terrible event seemed like dramatic material. But when Steven Spielberg made a movie about the massacre, it wasn't about the Jews as victims, but about the Jews as seeking justice (or, read differently, revenge) against those who had organized the massacre.

Raid on Entebbe (1976) was released originally in the United States as a television movie. In semi-documentary style, the film tells the stirring story of a real event that occurred on July 4, 1976, when Israeli soldiers in Operation Entebbe freed hostages held at Entebbe Airport in Uganda. The drama began when the hijackers, recruited and working for a terrorist group, the Popular Front for the Liberation of Palestine, hijacked an Air France plane and flew it to Uganda, where they were welcomed by the dictator Idi Amin.

Much of the film focuses on the painful, life-altering decisions made by the cabinet members. They were, after all, talking about a raid that took place on the Jewish Sabbath 2,500 miles away from Israel. But Israel had no intentions of surrendering to terrorist demands. Still, the uncertainty engendered arguments and a tense atmosphere.

> SHIMON PERES: Intelligence informs us they will begin killing hostages on Sunday.
> YITZHAK RABIN: The string has run out, Hmm?
> PERES: Then why are we debating the military plan? Let them go!
> RABIN: Because it is not perfect.
> PERES: Yitzhak, that's a joke! Here you are concerned with perfection, and... And we don't have a choice!
> RABIN: There will be two hundred of our best people on those planes... I damned well do have a choice!

As in real life, the Israelis pulled off the incredibly daring rescue with brilliant tactics and perfect follow-through of their plan. There was only one Israeli casualty. It is a hallmark of the Israeli Defense Forces that the leader leads from the front rather than staying in the rear. In this case the leader was Yonatan Netanyahu, whose younger brother Benjamin would eventually become Israel's Prime Minister. Three of the hostages were killed. Forty-five of Amin's soldiers perished in the attack. Still another hostage, an older woman named Dora Bloch, had been removed from the airport and taken to a hospital. After the raid, Amin ordered that she be killed, and the order was carried out.

The film is inspirational and provides a dimension to Jewish life not readily available in American Jewish films except in ones about Israel. There is a genuine hero in this story. It is a tale of physical and not just moral courage. It gives a body to the mind of Judaism. But not all movies about Israel were to be epic and heroic. After the Six-Day War and with increasing volume, there were voices raised that questioned the Israelis as pure heroes.

Munich (2005) was a new kind of film about Israel. No longer were the Jews struggling for their homeland. This time it's about Avner, the leader of a five-man team approved by Prime Minister Golda Meir to kill those involved with the Munich deaths. But these men aren't necessarily presented as heroes. The film, indeed, makes an explicit connection between the Israelis and the terrorists.

> EPHRAIM: We have 11 Palestinian names. Each had a hand in planning Munich. You're going to kill them, 11 men, one by one. They're all in Europe now. You'll stay there as long as it takes. Europe only, not the Arab countries. That's for us, not you. And not Eastern Bloc. Don't upset the Russians. Who needs it? You'll have no contact with us.
> AVNER: You're not going to give me any information?
> EPHRAIM: We deposit money from a fund that doesn't exist into a box we don't know about, in a bank we never set foot in. We can't help you because we never heard of you before. You'll do what the terrorists do. You think they report back to home base? They don't. We want them dead.

But the difference is that the Israelis have a conscience. As one of them says, "We are supposed to be righteous. That's a beautiful thing. And we're losing it. If I lose that, that's everything. That's my soul."

There is a new Israeli here, one American Jews are struggling with, one they can't fully identify with or they can't understand.

Munich is disappointing in failing to see the moral complexities of being an Israeli, of seeing Israel through only American eyes, of making conscience have to be easy or not useful. In this willful separation of an American Jewish identity and an Israeli one, *Munich* goes where other films about Israel haven't gone. If Mickey Marcus discovered his Jewish identity in Israel, in *Munich* Jewish identity is considered to be a morality that is too idealistic for reality and thus one the Israelis can't meet in the world in which they live. In that sense, *Munich* makes an Israeli identity impossible for American audiences. This is a far cry from previous films about Israel and cuts off questions of how Israel can contribute to an American identity.

Chapter Nine

The Dark Side: Jewish Criminals on Film

Despite an ethical religious system that has been sustained over several thousand years, and contrary to hope and expectation, not every Jew is a good person. Or, more precisely, not everyone Jewish by religious law is good. In theory at least, if someone obeys the moral precepts of Judaism, that person would be good. But there is much evidence that Jews are sometimes lacking in the moral character needed to be good. This ought to be obvious, and so there ought to be no particular problem in creating bad Jewish characters, such as Jewish criminals. There were, after all, such criminals in twentieth-century American history. Even in the late 19th century a man named Monk Eastman organized a Jewish criminal gang that rivaled and competed with the then-prominent Irish gangs in New York City. Later Jewish gangsters included Arnold Rothstein, who was, among other criminal enterprises, widely accused of fixing the 1919 World Series. It was especially during the Prohibition Era that Jews entered organized crime. Meyer Lansky and Ben "Bugsy" Siegel organized bootlegging operations. The Purple Gang, organized in Detroit by Abe Bernstein, engaged in an array of crimes, including murder. And there were many other famous Jewish criminals of the Prohibition Era, including Dutch Schultz, Abner "Longy" Zwillman, and others.

The relationship between Jews and Prohibition, and therefore Jews and criminality, is a complex one. Those who favored Prohibition were often the same people who opposed immigrants. And, though it may surprise some, Jews had a long relationship with making liquor. In Belorussia during the 19th century, for example, Jews owned between one third and two-thirds of all the distilleries. An 1890 census taken there showed that Jews ran 190,000 taverns. So Jews participated in the American liquor trade

Nine—The Dark Side

comfortably and were as upset as others when Prohibition arrived. The Prohibitionists attacked Jews as foreigners, for the supposedly corrupting influences of the popular entertainments that Jews helped shape, and for their participation in the alcohol trade. Jews, that is, were suddenly transformed in the minds of some White Anglo-Saxon Protestants who hadn't had a previous prejudice from hard-working and skilled entrepreneurs to criminal bootleggers.

Jews therefore generally opposed those in favor of Prohibition. Obviously this was partly because of social and economic self-interest. Alcohol had, after all, been at least part of the economic life of American Jews. But Jews also opposed Prohibition because they quite rightly viewed some in the leadership of the movement as intolerant and morally arrogant. Jews feared that as the Prohibitionists savored their political and legal victory against liquor, that would both inflame and empower them to turn their attention to increasing legal limits on the Jews. Prohibition became the law of the land in 1919 when the 18th Amendment passed.

There can be no denying the simple historical fact that Jews were involved in making, transporting, distributing, and selling illegal alcohol. Ironically, the Volstead Act, which had been passed to implement the ban on alcohol, allowed Jewish families to make and own ten gallons of kosher wine a year for religious purposes. There was no enforcement mechanism. That meant that Jews could distribute a lot of wine, and they did just that. In 1924, 2,944,764 gallons of "kosher wine" were distributed. It was the Jews prominent in making the wine who became the famous Jewish criminals. There were, it should be noted, also Jews very active in the fight against illegal alcohol. For example, Izzy Epstein, who worked on the Lower East Side in New York as a Prohibition agent, arrested many Rabbis for their work with liquor. As it turned out, some of these "Rabbis" were named Houlihan or Maguire.

All these criminals were used by those who opposed Jews entering America or opposed non–White Anglo-Saxon Protestants entering the country. The enemies of the immigrants did manage to eventually pass legislation that limited newcomers to America. People were scared of the foreigners to begin with. They were threatened by the new, by the rampaging change of history.

In the era leading up to the First World War it was much more possible to be optimistic. Starting with the mid–1870s and going to the start of World War I in 1914, consider the inventions: the telephone, the telegraph, the automobile, the phonograph, the motion picture camera and projector, the airplane, and so much more. Even the all-electric television tube, which over time allowed for that new invention, was invented by Vladimir Zworykin in 1909. That is to say, in the space of a single lifetime all changed. People could believe in the future, that all would be well. Sure, the Civil War had been devastating, but it was over, and the Industrial Revolution which swept across America was an economic dynamo. Manufacturing increased. National wealth increased. It looked, with all these inventions, as though the world would be a sort of paradise for one's children or at the very least one's grandchildren. And the foreign workers who didn't believe what other Americans believed, who didn't believe in Jesus at all, or accepted the rule of the Pope in Rome, or who were yellow people from Asia, or who couldn't speak English, and had terrible manners and odd customs, even these workers were accepted because they were needed to fuel the economy.

But the First World War changed all that. The Great War all too amply illustrated that paradise wasn't on the way. The takeover of the Bolsheviks in Russia in 1917 was scary. Foreign radicals could take over. And so, after the war, America changed. Prohibition came to power, and in its wake criminal elements learned to organize and grow to meet the drinking needs of a public openly willing to ignore the law. New immigrants were increasingly locked out. Without an ongoing belief in a great future, people who had been restraining their immoral impulses and working hard and delaying their gratifications just let go. The Roaring Twenties may have been a lot of fun, but it also marked the end of the last moment when great hope was possible. The era produced its own heroes. Some were writers or movie stars. And some were criminals, including Jewish criminals.

But the movies and the American Jewish community focused on the practical results of the criminality. They looked around and saw that there were Jewish criminals. Some observers blamed this on poverty or other social conditions. Some in the Jewish community were so ashamed of the relatively long list of Jewish criminals that they tried to pretend these men were simply aberrations who could be safely ignored while the health of the community continued to develop well. That is, every possible reason was considered by those who did the considering—except the most uncomfortable one, the most challenging one. Was it possible that America itself created Jewish criminals? Was it possible that assimilation had found another form beyond romantic love with Gentiles, beyond abandoning

Nine—The Dark Side

religious practices and beliefs and traditions, beyond refraining from work on the Sabbath? Unsurprisingly, this crucial question was not asked by American movies. Why, after all, make audiences uncomfortable? America was the Golden Land, not the garden for criminality. The question of America as a land of moral corrosion would have been a fascinating one for an American film, but none dared to go there. In part, this reluctance is revealing not just because movies were meant to be entertaining or movies didn't want to cause cognitive dissonance for the audience members' belief systems. The reluctance is also revealing because it shows how important religion was to Jewish survival. Religious films will be discussed later, but it is appropriate at this juncture to note that we might explain love interests as part of a natural human desire. We can explain the desire for fame and fortune and success as an understandable element of human beings even if those pursuits sometimes required the abandonment of tradition. But how is it possible to explain the attractions of sadistic criminality, of organized murder, robbery, and other crimes? These became acceptable because there was no longer a fear of punishment or even moral judgment by an absent or non-existent God. Once religion vanished from the life of American Jews, all the temptations remained but were now accompanied by a sense that there was no punishment waiting if any method at all was used to give in to those temptations. And, it should be recalled, it was the secular Jews, the young Jews, the most impressionable group, who ventured to the New World as immigrants. But, it must be concluded, it was America that offered the criminal life, the romance of the outlaw, the quick riches and quicker partners available to the criminals. Some Jews succumbed, but the lesson for all Jews was not learned. Religion did not make a comeback because of criminality, and, in some small part at least, that was because no films discussed the subject. Of course, only a very small portion of the blame can be ascribed to movies. Most of the blame can be assigned to the Jewish community itself, which did not clearly see what assimilation cost and how it might be tempered.

The very fact that the heroic Jewish criminals were real, even if that fact was manipulated by anti–Semites and anti-immigrant activists, posed a dilemma for the Jewish community, as well as journalists, writers, artists, and filmmakers. It was an act of moral cowardice to refuse facing the truth, but it was dangerous to emphasize Jewish criminality in an age when anti–Semitism in America was growing, when fascism, especially Nazism, was rising in Europe, and when Communism, which would end up killing an enormous number of Jews, was consolidating power in the new Soviet Union.

What happened with movies was interesting. Most of the films about criminals were about more famous criminals than Jews or about generic criminals without ethnic identification. Their rise was grounded in social comment, so that the films were as much about the evils of poverty or urban blight as about the moral choices of the criminals themselves.

Additionally, once Jews left organized crime in large numbers (the Jewish criminals being unwilling to pass on the family business to their children), and once Jews became much more widely accepted in American society, the idea of Jewish criminals became romanticized, much the same way American criminals had become romanticized. The brilliant folk singer Woody Guthrie, for example, wrote a historically inaccurate but stirring song about the bank thief Pretty Boy Floyd, turning him into a Robin Hood. Billy the Kid became a folk hero. People followed the adventures of John Dillinger. This mythologizing of the Jewish criminal was interesting for two reasons. The first reason is that the criminals soon enough discovered that they were rushing toward death or jail. They had discovered that America was opening up for Jews. They were succeeding in entertainment, in business, in education. There was, to put it simply, no benefit to making criminality a family business. The second reason the mythologizing is interesting is that it didn't lead to a revival of Jewish criminality or a reverence for criminals in the Jewish community. This fact, too, could have been the basis of an interesting film about Jews and criminality.

In post–World War II American Jewish life, especially starting with the revival of ethnic identity that began in the 1960s, the Jewish criminals were seen by some in the Jewish community as a healthy antidote to stereotypical portraits of Jews as weak and cowardly. The criminals' toughness was seen as positive.

But Jews had always prided themselves on their morality, their following laws. Their religious life for centuries had been grounded in following religious law. And however far American Jews had wandered from the notion of following such religious laws, and they had wandered very far indeed, the heritage of a respect for law was within them as they met the more lax American attitudes toward obeying laws.

Perhaps because of this dilemma, there were not a lot of big-budget serious films involving Jewish criminals. The small-budget movies didn't have the swaggering criminals of other American films. It was almost as though the movies were themselves conflicted and showed Jewish gangsters as conflicted as well. For example, Tony Curtis portrayed the Jewish criminal Louis "Lepke" Buchalter in the 1975 film *Lepke*, but Curtis portrayed the criminal as knowing a bad end would eventually arrive, as though some element of a conscience prevented the swagger necessary to be a criminal. Similarly, *King of the Roaring Twenties: The Story of Arnold Rothstein*, which was made in 1961, offers a character much tamer than the real Rothstein.

There were, though, more serious films (at least to some extent) made about Jews breaking the law. However, all the movies were external observers only. They looked at Jews from the outside. The more interesting internal questions were never probed. These questions included such dilemmas as how did criminals arise in a culture devoted to ethical behavior? Or how did the criminals reconcile their behavior with their background? Or did they even attempt such a reconciliation? Some of the films were very interesting, such as the black-and-white *The Plot Against Harry* (1989), which really had been made twenty years earlier but had gotten an inadequate release. It eventually found a second life through the film festival route. The movie is about Harry Plotnick, a middle-aged very-small-time crook. Harry is just released from prison as the film opens. He goes back to his roots but discovers that the entire world he once knew had changed, that the neighborhood, for example, is now filled with African Americans and Hispanics. Even his family is uninterested in his return, as he decides he wants to become a caterer. The whole world seems to be in a plot against Harry resuming a normal life. But what's interesting from a Jewish identity point of view isn't covered in the film. Harry is involved in a struggle with his conscience. Had that struggle more explicitly been tied to his being Jewish, and had it been given more explicit dramatic content, this movie would have been much more important.

But, like with many other films, the Jewish content just didn't make an adequate appearance. A prime example of this absence of Jewish content was in *Compulsion* (1959). The movie was about the Leopold and Loeb case, one of the most well-known murder trials in America. The film was based on the writing of Meyer Levin, especially his play. The picture's director, Richard Fleischer, kept Levin's changed names, which were Artie Strauss and Judd Steiner. These were still Jewish names, but now the story inhabited a fictional world, as though Fleisher was unwilling to remind viewers exactly who had committed the crime of murdering a boy. The story is the same, however. Two very bright college students think they are far more intelligent than those around them and seek to demonstrate that intelligence and that dismissal of others by committing what they assume will be a perfect crime. They murder a fourteen-year-old boy named Bobby Franks. The two men receive life sentences thanks to the defense provided by their nationally famous lawyer, Clarence Darrow. The murder had also inspired Alfred Hitchcock's film *Rope* (1948), but *Compulsion* was even more clearly based on this case.

The film seems to go out of its way to avoid mentioning the fact of Leopold and Loeb's Jewishness or discussing the role that Jewishness may have played in the crime. Meyer Levin was a novelist and playwright. He cared passionately about American Jewish life. And he deeply believed that the pair suffered from Jewish self-hatred, and that had been a crucial factor in the crime. The filmmakers, however, completely eliminated Jewish issues from the movie.

This decision was a matter of choice, because Levin provided the material. Here is the pertinent exchange in Levin's play, which was not included in the film. It is a conversation between Ruth, a young woman Judd has dated, and Jonathan Wilk, the defense attorney for Leopold and Loeb:

> RUTH: He had no childhood, nothing normal…. There was something else — it's hard to explain. We're Jewish — oh, it's so hard to explain. Some are proud and some — it torments them, twists them. It's called self-hatred. They hate themselves for being somehow ashamed of being Jews. Judd had this trouble.
> WILK: What makes you think that?
> RUTH: Being called a sheenie and other dirty names. It affected him deeply. When he was small the neighborhood boys — not Jewish — tormented him, even tore down his trousers. He hated them. He hated himself. He wanted to be like Artie, a tall blonde type who doesn't look Jewish. That was one reason he idolized him.
> WILK: In speaking of this Jewish trouble here, this self-hatred, it's not a religious matter?
> RUTH: No. But maybe religion is mixed up in it. Because of the social troubles about being a Jew, children get to hate their religion. Judd told me he dreamed of his mother as the Christian Madonna. It's another way of not wanting to be Jewish, of running away from it…. My father once showed me a prayer, the deepest prayer of the whole year. Atonement. And there is a line. We ask for forgiveness for the sins of free will and the sins of compulsion.[1]

Nine—The Dark Side

It is a shame this exchange was not in the film. It would have added a significant and revealing dimension. Its absence, though, offers its own revelation. Using a charitable interpretation, the filmmakers didn't want to provoke anti–Semitism. They were afraid of discussing Jewish issues from a Jewish point of view in an open way. This self-censorship, this artistic repression, reduced the power of Jewish films and prevented greater ones from being made.

In a way, then, *Compulsion* is a metaphor for all American Jewish films. The filmmakers are unable or unwilling to probe the Jewish psyche deeply. Perhaps it is a fear that American audiences won't watch the movies, or that the Jewish community will rush to condemn uncomfortable subjects, or that the material is difficult to present dramatically. Whatever the reason, Jewish films have not examined Jewish life the way more broadly American films have unsentimentally examined American life.

Once Upon a Time in America (1984) is about two Jewish hoodlums, but perhaps because filmmaker Sergio Leone is not American the movie seems to have no Jewish moorings. Artistically, the film is extremely interesting. Leone takes chances. He has long scenes without any dialogue. The story covers time and has a large cast of characters, centering on Noodles and Max, the Jewish hoods, played astonishingly well by Robert De Niro and James Woods. Neither one of the hoods, like the movie, is grounded in reality. This is a fantasy film, or, to be fairer, a mythic movie rather than a film truly about Jewish gangsters. There are mentions of Jewishness but no examination beyond the superficial. In that sense, despite the definition offered to the characters, this is much more a film about gangsterdom than about Jews.

Perhaps the biggest Hollywood attempt to portray a Jewish gangster came in *Bugsy* (1991). The story, at least in theory, is about the gangster Benjamin "Bugsy" Siegel. Directed by Barry Levinson, the film attempts a bit of magic. Bugsy is not merely a gangster; he's a charming gangster. Perhaps every character played by Warren Beatty ends up being charming, even a criminal (think of, most obviously, Clyde Barrow in *Bonnie and Clyde*). The Bugsy Siegel in this movie is not the Bugsy Siegel of the real world. This Bugsy is genuinely in love, though this love is doomed to fail. The dialogue in the film is meant to generate heat. Here is an exchange with the woman he loves, Virginia Hill:

> "Bugsy" Siegel: Got a light?
> Virginia: The way you were looking at me, I thought you were going to ask for something more interesting.

BUGSY: Like what?
VIRGINIA: Use your imagination.
BUGSY: I'm using it.
VIRGINIA: Let me know when you're finished.

The Bugsy of this film is a grand dreamer, a planner, a visionary, a man who built Las Vegas. It should be noted that Bugsy's plan to build The Flamingo was not original in any real sense of the word. The El Rancho and Last Frontier already existed on the Las Vegas Strip when Bugsy started, and it was Billy Wilkerson, a gambler, who had the idea. Wilkerson had Los Angeles nightclubs and intended to make a comparable club out on the Strip. Siegel became Wilkerson's partner and ultimately gained control. It should also be noted that, to be fair, Siegel did dream big, much bigger than Wilkerson ever imagined. Casting Beatty in the role was typical Hollywood. He wasn't Jewish and was ten years older than Siegel was at the time of Siegel's death.

Perhaps *Bugsy* works so well as a film (it was nominated for ten Academy Awards) because it wasn't really about a gangster but about a love affair, a dream, and Las Vegas. And it had great original material. The real Bugsy Siegel was a ladies man. He was someone who enjoyed being around celebrities, and was, to some extent at least, a minor celebrity himself. In real life the actor George Raft had come from Bugsy's childhood neighborhood and knew a lot of the gangsters. Bugsy knew and was even friends with a whole variety of Hollywood A-list actors. He knew Gary Cooper, Clark Gable, Cary Grant, Jean Harlow, Howard Hughes, and others. But the real Bugsy was an amoral murderer, a man incapable of genuine empathy. In real life he had been part of a gang on the Lower East Side's Lafayette Street. Eventually he went into the protection racket. The poor Jewish pushcart owners had to pay him a dollar for protection, or else he would set their merchandise on fire. Siegel, as a youth, engaged in rape, armed robbery, and murder, all while still a teenager. There was nothing at all romantic or attractive about him, only morally repulsive.

Later, the real Benjamin Siegel was supposed to be in charge of the crime syndicate's interest in Los Angeles. He was a clever and forceful salesman of his Las Vegas plan to the mob, but the costs beyond expectations and the sheer amount he was cheated eventually led to his gangland execution on June 20, 1947.

As he had done with some of his films prior to *Bugsy*, Levinson took out most of the Jewish references. Only once does the word "Jew" appear in the film, but the context is interesting. Siegel plans, in his typical grandiose fashion, to murder Mussolini because the Italian dictator, along with Hitler, were "trying to knock off every Jew in the world." This is a potentially revelatory part of the Siegel make-up, but, unfortunately it is never fully explored. And neither was it in two other films also released in 1991 that had Bugsy Siegel as a character: *Mobsters* and *The Marrying Man*. The character as gangster was intriguing to Hollywood much more than the character as Jewish gangster. All the other Jewish gangsters followed this pattern, even when portrayed by great actors. Dustin Hoffman, for example, played Dutch Schultz in *Billy Bathgate*, and Robert De Niro played a character based on Lefty Rosenthal in the movie *Casino*.

Bugsy is the great attempt to make a film about a Jewish gangster. But it is not a film about a Jewish gangster at all. And so, the dark side of Jewish life, at least in the dimension of criminality, is left essentially unexplored at the deepest levels.

Bugsy is a paradigmatic example of how extraordinary Hollywood talent still cannot probe the darkest contours of the American Jewish mind. As with other films, there is a growing amount of evidence that cinema as a form has its limits for several reasons. It is a business and must attract a very large, diverse audience uninterested in an intellectual experience or pondering any sociological implications, or walking in with the necessary knowledge to seek, assess, enjoy, and learn from complex films. But a still deeper question emerges. Is it the art form, the very nature of film, that limits what we can learn about Jewish life, among many other subjects?

CHAPTER TEN

Faith on Film

There have been several different approaches to try to portray the complex inner life of religious belief on film. This has not been an easy task. Film, like drama, is an external experience. We in the audience use our five senses to apprehend what is going on up there. We need to have it in front of us. The actors can express rather than state thoughts through their vocal intonations, their costumes, their expressions, and their behaviors. But all of these are still external to what is the most important part of a human being: the internal life. Unless we assume that a character's every thought or whim, every passing moment of consciousness, can be and is translated into external action, we miss a great deal about what is going on inside the character.

This is particularly true of the religious life. Consider the basic religious actions of praying silently to God. To show this is to show a person sitting still or, in the case of traditional Jews, swaying. But struggling with faith, thinking through one's belief system, trying to sort out the intricacies of a moral dilemma, all these cannot be in a film because they are static images.

Some movies seek to overcome this limitation by having the character simply narrate inner thoughts. This approach is more popular in Europe than the United States. In a sense it resembles reading a book written in the first person. But that isn't most American films. That is too bad. It would be very provocative to see a movie with a narration that consists of the protagonist's thoughts as the person is going through a religious experience involving the internal use of language. Even this approach, however, cannot get at the silence that accompanies many religious experiences. Neurologists have begun examining the brain activity of those undergoing spiritual and mystical experiences, but so far no one has been able to translate these into cinematic representations.

Ten—Faith on Film

And normal religious activities aren't usually the subject of sustained filming. A Bar Mitzvah or Bat Mitzvah is often included in films, but the ceremony, long and Hebrew-filled in real life, is represented chiefly by the post-ceremonial party rather than the religious event. How then to represent such religious moments?

This problem doesn't arise for most films. Audiences want to be entertained, and American filmmakers have figured out how to do this on a grand scale. There needs to be lots of action (a euphemism for violence), suspense, romance, simple emotion, and danger, all mixed in a brew that contains an interesting locale, attractive actors, and relatively little dialogue.

While this approach works well to sell most films, it is a dismal failure in creating serious movies. The problem is compounded in making films about the most serious of examinations of Jewish identity: a religious world view.

It is easy to see why filmmakers seeking to make a movie about a Jewish subject shy away from religious subjects. The material is potentially controversial. The limited number of American Jews means the subject matter might not be of widespread enough interest to the mass audience needed to sustain a film. Religion, or at least the spiritual aspects of it, is made up of subjective, internal experiences that are difficult to portray onscreen. Rather, the filmmakers have focused on the Holocaust or anti-Semitism, highly dramatic subjects with stories that can be filmed.

One way around this problem is to make movies about Biblical subjects. American Christians, no less than American Jews, embrace the stories (and religious import) of the Hebrew Bible (what in Christian theology is called the "Old Testament"). This approach seems to ensure at least a potentially large audience. The problem with it, ironically, is that in telling the Biblical stories there has been little interest in exploring the internal religious questions posed by said stories. Instead, the Bible has been the source of adventure, romance, and conflict, just like any other source of cinematic material.

That is a shame because a religious identity is the most basic of Jewish identities, the one that should be the most closely examined, the one most likely to yield insights into Jewish life. A religious identity is traditionally grounded in a belief in a supernatural Being. In Judaism's case, a religious identity focuses on a unified, moral God who has communicated to humans and wants humans to act morally. This core Jewish identity should shape character actions and conflicts. But most descriptions of moral choices focus on the individual case and personal moral inclinations, and do not invoke religious teachings.

Take a hypothetical case involving a moral decision, one involving an external action that might be filmed. This case is inspired by Bernard Malamud's mesmerizing and beautifully-written novel *The Assistant*. A man works in a grocery story owned by an elderly Jewish man. The young man learns that he can easily embezzle money that won't be missed for many months. The grocer's daughter loves the man but discovers what he is doing. The moral puzzle is: should she tell her father or instead seek to transform the man so that he sees the error of his ways. Most films would focus on the theft and romance. Any moral choice would ordinarily focus on the implications of the decision on the romance as much as the actual theft. A genuinely Jewish response to this moral dilemma would take Jewish ethical teachings into account. Ethics trumps romance, which is why Jewish religious thought isn't the basis of films. Except, it is a religious quest to try to redeem the man, but that redemption must include the recognition of his guilt, his confession of his sins, and his transformation into a good person. It is, however, the internal quest for religious information, the examination of Jewish sources for contemplating the moral strategy employed, and the psychological choice based on a religious view that cannot, by their very nature, be externally displayed.

As long as movies have been produced there were religious epics in the sense of Biblical films. They were sometimes useful in evading censure. The filmmakers (Cecil B. DeMille being the prime example) could spend most of the movie lavishly displaying sins. There were the gyrating women, the drunken men, the evildoers making plots as easily as they breathed. Some of this might have caught the eye of the Hays Office, the censoring body, because of the scanty costumes or the lewd behavior. But how could they complain if the material came from the Bible? And DeMille had his own solution. All those that did bad were punished, so that sin never triumphed. The movie audiences got it all: the exciting scenes of sin they enjoyed tempered with a punishment for those sins, so those in the audience didn't feel guilty about enjoying the sins too much.

It is impossible to discuss every Biblical film produced. Some, though, will have to be considered representative of all the rest, and one, *The Ten Commandments*, continues to be shown on television during the weeks of Easter and Passover, so powerful is its story.

Ten—Faith on Film

David and Bathsheba (1951) is a dramatic re-telling of the great King David. The story begins as David is King of Israel, and as such has great power and wealth. But he is overcome by desire for Bathsheba, who is married to one of David's soldiers. Her husband is dedicated to battle and ignores his wife. David and Bathsheba's ensuing illicit affair results in her becoming pregnant. David then decides to arrange to have her husband killed so that Bathsheba will be available to become his wife. But his immorality brings ruin to the people, and David has to struggle to reassert and understand his faith.

The major problem with the film starts with the stilted screenplay. Here are some examples of the dialogue:

> BATHSHEBA [David is trying to kiss her in a field where they can be spotted]: No, David! The boy! He'll see us!
> KING DAVID [David stares at the shepherd boy]: No matter. Shepherd boys learn early about life.
> BATHSHEBA: Did you, David?
> KING DAVID: Did I what?
> BATHSHEBA: Learn about life early?
> KING DAVID: Before I was 12, I knew everything there was to know about life. At 12 I'd killed wolves ... at 13 a man.

And:

> KING DAVID: That soldier who laid his hands on the Ark—he was only trying to be helpful.
> NATHAN: It is not for us to question the ways of the Lord.
> KING DAVID: I question nothing, yet the sun was hot that day, the man had been drinking wine, all were excited when the Ark began to fall. Is it not possible that the man might have died naturally from other causes?
> NATHAN: All causes are from God!

The even deeper problem with the film is that the poor writing and the inability to get at deep psychological problems only by showing external actions reduce the profound message of the Biblical text—that even the great King David was subject to human desires, that we need to learn that all such actions have profound consequences, that leaders affect not only themselves when they sin but everyone who is a citizen—to a tale of lust. The story is an excellent one to confront the clash between duty and desire, between power and the personal. Instead, the film squanders this opportunity. More of David writing psalms in which he gives voice to his struggles, or pleading with God, or more explanations of his plight would have helped, but as it is, the movie is an ironically good example of why Biblical films have generally not been very moving.

There is, however, one great counterexample to this thesis.

The Ten Commandments (1956) had the advantage of telling a story that was virtually universally known. As with other historical films, this one should be seen as a stand-in for current events. In particular, the Holocaust, with all its horror and evil, was so fresh in the audience's mind that they were unable to deal with it. Hollywood dealt with this in various ways, including making movies about anti–Semitism. In this case, Jewish suffering, the continuing pride of the people, and their fierce attachment to their tradition are all on display in *The Ten Commandments*. At one point in the film Moses is asked why he is leading the Israelites out of

Charlton Heston (right) as Moses pleads for his peoples' freedom in *The Ten Commandments* (Paramount, 1956). Yul Brynner, seated, plays Rameses II, and, standing next to him, Anne Baxter plays Nefretiri. The Biblical epic, with its stunning depiction of the Israelites crossing the Red Sea, remains powerful for its themes of freedom and escape from enslavement.

Ten—Faith on Film

Egypt. What, his inquisitor wants to know, has been done to him? Moses responds with a stirring call for human freedom: "The evil that men should turn their brothers into beasts of burden, to be stripped of spirit, and hope, and strength only because they are of another race, another creed. If there is a God, he did not mean this to be so."

The Ten Commandments, virtually alone in the 1950s, dealt with Jewish religious beliefs. There are Jewish prayers in the film. There is also, for example, the remarkable scene of Moses at the Burning Bush talking with God:

> GOD: Moses. Moses.
> MOSES: I am here, Lord.
> GOD: Put off thy shoes from off thy feet, for the place thou standest is holy ground. I am the God of your fathers, the God of Abraham, the God of Isaac and the God of Jacob.
> MOSES: Lord ... Lord, why do you not hear the cries of their children in the bondage of Egypt?
> GOD: I have surely seen the affliction of my people which are in Egypt and I have heard their cry by reason of their taskmasters, for I know their sorrows. Therefore, I will send thee, Moses, unto Pharaoh, that thou mayest bring my people out of Egypt.
> MOSES: Who am I, Lord, that you should send me? How can I lead this people out of bondage? What words can I speak that they will heed?
> GOD: I will teach thee what thou wilt say. When thou hast brought forth the people. They shall serve me upon this mountain. I will put my laws into their hearts, and into their minds will I write them. Now, therefore, go and I will be with thee.
> MOSES: But if I say to your children that the God of their fathers has sent me, they will ask "What is his name?" How shall I answer them?
> GOD: I am, that I am. Thou shalt say "I am" hath sent me unto you.

Only later in his life did leading actor Charlton Heston, who played Moses, admit that in this scene he also supplied the voice of God.

It is a legitimate question to ask why the deep faith and epic grandeur of this film wasn't applied where it was most psychologically needed — to the Holocaust itself. That ability to face what had happened would take time.

No one, however, can accuse the makers of *The Ten Commandments* of sparing any effort to tell the story they did tell. The exodus scene included 12,000 people and 15,000 animals. Director and producer Cecil B. DeMille hired members of the Egyptian army to get into chariots to chase the fleeing Israelites. Twenty assistant directors, speaking both English and Arabic, were on the set. There is a sandstorm in one scene, and to create it DeMille had several Egyptian Air Force planes tied down. Then he had their engines blasting so that sand was blown wildly around behind them.

DeMille had filmed a silent version of the movie in 1923 and replicated various shots from that film for the 1956 remake. He also learned some lessons from the earlier experience. For example, to lend authenticity to the Israelites' appearance, several hundred Orthodox Jews from Los Angeles were hired as extras for the Exodus scenes in the 1923 film. When dinner was served to the extras on the first evening, the strictly kosher extras were shocked to discover that they were being served ham. DeMille set up a kosher kitchen. He remained delighted with his choice of extras.

DeMille was 73 when he made the 1956 film, his last, and many in Hollywood were shocked by his choice of material. DeMille was not widely known for his religious fervor; his interests were widely known to be focused much more on young women. For whatever reason, though, DeMille finished with a film that has spanned the generations.

In terms of identity, *The Ten Commandments* provided support for those with traditional religious beliefs and for those who relished Biblical history as part of their ethnic identity. But it did not propose to or claim to provide any new insights into what it meant to be an American Jew.

Solomon and Sheba (1959) has the dubious distinction of being included in *The Fifty Worst Films of All Time (And How They Got That Way)* by Harry Medved and Randy Lowell. The film is reminiscent of *David and Bathsheba* in focusing on a Biblical king, in this case David's son Solomon, and how his attraction to a woman undermined his rule. At least the movie is not afraid to have God as one of the characters. At one point God says:

> But if he turn away and forsake my statutes, then I will pluck them up by the roots out of my land which I have given, and this house which is high shall be an astonishment to everyone who crosseth it, so that he shall say, "Why has the Lord done naught onto this land and onto this house?" And it shall be answered, "Because they forsook the Lord God of their fathers, which brought them forth out of Egypt, and raised them on hallowed grounds, and worshiped them, and served them — therefore has he brought all this evil upon them.

The film begins with David's vision from the Lord stating that Solomon should be his successor. However, Adonijah, another son, is understandably displeased with this proclamation and decides he should be the one who is king. While this struggle for power is occurring, the Pharaoh in Egypt helps the Queen of Sheba in her plot to destroy Solomon. After all, his wise approach to governing makes the other regional rulers look bad in comparison. Sheba tries to tempt Solomon, and his impressive array of enemies makes life difficult for him.

The movie is marred in many ways. Consider a significant historical mistake. The Magen David, the six-pointed Star of David, is constantly used as a symbol of power. It is on army shields, and adorns clothing worn by Solomon as well as members of his court. That would be fine except for the small fact that the Star of David did not make its first appearance in the literature of the Jews until the twelfth century of the Common Era, and only became a widespread symbol representing Judaism five centuries later. Perhaps if this were the only historical error, it might be forgiven as cinematic license. It is not, however, the only error. The Ark of the Covenant had poles by which it could be carried. The film shows it without poles. The Temple is shown as being destroyed by lightning. That never happened. There are other mistakes as well.

Unfortunately, the dialogue is as bad as the errors. Here are some examples of plainly silly exchanges:

> PHARAOH: And how will you destroy Solomon?
> SHEBA: It is said that Solomon is wise. But no matter how wise he may be, he is still human, with a human weakness.
> PHARAOH: Surely the way of a woman is beyond understanding.
> SHEBA: The way of a woman is simple, my lord. It is always to follow the way of a man.

And:

> ABISHAG: How interesting your encampment is. Are your people always so carefree and gay?
> SHEBA: We enjoy life and pleasure. Don't you?
> ABISHAG: Oh yes, we do. But we are ... an austere people. We tend to be more serious.
> SHEBA: And your king ... is he also serious?
> ABISHAG: King Solomon has a great responsibility.

It is not clear why Biblical pictures in particular are subject to such problems. Perhaps it is thought by Hollywood executives that the story is already known and it is not necessary to have a great screenplay. After all, a provocative screenplay might cause some viewers to complain about how the original text had been altered.

The deeper problem is that religion deals with the most fundamental, the most significant, of all human questions in regard to their meaning. Either there is a God or there is not. The human answer to that question shapes a good deal about how one deals with life. Perhaps the very difficulty of the question makes producers shy away from the subject or makes writers unable to confront its enormity.

The other Bible picture that has some artistic value is *Ben-Hur* (1959). Ultimately, this is a Christian story, but for its beginning at least it is an interesting story of the era in which Rome controlled the Land of Israel. It is the story of Judah Ben-Hur, a well-to-do Jewish merchant living in Jerusalem. The setting is the beginning of the first century of the Common Era. The time is significant and full of potential drama. A people is under foreign control. There is widespread religious sentiment that the foreign rule must end. Into this explosive situation Ben-Hur's friend Messala arrives in Jerusalem as part of the Roman controlling forces. Indeed, Messala is in charge of the Roman legions, the powerful armed forces keeping the people of Israel under tight control. The friendship between Ben-Hur and Messala brings them together originally, but eventually the inevitable political frictions undermine their friendship. There is a parade to welcome the Romans, and some roof tiles fall from Ben-Hur's home and injure the Roman governor. Messala is well aware that his friend did not cause the tiles to fall but nonetheless has Ben-Hur sent to the galleys while his mother and sister are sent to prison. Ben-Hur vows revenge.

The film's script is good, and its justly famous chariot race scene is dramatically done. But when all is said and done, this is only in part a Jewish film. It cannot finally be seen as contributing to a Jewish identity when its very focus is the transformation of that religious identity. Here is a bit of dialogue to illustrate that:

> ESTHER: Oh, Judah, rest. Sleep. For a few hours of the night, let your mind be at peace.
> JUDAH BEN-HUR [in a bitter tone]: Peace! Love and peace. Do you think I don't long for them as you do? Where do you see them?
> ESTHER: If you had heard this man from Nazareth...
> JUDAH BEN-HUR: Balthasar's word.
> ESTHER: He is more than Balthasar's word. His voice traveled with such a still purpose.... It was more than a voice ... a man more than a man! He said, "Blessed are the merciful, for they shall obtain mercy. Blessed are the peacemakers, for they shall be called the children of God."

Ten—Faith on Film

> Judah Ben-Hur: Children of God? In that dead valley where we left them? I tell you every man in Judea is unclean, and will *stay* unclean until we've scoured off our bodies the crust and filth of being at the mercy of tyranny. No other life is possible except to wash this land clean!
> Esther: In blood?
> Judah Ben-Hur: Yes, in blood!
> Esther: I know there is a law in life, that blood gets more blood as dog begets dog. Death generates death, as the vulture breeds the vulture! But the voice I heard today on the hill said, "Love your enemy. Do good to those who despitefully use you."
> Judah Ben-Hur: So all who are born in this land hereafter can suffer as we have done!
> Esther: As you make us do now! Are we to bear nothing together? Even love?
> Judah Ben-Hur: I can hardly draw breath without feeling you in my heart. Yet I know that everything I do from this moment will be as great a pain to you as you have ever suffered. It is better not to love me!
> Esther: It was Judah Ben-Hur I loved. What has become of him? You seem to be now the very thing you set out to destroy, giving evil for evil! Hatred is turning you to stone. It is as though you had become Messala!
> [Judah looks over at Esther. He is shocked.]
> Esther [in a sad voice]: I've lost you, Judah.

And so, one potentially excellent Jewish film turns out not to be appropriate for the category after all.

There have been other movie based on the Bible, but none with any great success.

The Bible: In the Beginning (1966) is partially misleading. The subtitle, however, is more revealing. The film covers just the first part of the Book of Genesis. In a way, this narrative arc undercuts the story because, unless we include God as a character, there is no protagonist. And God doesn't make a good film protagonist because such a character needs a lot of internal and external conflicts, a lot of confusion. Looking at the film, it seems possible to draw out of it a possible movie that doesn't exist in this film or anywhere else. It is the character of Abraham who is compelling. His mysticism, his direct connection to God, his confrontation of his father's idol worship, his willingness to leave his home and follow God's command, and his unparalleled role in history all combine to make him a potentially exciting protagonist. It is surprising that no film specifically about Abraham's religious quest has been made.

King David (1985) was one more failed attempt to make a Biblical film. Perhaps there is a hint of where these movies go wrong in the following dialogue:

> SAMUEL: God is not a man that He should deceive you.... The Lord does not see as man sees. Men judge by outward appearances, but the Lord judges by the heart alone.
> [speaking to David]
> SAMUEL: You kneel before me as the shepherd of your father's flock, but God has chosen you ... to be the shepherd of His people Israel, to unite His scattered tribes into one nation ... and to send the heathen from His promised land.
> YOUNG DAVID: My brothers are all soldiers. Why not choose one of them?
> SAMUEL: It was not I who chose you. It was the Lord God of Israel.
> YOUNG DAVID: I am the least in my father's house.
> SAMUEL: You are a child after God's own heart.
> YOUNG DAVID: If I stand so well in His sight, why not let Him command me face to face?
> JESSE: Because no man may see God face to face and live. God speaks to man through the mouths of His prophets.
> SAMUEL: So be it. When I have gone the way of all flesh, you shall be brought before the king by one of his sons. Then shall the Lord challenge you, even as you have challenged Him, to defend His name and His honor. Have no fear, David. The Lord shall not forsake you so long as you keep His laws and obey His prophets without question.

The stilted language comes from trying to copy the Bible, at least as rendered by the translators who constructed the King James Bible. But they were writing Elizabethan English, which is not always congenial to a contemporary ear. And yet, if the screenwriter wrote in a more contemporary language — that is, created a more contemporary translation — the screenplay might appear to be inauthentic. It would be an interesting exercise for a screenwriting student to take a section of dialogue from this film, even a moderately clever bit of dialogue, and render it into more contemporary language. Doing so would have made the movie much better. As it is, this is just one more bit of proof that Hollywood and the Bible have, at best, an uneasy relationship.

And yet audiences crave these films, as made evident by the perennial popularity of *The Ten Commandments*.

Consider one more case of an attempt to make a film based on Biblical materials. *The Prince of Egypt* (1998) is interesting in its efforts to create an animated film based on the Bible targeted at more than an audience of children. The movie is mostly well-done, but again the dialogue is revealing of a seemingly inherent weakness in Biblical films:

> GOD [whispers]: Moses...
> MOSES: Here I am.
> GOD: Take the sandals from your feet, Moses, for the place on which you stand is holy ground.
> MOSES: Who are you?
> GOD: I am that I am.
> MOSES: I don't understand.
> GOD: I am the God of your ancestors, Abraham, Isaac, and Jacob.
> MIRIAM [disembodied presence]: You are born of my mother Yocheved! You are our brother!
> MOSES [removes his sandals and tosses them behind]: What do you want with me?
> GOD: I have seen the oppression of my people in Egypt, and have heard their cry.
> [There is a sound of screams and whips cracking.]
> GOD: So I shall stretch forth my hand, and lead them out of Egypt, into a good land. A land flowing with milk and honey. And so, unto Pharaoh, I shall send ... you.
> MOSES: Me? W-who am I to lead these people? They won't follow me, they won't even listen!
> GOD: I shall be with you, and teach you what to say.
> MOSES [a disembodied voice]: Let my people go!
> MOSES: But I was their enemy. I was the prince of Egypt, the son of the man who slaughtered ... their children. You've chosen the wrong messenger! H-how can I even speak to these people?
> GOD: *Who made man's mouth? Who made the deaf, the mute, the seeing or the blind? Did not I? Now Go!*
> [Moses falls to the ground.]
> GOD [in a soothing voice as Moses is lifted up]: Oh, Moses, I shall be with you when you go to the king of Egypt. But Pharaoh will not listen. So I will stretch forth my hand and smite Egypt with all my wonders! Take the staff in your hand, Moses. With it, *you* shall do my wonders.
> [a whisper]
> GOD: I will be with you.

This dialogue is certainly faithful enough. No one can accuse of filmmakers of tinkering with the words or intentions of the Bible. Perhaps that is part of the problem. Unlike many films with awkward dialogue, this one is accurate, but the material does not go beyond the Bible. It offers no new interpretation, no new lesson. It may well be asked: what, then, is the justification for making the film in the first place? *The Prince of Egypt* is so well-made technically, such an artistic achievement in animation, that it never seemed to occur to anyone that all that skill should be with a purpose beyond re-telling a familiar story.

The ineluctable conclusion seems to be that for a high-quality Biblical film, there has to be a clear protagonist and there has to be a novel interpretation of that Biblical protagonist's life without violating the traditions or history of the Biblical text. An extension of it is needed, not a replacement. It is therefore particularly important that a great effort needs to be made to prepare an excellent screenplay.

Such a Biblical film has yet to be made.

There have been attempts at religious films about Judaism, but they have been relatively few. They did have potential problems in attracting a wide audience, and in a way they faced the same problems as Biblical pictures, portraying religion in a provocative and challenging new way. There have been only two unquestionably successful attempts at making such religious movies.

The Chosen (1981) is an engaging film based on the bestselling novel by Chaim Potok. The story is set entirely within the world of Orthodoxy and features an interesting struggle between a modern Orthodox teenager, Reuven Malter, and Danny Saunders, whose austere father is a Hasidic Rebbe. The two meet at a baseball game in which one injures the other with a pitch. At the hospital, recovering, they confront each other's differences:

> REUVEN MALTER: You are weird.
> DANNY SAUNDERS: *I* am?
> REUVEN: Yeah, you are. You look like you walked out of another century. You play baseball like Babe Ruth. You talk like you're from another planet.
> DANNY: Thanks for the compliment.

The dialogue may or may not sound realistic, but the two boys in this case each have extraordinary minds and a profound passion to explore the purposes their selves have in the world. It's the excitement of life, the very possibilities of what can be done within the boundaries given to us by our families, our communities, our own selves, that are explored in the film. There are interesting religious possibilities, but the two boys talk

Ten—Faith on Film

Robby Benson (left) as Danny Saunders and Barry Miller as Reuven Malter play baseball, but the game is really a symbolic struggle between two views of what it means to be an Orthodox Jew. The boys' friendship and the struggle within their souls is played out in *The Chosen* (Chosen Film Company, 1981).

about settled religious texts and don't ever match the passions of the youth with questions that go beyond received opinion. They question all except what they most need to question. This is not explored in the movie, unfortunately, because such a discussion would have added an important element to the film.

The movie follows their developing friendship. It is a fascinating encounter for both of them, but it is Danny who travels the farthest. He goes to see the first movie of his life. He suddenly desires some nice looking eyeglasses. And a woman he doesn't know celebrates the war's end by planting a kiss on Danny, the first time he has ever been kissed by a strange woman. In turn, Danny invites Reuven to the Rebbe's house, and Reb Saunders starts drilling Reuven about halachah (the intricacies of Jewish law, especially as presented in the Talmud), as well as Jewish history. But Reuven's father is a great scholar and has taught Reuven well, and so he becomes a welcome guest in the Malter household. But Reuven is only drawn into the stricter life up to a point. He goes to college and does not enter into his friend's world.

Because the story is set in Brooklyn right after the end of the Second World War, there are intense historical outside circumstances, particularly the Holocaust and the birth of the modern nation of Israel. Reuven's father uses modern methods to look at sacred texts. He is a deeply-committed Zionist. Danny's father, in contrast, has the responsibility to lead his followers and follows all the traditions. He is anti–Zionist, believing that only the return of the Messiah can justify a return to the land of Israel. One particularly moving part of the story is that Danny's father believes that by not speaking to his son except in studies he is building the boy's character. In contrast, without knowing it, Reuven's father helps Danny with modern studies. But, as Joel Samberg notes, Danny's father also has a profound effect on Reuven:

> Ironically, Reuven, who is curious and slightly skeptical of the ways of the Hasidim, thinks he may want to become a rabbi. "I never realized how full the life of a rabbi could be," he tells Danny. "Babies to be blessed, boys to be bar mitzvah, disputes to be settled." He also happens to notice the fire of passion in just about everything Danny's father says and does, and it is a passion he himself would love to possess.[1]

But Reuven's father precisely understands this passion. He tells his son, "In a way it is that kind of fanaticism that has kept us alive."

The film is a model of how to create realistic atmosphere. But its drama is limited to inter–Orthodox ideological struggles and father-son squabbles. This makes the movie unusual. The standard Jewish film is about Jews and Gentiles. The relationship might involve romance or friction or a narrative arc that leads to understanding. *The Chosen* is about how Jews can understand each other. It is somewhat valuable in that respect, except that the Hasidic sect of the Saunders family is so far outside the American Jewish mainstream that it is unlikely that audience members will even meet members of comparable groups, especially the anti–Zionist Hasidic groups. Had the film instead been about a secular and a religious Jew coming together in friendship, some of the exoticism and atmosphere might have been lost (along with the jaw-dropping custom of raising a son in silence), but the film would have been much more valuable for American Jews in a search for their identity.

But *The Chosen* is an interesting movie, enjoyable to watch, valuable in its admirably careful depiction of the world it portrays. It is a good film but not a great film. It lacks dimension. It tells a story and the screen shows all. We may be left thinking about the characters' fates afterwards, but we are not left pondering the mysteries of the cosmos, which is, after all, the ultimate purpose of a movie about religion.

Still, the very intelligence with which the film was made, the very care that was taken to be authentic, the very quality of the acting all combine to create a well-made movie with an interesting story that has no effect on the lives of most American Jews. The commercial success of the book and the film is an indication that there was a hunger for a deeply satisfying artistic creation about American Jewish life. It was clever to begin the picture at a baseball game, but the limits of how much of America is present in the film are carefully proscribed. It is not America that tempts the boys in this movie. It is knowledge, especially secular knowledge.

Either oddly or interestingly, there were other, later Hollywood films set in the arcane world of Hasidim. *A Stranger Among Us* (1992) is about an undercover woman police officer who enters the community to solve a crime. She finds herself in love with Ariel, a good-looking rabbinical student. He has tradition behind him. He tells her, "Kabbalah says women are on a higher spiritual plane than men. Therefore it would be foolish of me not to trust you." Poor Melanie Griffith was truly out of her depth, as she failed to give dramatic power to the film. The story is poor. More could have been made of the relationship, however. Samberg concludes:

> She wants him because he makes her feel safe, closer to a family than she has ever felt before, and open to all the wonderful possibilities of devotion. And he has grown to respect her as well. But she knows she'll never fit in because she is who she is, and besides, she's too late: Ariel is engaged to be married to a French student.... He's already made all of his life's choices.[2]

There were other efforts to explore such a world. For example, *A Price Above Rubies* (1998) is another failed attempt about a young woman married to a religious man. The woman feels trapped.

Finally, though, we come to a deeply religious film that is about a suburban scientist. The movie uses some laws of modern physics to get at the most profound of religious questions. It is a multi-layered film about Jewish identity and what it means to be religious in the modern world. *A Serious Man* (2009) is the American Jewish film that deserves the most extensive analysis. It is a dark comedy, a tragic analysis of a man's falling

American Jewish Films

apart. The movie was written, produced, and directed by the Coen brothers, Joel and Ethan.

The film begins in a shtetl, a small Jewish village in Poland, back at the beginning of the last century. A man arrives home and announces to his wife that he received aid on the journey from Treitle Groshkover and, in thanks, has invited the helper home on the cold night for a bowl of soup. But Dora, the wife, is horrified. She tells her husband that Treitle is no longer alive, that the visitor must be a dybbuk, a creature from Jewish folklore that is an evil spirit, part of the wandering soul of someone who has died. For an understanding of the film, the crucial point is that a dybbuk seems simultaneously to be both alive and dead. Treitle (or is it a dybbuk?) arrives and mocks the accusation that he is not alive:

> DYBBUK?: I shaved hastily this morning and missed a bit — by you this makes me a dybbuk? It's true, I was sick with typhus when I stayed with Peselle, but I recovered, as you can plainly see, and now I — ugh!
> [She stabs the dybbuk with an ice pick straight into his heart.]
> DYBBUK?: What a wife you have!
> SHTETL HUSBAND: Woman, what have you done?
> DYBBUK?: Why would she do such a thing? I ask you, Velvel, as a rational man: which of us is possessed?
> SHTETL WIFE: What do you say now about spirits? He is unharmed!
> DYBBUK?: On the contrary! I don't feel at all well.
> [Blood begins to trickle from the dybbuk's chest.]
> DYBBUK?: One does a mitzvah and this is the thanks one gets?
> HUSBAND: Dora! Woe, woe! How can such a thing be!
> DYBBUK?: Perhaps I will have some soup. I am feeling weak. Or perhaps I should go. One knows when one isn't wanted.
> HUSBAND: Dear wife. We are ruined. Tomorrow they will discover the body. All is lost.
> WIFE: Nonsense, Velvel. Blessed is the Lord. Good riddance to evil.

Groshkover/the Dybbuk gets up, still bleeding, and walks off into the night.

After this prologue to the movie, the main story begins. The setting is in Minnesota in 1967. Larry Gopnik is the protagonist. He is, very significantly, a professor of physics who is up for tenure. His career, that is, hangs in the balance. He is in limbo, between working as a professor and being out of work. This is much like the dybbuk was in a limbo between life and death. Poor Larry also is in trouble on the domestic front. His wife Judith tells them that the couple needs a get (an official bill of divorcement according to Jewish law) which will free her to marry another man, Sy Ableman. Here, too, there is a limbo, in this case between being married and being single. Sy and Judith try to convince Larry not to argue too much about the upcoming divorce and simply accept it.

Sy is called, and calls himself, "a serious man." Larry also says, "I've tried to be a serious man." Being serious involves not only the deep thought required of a physicist, who, after all, considers the basic constituents of the natural world, but also being sincere. Many of the characters, including Sy, who has cheated with Larry's wife, as well as the Rabbis encountered later, believe they are serious, but they are not. They have deceived themselves and others. But Larry does not deceive anyone. The film is titled *A Serious Man*, as though there is only one such man in the movie, and that is Larry. Why is he serious? Because he is honest with others and with himself. He genuinely cares about the world. He wants to do what is right, even if he is not sure exactly what that is. He is serious because he is always between the right and the real, between an idealistic morality and the frightening constraints required to live in the real world.

Larry's son, Danny, is in the middle of preparing for his bar mitzvah. He also owes a very mean Hebrew school classmate twenty dollars as a payment for marijuana. Danny can't pay because he has hidden the money in the back compartment of a transistor radio that his teacher confiscated because Danny was playing the radio in class. Larry's daughter, Sarah, doesn't get along with her brother and is focused on her appearance, especially her hair. The two youngsters are in limbo as well, in their case between childhood and adulthood, with Danny's being the more direct example because the bar mitzvah ceremony is the gateway into Jewish adulthood. Larry's brother, Arthur, is the final member of the household. Arthur has no home of his own; he stays on the Gopnik couch and seemingly fills his days with arcane numbers supposedly charting "a probability map of the universe."

The crises in this world begin to emerge. One of the problems involves Larry's tenure. The head of the physics department, who seems to be Larry's friend, says that some anonymous letters have been received. The letter writer urged that tenure be denied. Larry has a problem with an Asian student, Clive Park:

> LARRY GOPNIK: So, uh, what can I do for you?
> CLIVE PARK: Uh, Dr. Gopnik, I believe the results of physics mid-term were unjust.

LARRY: Uh-huh, how so?
CLIVE: I received an unsatisfactory grade. In fact, F, the failing grade.
LARRY: Uh, yes. You failed the mid-term. That's accurate.
CLIVE: Yes, but this is not just. I was unaware to be examined on the mathematics.
LARRY: Well, you can't do physics without mathematics, really, can you?
CLIVE: If I receive a failing grade I lose my scholarship, and feel shame. I understand the physics. I understand the dead cat.
LARRY: You understand the dead cat? But ... you ... you can't really understand the physics without understanding the math. The math tells how it really works. That's the real thing; the stories I give you in class are just illustrative; they're like, fables, say, to help give you a picture. An imperfect model. I mean — even I don't understand the dead cat. The math is how it really works.

After Park leaves, Larry discovers an envelope in his office. He opens the envelope and finds it filled with cash. Larry understands this for the attempted bribe it is and tries to return it, but Clive's father shows up at Larry's house and says he will sue Larry for defamation if Larry persists in claiming that Clive tried to bribe him or for holding on to the money in the face of a failing grade.

Larry and Arthur leave the house together and go to a motel. Larry is left without money because his wife has taken all the couple's money from their bank account. Larry needs help from a divorce attorney, but his troubles aren't over. Arthur is facing charges of solicitation. Overwhelmed by life's crises, Larry tries to find an answer in Judaism. He consults two rabbis, neither of whom are very helpful. One is a junior Rabbi who is fixated on the synagogue parking lot.

More interesting is the case of Rabbi Marshak. He gives Danny back the radio. But, almost overlooked, there is a portrait of Groshkover/the dybbuk on Rabbi Marshak's office wall. Larry, though, can't get in to see this Rabbi with a reputation for wisdom:

LARRY GOPNIK: Please. I need help. I've already talked to the other rabbis. Please. It's not about Danny's bar mitzvah — my boy Danny, this coming Shabbos, very joyous event, that's all fine. It's, it's more about myself, I've ... I've had quite a bit of tsuris lately. Marital problems, professional, you name it. This is not a frivolous request. This is a ser- I'm a ser- I'm, uh, I've tried to be a serious man, you know? Tried to do right, be a member of the community, raise the- Danny, Sarah, they both go to school, Hebrew school, a good breakfast.... Well, Danny goes to Hebrew school, Sarah doesn't have time,

Ten—Faith on Film

she mostly ... washes her hair. Apparently there are several steps involved, but you don't have to tell Marshak that. Just tell him I need help. Please? I need help.

[The secretary stands up, walks over to the door behind her, opens the door, walks in to speak in hushed tones to the Rabbi, who sits idly. She walks back, closes the door and sits down again.]

MARSHAK'S SECRETARY: The Rabbi is busy.

LARRY: He didn't look busy!

SECRETARY: He's thinking.

Unable to find relief from traditional religious authorities, Larry almost falls apart when he is in a car crash. Oddly, Sy is involved in a crash that occurs almost exactly at the same time. Larry emerges without any injuries, but poor Sy dies from his crash. Larry finally finds some solace from his son's bar mitzvah. Larry does receive some good news from his department head, who suggests that Larry will win tenure. Just when all seems to be back on the right track, Larry's doctor calls saying Larry must come in immediately to learn the results of a chest x-ray. Larry, too, is in limbo between life and death. Just then, Danny and his classmates are rushed to an emergency shelter to escape a tornado heading right for them. But Danny's teacher cannot get the emergency door open as the film ends, once again leaving people between life and death.

The movie's many Biblical allusions mark it as a struggle of faith. Larry himself is clearly similar to Job in the Bible, a good man who for inexplicable reasons suffers a variety of terrible crises. At one point Larry is on the roof and spots a woman neighbor stretched out on a chair naked in her yard. This is a reference to King David seeing Bathsheba. Danny sees the looming tornado. It is like the whirlwind in Job from which God speaks. The voice says that God has no intention of offering an explanation of why all the terrible events have occurred to Job.

But for all the appearances of feckless Rabbis, and talks of a get, and the story line of Danny's bar mitzvah, and the opening all in Yiddish, the real religious quest in the film emerges from physics. In his argument with Larry, Clive Park mentions that he understood the "dead cat." This is a reference to an important concept in physics known as "Schrodinger's Cat." It is a well-known theoretical experiment illustrating a principle in quantum theory. Erwin Schrodinger suggested it in 1935. According to this mental exercise, we put a living cat in a steel chamber. Along with the cat we put some device that has a vial of hydrocyanic acid. There is also a radioactive substance. If just one atom of the substance decays while the cat is inside, a relay mechanism is triggered to trip a hammer that will break the vial and end up with the cat being killed. Of course, any observer cannot determine whether or not that atom has decayed. Because of this lack of knowledge, there is, in Schrodinger's argument, a quantum contradiction. The cat is in a superposition of states; in non-scientific terms, the cat is simultaneously both alive and dead. Only when we break open the box and in fact see the status of the cat does the cat become either alive or dead. This quantum interderminacy also illustrates the effect of the observer because without the observer there is no outcome. The cat remains in limbo between life and death.

In the film Larry also teaches about Heisenberg's Uncertainty Principle. Again put in simple terms, in classical mechanics there is the possibility to measure exact simultaneous values to all physical quantities. Quantum mechanics claims this is not accurate. In the latter theory, the more precisely the position of a particle is provided, the less precisely an observer can also state its momentum. We can't, that is, ever be certain about reality in the quantum world — and, consequently, in the world in which we live.

These two physical ideas, Schrodinger's Cat and the Uncertainty Principle, guide the viewpoint offered in *A Serious Man*. As a line in the film goes, "Everything that I thought was one way turns out to be another." This is a film with a God who doesn't make understanding the ways of the Divine very easy to grasp.

Larry's and Sy's attempts to be "a serious man" make them the alive and dead side of the same person. They provide the only possible spiritual guidance there is. We can't tell if we are even alive or dead. We can't comprehend how the world works or what will happen one minute from now. The great Jewish thinker Rashi is quoted as saying, "Receive with simplicity everything that happens to you." This is not a plea for passivity. It is a plea for seriousness. The film urges us to question life, to probe it, to turn it over and look at it, never to take it for granted, never to think we understand it. We are all called upon to be serious. It is just a fact that the mystery of life is its unnerving uncertainty about life and death and love and, of course, God. We suffer with that uncertainty. It is the human condition.

One interpretation of the film is more bluntly theological. According to this view, God is Schrodinger's cat, both alive and dead, depending on the observer. We can look at the world and believe God is alive or believe

God is dead. Presumably, our death will involve our opening the box to see which is the case.

It's also possible to see Larry as Schrodinger's cat, or the Hebrew school children or the dybbuk. For it is the observers of the film, the people in the audience, who will decide what Larry will learn when he goes to the doctor; who will determine whether the teacher could or could not unlock the door, allowing the children to escape the wrath of the tornado; and to decide if the dybbuk was a wronged human or some mysterious soul of a departed scholar.

At the conclusion of the film's credits is a line that announces to viewers that "No Jews were harmed in the making of this motion picture." (This is an example of what in entertainment is called an "Easter Egg," an in-joke or sometimes a hidden message in, for example, a film, book, website, or computer program.)

This mock reassuring message is more serious than it seems. Questioning as deeply as the Coen brothers have done can be troubling to some viewers, can cause them spiritual if not physical harm. But the message is exactly correct. The film not only doesn't harm any Jews, it helps them.

For, in the end, it is the observers themselves, the Jews in the audience struggling with their identity, who are Schrodinger's cat. We are, like so many of the characters in the film, between life and death, between hope and despair, between faith and bleak emptiness. But there is an interesting aspect to our situation. We are not only the cat; we are also the observers. We can look at ourselves and decide whether we wish to look at life and find hope, to embrace God, to choose life. This is an empowering message of human possibility.

What it says to American Jews, an idea that other films have not gotten at, is that given all the identity options, we are free to choose. We decide whether we live or die spiritually. We conclude what kind of Jews we will be.

CHAPTER ELEVEN

An American Jewish Identity

For all its greatness, *A Serious Man* finds its answers in physics and finds Jewish religious tradition vacuous, although Jewish folklore revealing. An examination of the film leads to the painful conclusion that no great Jewish religious movie has been made. It is unclear whether this is a failure of filmmakers' imagination, a realistic acknowledgment that mass audiences won't pay to see such a picture, the inherent limits of film as an art form, or some combination of these.

But religion is only one form of Jewish identity, and not the most prominent one among a vast number of American Jews. There are a lot of competing and mixed identities. The focus in this book has been on the variety of Jewish identities in the overall American Jewish identity. But this confusing mix, this hybrid of potential Jewish selves, should be supplemented by the confusing mix of possible American identities as well. After all, what does it really mean to be an American other than to live in the country? There is no religious test, no racial test, no ideological or political or cultural or ethnic test. Americans come in an amazing array of identities.

What is telling about an American Jewish identity is that it has one unclear side mixed with another unclear side. No wonder it has been so difficult for American Jews to sort out their identity, to determine a clear definition of who they are and what they believe to be true so that they can define a clear and precise mission. In brief, so they can define a clear identity.

A tentative conclusion suggested at the beginning of this book now appears to be true after having been tested against all the films discussed. One of the missions of an American Jewish identity seems to be to test out, uniquely in Jewish history, what an unrestrained pluralistic and free Judaism would look like. That is, in a sense American Jews have been

Eleven—An American Jewish Identity

explorers searching to explore and expand the very borders of what it means to be a Jew in America.

The Jews came here as immigrants, but they quickly dispersed. It was clear that crowds and poverty, isolation and communal restraints, were not attractive to America's Jews. They wanted to stretch. They wanted success. They wanted the freedom to go where they wanted to go and do what they wanted to do. They wanted to become Americans because they admired the spirit of America.

So America has been a success for America's Jews. They have accomplished far more than they might reasonably have been expected to in a very few generations. But has America been a success for American Judaism? That is a very different question.

The very failure of films to define a clear American Jewish identity is one indication that Judaism's borders aren't capable of being moved to an infinite limit. The individualism, the defiance of communal expectations, the rebellion generally against authority, and other parts of the American character have failed to produce an American Judaism that can authentically be called Jewish. Sometimes there is a magic trick attempted. We can say all the American values we admire are really Jewish values. We can stare at the American Idea and call it congruent with Judaism. But, of course, it is not. Calling American values Judaism means it is not necessary to be Jewish, just to be an American. That is the very definition of a formula for the assimilatory disappearance of American Jews, or, as suggested earlier, the de facto elimination of a distinctive culture and a potential reduction of their political influence.

Put simply, the exploration of new borders of an identity cannot at the end form the moral basis for a definition of Judaism. It is a mission too ill-defined, too diffuse, too easy to be subsumed under secular missions.

American Jewish films are, like any other cinematic subset, sometimes enormously entertaining. They are sometimes emotionally captivating. We see ourselves in the characters and the situations in which they find themselves. But the crisis of American Judaism is no longer immigration or anti–Semitism on a large scale, or one that is socially accepted. The crisis is no longer that Jews are not accepted by Americans as neighbors, romantic or marital partners, business associates, or common citizens. American Jews don't want to return to communal isolation. The Lower East Side and the Borscht Belt hotels and resorts are romanticized as happy

Edens, but they were not always. The Lower East Side certainly was disease-ridden, poor, riddled with poverty and crime and crowds and horrible working conditions. For all the laughter and endless food in the Borscht Belt, the hotels were a reminder of restraints. The Borscht Belt was a velvet prison because Jews weren't accepted in Gentile resorts. American Jews, apart from some Hasidic groups, have not voted with their feet for self-segregation.

Neither have American Jews voted with their feet to move to Israel. American Jews admire Israel. They are fans. They root for it and like to see stories about it. A relatively small number have even visited Israel. A small number, though, question its policies. A larger number, especially among the young, are indifferent to it.

Certainly, crime is not an identity to which American Jews aspire. Americans have made heroes out of outlaws, and it was inevitable in some quarters that Jewish criminals would be seen as having some special quality missing in the general Jewish population. But obviously criminality is not an acceptable identity. It is a subject to make a movie about.

And American Jews are neither very knowledgeable nor very interested in Jewish history. Again, this is partly an inheritance of an American identity that is indifferent or hostile to history, at least non–American history. American Jews, like all Americans, want stories that tell them about their lives now. That is why the successful historical films were made a long time ago when Jewish audiences knew and cared more about their history.

And, finally, American Jews are so befuddled about their religion and their role in it that they can't clarify adequately their own religious identities, at least enough to put on film.

For all their charm and entertainment, American Jewish films haven't been able to talk about an American Jewish identity because American Jews haven't been able to decide on such an identity.

There is no definitive approach to improve the situation. Surely it would help if more excellent films, such as *A Serious Man*, were produced and discussed within the Jewish community. But the answer seems to require a religious communal introspection prior to any films. Perhaps because Judaism has focused its communal identities on behaviors, culture, and so on, and has ignored religious beliefs, it has not been able to form an ideologically coherent message. Religious beliefs, not behavior, might be needed to provide meaning, and that meaning to provide purpose, as made concrete through actions that flow from the beliefs.

Such a conversation might, ironically, logically start outside the Jewish community. That is the role for future Jewish films: to find compelling stories with interesting characters struggling to define the nature of their beliefs. Armed with a Jewish world view, they will define their Jewish identities.

There is, then, a potentially enormously meaningful future for American Jewish films if they decide they are willing to take on the task. It's not called the big screen for nothing.

Chronology of Films

This chronology does not include all American Jewish films. I have included the most important ones in this book and a few others. For the first seven decades of such films, see the Stuart Fox book in the bibliography.

1922 *Hungry Hearts*
1925 *The Rag Man*
1925 *His People*
1927 *The Jazz Singer*
1928 *Abie's Irish Rose*
1929 *Disraeli*
1931 *The Yellow Ticket*
1931 *Street Scene*
1932 *Symphony of Six Million*
1933 *Counsellor-at-Law*
1934 *The House of Rothschild*
1934 *Little Man, What Now?*
1937 *Green Fields*
1937 *The Life of Emile Zola*
1940 *You Nazty Spy*
1940 *The Great Dictator*
1940 *The Mortal Storm*
1941 *Pimpernel Smith*
1942 *Hitler's Children*
1942 *To Be or Not to Be*
1944 *The Purple Heart*
1947 *Gentlemen's Agreement*
1947 *Crossfire*
1947 *Body and Soul*
1948 *The Last Stage*
1948 *The Search*
1949 *Sword in the Desert*
1950 *Molly*
1953 *The Juggler*
1956 *The Ten Commandments*
1958 *Marjorie Morningstar*
1958 *Me and the Colonel*
1958 *The Young Lions*
1958 *I Accuse*
1959 *The Diary of Anne Frank*
1959 *Compulsion*
1960 *Exodus*
1960 *Conspiracy of Hearts*
1961 *Judgment at Nuremberg*
1961 *A Majority of One*
1965 *The Pawnbroker*
1965 *Ship of Fools*
1966 *Cast a Giant Shadow*
1967 *Enter Laughing*
1968 *Funny Girl*
1968 *The Producers*
1968 *The Fixer*
1968 *No Way to Treat a Lady*

Chronology of Films

1969 *Goodbye, Columbus*
1969 *Me, Natalie*
1970 *I Never Sang for My Father*
1970 *The Angel Levine*
1971 *Fiddler on the Roof*
1972 *The Heartbreak Kid*
1973 *The Way We Were*
1974 *Blazing Saddles*
1974 *The Apprenticeship of Duddy Kravitz*
1975 *Hester Street*
1975 *The Man in the Glass Booth*
1975 *The Sunshine Boys*
1976 *The Front*
1976 *Marathon Man*
1977 *Annie Hall*
1977 *Madame Rosa*
1977 *Raid on Entebbe*
1977 *Julia*
1979 *The Frisco Kid*
1979 *Boardwalk*
1980 *Tell Me a Riddle*
1980 *Private Benjamin*
1981 *The Chosen*
1981 *Eyewitness*
1981 *Chariots of Fire*
1982 *Sophie's Choice*
1983 *Yentl*
1983 *Zelig*
1983 *Daniel*
1984 *Broadway Danny Rose*
1985 *Lost in America*
1987 *Dirty Dancing*
1987 *Sweet Lorraine*
1987 *Au Revoir Les Enfants*
1988 *Crossing Delancey*
1988 *Biloxi Blues*
1989 *Enemies: A Love Story*
1989 *Driving Miss Daisy*
1989 *Crimes and Misdemeanors*
1990 *Avalon*
1990 *Europa Europa*
1991 *Homicide*
1992 *School Ties*
1992 *A Stranger Among Us*
1993 *Schindler's List*
1998 *Pi*
1999 *Liberty Heights*
2001 *The Believer*
2002 *The Pianist*
2003 *Marci X*
2005 *Munich*
2005 *Everything Is Illuminated*
2008 *Defiance*
2009 *A Serious Man*
2009 *Inglourious Basterds*
2009 *Taking Woodstock*

Chapter Notes

Chapter Two
1. Carringer, *The Jazz Singer,* 144.

Chapter Three
1. Erens, *The Jew in American Cinema,* 159.
2. Friedman, *Hollywood's Image of the Jew,* 78.
3. *Ibid.,* 242.
4. Bernheimer, *The 50 Greatest Jewish Movies: A Critic's Ranking of the Very Best,* 186.

Chapter Four
1. Erens, *The Jew in American Cinema,* 149.
2. Bartov, *The "Jew" in Cinema: From The Golem to Don't Touch My Holocaust,* 128.
3. *Ibid.,* 129.
4. Insdorf, *Indelible Shadows: Film and the Holocaust,* 68.
5. Bartov, *The "Jew" in Cinema,* 131.
6. Samberg, *Reel Jewish,* 87.
7. Friedman, *Hollywood's Image of the Jew,* 128.
8. *Ibid.,* 129.
9, Bernheimer, *The 50 Greatest Jewish Movies,* 40.
10. http://www.tabletmag.com/100-films/84314/no-100-schindler%E2%80%99s-list/.
11. Bernheimer, *The 50 Greatest Jewish Movies,* 12.
12. Bartov, *The "Jew" in Cinema,* 142.

Chapter Five
1. Desser and Friedman, *American Jewish Filmmakers,* 27.
2. Epstein, *The Haunted Smile: The Story of Jewish Comedians in America,* 90.
3. Bernheimer, *The 50 Greatest Jewish Movies,* 83.
4. As quoted in Epstein, *The Haunted Smile,* 210.
5. *Ibid.*
6. Erens, *The Jew in American Cinema,* 337.

7. Rosenberg, "Coming Out of the Ethnic Closet: Jewishness in the Films of Barry Levinson," *Shofar*, 41.
8. Desser and Friedman, *American Jewish Filmmakers*, 295–296.
9. Rosenberg, "Coming Out of the Ethnic Closet," 42.

Chapter Six

1. Friedman, *Hollywood's Image of the Jew*, 136.
2. Bernheimer, *The 50 Greatest Jewish Movies*, 146.
3. As quoted in Erens, *The Jew in American Cinema*, 269.
4. Ibid., 277–278.
5. Friedman, *Hollywood's Image of the Jew*, 256.
6. Erens, *The Jew in American Cinema*, 323.

Chapter Seven

1. Epstein, *The Haunted Smile*, 196.
2. Ibid., 197.
3. Ibid., 219.

Chapter Eight

1. Erens, *The Jew in American Cinema*, 217.
2. Friedman, *Hollywood's Image of the Jew*, 192.
3. Erens, *The Jew in American Cinema*, 220.

Chapter Nine

1. As quoted in Friedman, *Hollywood's Image of the Jew*, 147.

Chapter Ten

1. Samberg, *Reel Jewish*, 128.
2. Ibid., 130.

Bibliography

Altman, Sig. *The Comic Image of the Jew.* Rutherford, NJ: Fairleigh Dickinson University Press, 1971.
Antler, Joyce, ed. *Talking Back: Images of Jewish Women in American Popular Culture.* Waltham, MA: Brandeis University Press, 1998.
Baron, Lawrence. *Projecting the Holocaust into the Present: The Changing Focus of Holocaust Feature Films Since 1990.* Lanham, MD: Rowman and Littlefield, 2006.
Bartov, Omer. *The "Jew" in Cinema: From The Golem to Don't Touch My Holocaust.* Bloomington: Indiana University Press, 2005.
Baumgold, Julie. "The Persistence of the Jewish American Princess." *New York,* March 22, 1971, 25–31.
Beaver, James N. *John Garfield: His Life and Films.* South Brunswick, NJ: Barnes, 1978.
Belth, Nathan C. *A Promise to Keep: A Narrative of the American Encounter with Anti-Semitism.* New York: Times Books, 1979.
Bergman, Andrew. *We're In the Money.* New York: NYU Press, 1971.
Berlin, Charles. *Jewish Film and Jewish Studies.* Cambridge, MA: Harvard University Library, 1991.
Bernheimer, Kathryn. *The 50 Greatest Jewish Movies: A Critic's Ranking of the Very Best.* Secaucus, NJ: Carol, 1988.
Bernstein, Matthew H. *Screening a Lynching: The Leo Frank Case on Film and Television.* Athens: University of Georgia Press, 2009.
Bial, Henry. *Acting Jewish: Negotiating Ethnicity on the American Stage and Screen.* Ann Arbor: University of Michigan Press, 2005.
Birdwell, Michael. *Celluloid Soldiers: The Warner Bros. Campaign Against Nazism.* New York: NYU Press, 2000.
Brook, Vincent. *Driven to Darkness: Jewish Émigré Directors and the Rise of Film Noir.* New Brunswick, NJ: Rutgers University Press, 2009.
_____, ed. *"You Should See Yourself": Jewish Identity in Postmodern American Culture.* New Brunswick, NJ: Rutgers University Press, 2006.
Buhle, Paul. *From the Lower East Side to Hollywood: Jews in American Popular Culture.* New York: Verso, 2004.
Carr, Steven Alan. *Hollywood and Anti-Semitism: A Cultural History up to World War II.* Cambridge, UK: Cambridge University Press, 2001.
Carringer, Robert, ed. *The Jazz Singer.* Madison: University of Wisconsin Press, 1979.
Cohen, Sarah Blacher, ed. *From Hester Street Hollywood: The Jewish-American Stage and Screen.* Bloomington: Indiana University Press, 1983.

Bibliography

Cripps, Thomas. "The Movie Jew as an Image of Assimilation, 1903–1927." *Journal of Popular Film* 4 (1975): 190–207.
Davka. Special Issue: The Hollywood Jew, V, No. 33, 1975.
Desser, David, and Lester D. Friedman. *American Jewish Filmmakers*, 2d ed. Urbana: University of Illinois Press, 2004.
Dinnerstein, Leonard. *Anti-Semitism in America*. New York: Oxford, 1995.
Doneson, Judith E. *The Holocaust in American Film*, 2d ed., Syracuse: Syracuse University Press, 2002.
Epstein, Lawrence J. *At the Edge of a Dream: The Story of Jewish Immigrants on New York's Lower East Side, 1880–1920*. San Francisco and New York: Jossey-Bass and the Lower East Side Tenement Museum, 2007.
_____. *The Haunted Smile: The Story of Jewish Comedians in America*. NY: Public Affairs, 2001.
Erens, Patricia. *The Jew in American Cinema*. Bloomington: Indiana University Press, 1988.
Erens, Patricia Brett. "Film." *Jewish-American History and Culture: An Encyclopedia*. Eds. Jack Fischel and Sanford Pinsker. New York: Garland, 1992. 174–181.
Finkelstein, Norman H. *American Jewish History*. Philadelphia: Jewish Publication Society, 2007.
Fishman, Sylvia, Barack. *I of the Beholder: Jews and Gender in Film and Popular Culture*. Waltham, MA: Brandeis University, International Research Institute on Jewish Women, 1998.
_____. *Real Americans: The Evolving Identities of American Jews*. New York: Jewish Media Fund, 1996.
Fox, Stuart. *Jewish Films in the United States: A Comprehensive Survey and Descriptive Filmography*. Boston: G. K. Hall, 1976.
French, Philip. *The Movie Moguls: An Informal History of the Hollywood Tycoons*. Chicago: Regnery, 1971.
Friedman, Lester D. *Hollywood's Image of the Jew*. New York: Ungar, 1982.
_____. *The Jewish Image in American Film*. Secaucus, NJ: Citadel, 1987.
_____. *Unspeakable Images: Ethnicity and the American Cinema*. Champaign: University of Illinois Press, 1991.
Friedman, Norman L. "Hollywood, the Jewish Experience, and Popular Culture," *Judaism* 19, No. 4 (1970): 482–487.
Furnish, Ben. *Nostalgia in Jewish-American Theatre and Film, 1979–2004*. New York: Peter Lang, 2005.
Gabler, Neal. *An Empire of Their Own: How the Jews Invented Hollywood*. New York: Anchor, 1989.
Gertel, Elliot B. *Over the Top Judaism: Precedents and Trends in the Depiction of Jewish Beliefs and Observances in Film and Television*. Lanham, MD: University Press of America, 2003.
Goldman, Eric A. *Visions, Images and Dreams: Yiddish Film Past And Present*, rev. ed. Teaneck, NJ: Holmes & Meier, 2011.
Haggith, Toby, and Joanna Newman, eds. *The Holocaust and the Moving Image*: West Sussex, England: Wallflower Press, 2005.
Hecht, Ben. *A Child of the Century*. New York: Simon & Schuster, 1954.
Hirsch, Joshua. *Afterimage: Film, Trauma, and the Holocaust*. Philadelphia: Temple University Press, 2003.
Hoberman, J., and Jeffrey Shandler. *Entertaining America: Jews, Movies, and Broad-*

casting. New York and Princeton, NJ: Jewish Museum and Princeton University Press, 2003.
Howe, Irving. *World of Our Fathers: The Journey of the East European Jews to America and the Life They Found and Made*. New York: Harcourt Brace Jovanovich, 1976.
Insdorf, Annette. *Indelible Shadows: Film and the Holocaust*, 3d ed. New York: Cambridge University Press, 2003.
Joselit, Jenna Weissman. *The Wonders of America: Reinventing Jewish Culture 1880–1950*. New York: Picador, 2002.
Kanin, Josh. "The Portrayal of the Jew in American Cinema 1900–1953." Master's Thesis, University of Southern California, 1973.
Kellerman, Henry. *Greedy, Cowardly, and Weak: Hollywood's Jewish Stereotypes*. Fort Lee, NJ: Barricade Books, 2009.
Kerner, Aaron. *Film and the Holocaust: New Perspectives on Dramas, Documentaries, and Experimental Films*. New York: Continuum, 2011.
Loshitzky, Yosefa. *Spielberg's Holocaust: Critical Perspectives on Schindler's List*. Bloomington: Indiana University Press, 1997.
Lyman, Daryll. *Great Jews on Stage and Screen*. Middle Village, NY: Jonathan David, 1987.
May, Lary. *Screening Out the Past: The Birth of Mass Culture and the Motion Picture Industry*. New York: Oxford University Press, 1980.
Meltzer, Milton. *Remember the Days: A Short History of the Jewish American*. Garden City, NY: Doubleday, 1974.
Merwin, Ted. *In Their Own Image: New York Jews in Jazz Age Popular Culture*. New Brunswick, NJ: Rutgers University Press, 2006.
Miller, Randall, ed. *Ethnic Images in American Films and Television*. Philadelphia: The Balche Institute, 1978.
Quinley, Harold E., and Charles Y. Glock. *Anti-Semitism in America*. New York: The Free Press, 1979.
Rischin, Moses. *The Promised City: New York's Jews, 1870–1914*. Cambridge, MA: Harvard University Press, 1962.
Rogin, Michael. *Blackface, White Noise: Jewish Immigrants in the Hollywood Melting Pot*. Berkeley: University of California Press, 1998.
Rosenberg, Joel. "Jewish Experience on Film — An American Overview." *American Jewish Year Book*, 1996, 3–50.
Rosenberg, Warren. "Coming Out of the Ethnic Closet: Jewishness in the Films of Barry Levinson." *Shofar* 22.1, Fall 2003, 29–43.
Samberg, Joel. *Reel Jewish*. Middle Village, NY: Jonathan David, 2000. Sarna, Jonathan. *American Judaism: A History*. New Haven: Yale University Press, 2005.
Shavelson, Melville. *How to Make a Jewish Movie*. Englewood Cliffs, NJ: Prentice-Hall, 1971.
Sklar, Robert. "Jews and Hollywood." *Encyclopedia of American Jewish History*. Eds. Stephen H. Norwood and Eunice G. Pollack. Santa Barbara, CA: ABC-CLIO, 2008. vol. 2. 460–467.
Sklare, Marshall. *America's Jews*. New York: Random House, 1971.
_____. *The Jews: Social Patterns of an American Group*. Glencoe, IL: Free Press, 1958.
Stern, Bill. *You Don't Have to be Jewish: Commentaries on a Selection of Jewish Content Films* Toronto: Lugus, 2002.
Suber, Howard. "Politics and Popular Culture: Hollywood at Bay, 1933–1953." *American Jewish History*, LXVII, June 1979, 517–533.

Bibliography

Taub, Michael, ed. *Films about Jewish Life and Culture*. Lewiston, NY: Edwin Mellen Press, 2005.

Weinberg, David. "The 'Socially Acceptable' Immigrant Minority Group: The Image of the Jew in American Popular Film." *North Dakota Quarterly*, Autumn 1972, 60-68.

Welky, David. *The Moguls and the Dictators: Hollywood and the Coming of World War II*. Baltimore: Johns Hopkins University Press, 2008.

Whitfield, Stephen J. *In Search of American Jewish Culture*. Waltham, MA: Brandeis University Press; 2001.

Wisse, Ruth R. *The Schlemiel as Modern Hero*. Chicago: University of Chicago Press, 1971.

Zierold, Norman. *The Moguls*. New York: Coward-McCann, 1969.

Websites

Ergo Media http://www.ergomedia.com/.

The Jewish Image in American Film http://www.jhvc.org/courses/course_notes/jimg_web/JIMG_Guide.pdf.

JewishFilm.com http://www.jewishfilm.com/.

The Jewish Film Club http://www.jewishfilmclub.com/index.asp?gclid=COP3h67mlqoCFcpM4AodcVtH-g&.

The National Center For Jewish Film http://www.brandeis.edu/jewishfilm/about.htm.

Index

Abie's Irish Rose 118
Allen, Woody 8, 91, 95–97, 101–106, 109, 125, 128–129, 131, 137–141
Annie Hall 128–132
anti–Semitism 12, 15, 29, 36–39, 48
Arliss, George 36–37
Avalon 112–113

Bartov, Omar 52–53, 56, 76
Ben-Hur 182–183
Benny, Jack 31, 51, 54, 87
Bernheimer, Kathryn 40, 62, 75, 121
The Bible: In the Beginning 183
Biloxi Blues 106–107
Blazing Saddles 95–96
Body and Soul 90–91
Broadway Danny Rose 140–142
Brooks, Mel 91–95
Bugsy 171–173
Burns, George 31

Cahan, Abraham 31
Cast a Giant Shadow 160–161
Chaplin, Charlie 20, 23, 50–52
The Chosen 186–189
Clift, Montgomery 63
The Cocoanuts 84
Coen Brothers 190, 195
Cohen, Leonard 14
The Cohens and the Kellys 16–17
Compulsion 169–171
Conspiracy of Hearts 67
Coogan, Jackie 20
Counsellor-at-Law 29
Crimes and Misdemeanors 109–112
Crossfire 62–63 94–95, 143
Crossing Delancey 32–33
Crystal, Billy 144–145

David and Bathsheba 177–178
Davidson, Max 16, 20
Defiance 77–78
The Diary of Anne Frank 65–67
Dirty Dancing 142–143
Disraeli 35–36
Douglas, Kirk 149, 160
Driving Miss Daisy 107–108
Duck Soup 88–89
Dylan, Bob 14

Erens, Patricia 49, 99, 124, 127, 152, 157
E.T.: The Extra-Terrestrial 101
The Eternal City 11
ethnic stereotypes 11, 16
Everything Is Illuminated 77
Exodus 152–159

Fiddler on the Roof 39–44
Friedman, Lester 38, 44, 61, 83, 113, 120, 125, 156, 203–204, 206
The Frisco Kid 99–100
The Front 97–98
Funny Girl 121–123

Gentleman's Agreement 57–62
Goldwyn, Samuel 9–12, 16, 18–19
Goodbye, Columbus 94–95, 143
The Great Dictator 50–53

Hawn, Goldie 100–101
Hays Office 50, 176
The Heartbreak Kid 124–125
Hester Street 30–31, 41–42
His People 21, 26
Hobson, Laura Z. 59
the Holocaust 7, 12, 48, 51, 57–58, 61, 63, 65, 67, 69–78, 90, 110, 148–150, 158–161, 175, 178–179, 188, 203, 205–206

Index

Horse Feathers 85
The House of Rothschild 37–38
Hungry Hearts 18–19

In Hollywood with Potash and Perlmutter 16
Inglourious Basterds 78

The Jazz Singer 21–28, 43
Jewish identity 13–15
Jolson, Al 23–28
Judgment at Nuremberg 67–69
Judith 160
The Juggler 149–152

Kane, Carol 30
King David 184

Laemmele, Carl 21
Leibovitz, Liel 73
Levinson, Barry 112–116
Liberty Heights 113–116
The Life of Emile Zola 38–39
Lower East Side 17–34

Malamud, Bernard 176
The Man in the Glass Booth 96–97
Marjorie Morningstar 118–120
A Majority of One 120–121
Marx, Groucho 83–90
Marx Brothers 83–90
Matthau, Walter 31
Mr. Saturday Night 144–145
The Mortal Storm 53–54
Mostel, Zero 92, 97
Muni, Paul 38
Munich 163

Newman, Paul 153
A Night at the Opera 89
No Way to Treat a Lady 123–124

Oedipus Wrecks 139
Once Upon a Time in America 171

Partners Again with Potash and Perlmutter 16
The Pawnbroker 69
Peck, Gregory 59

personal identity 13
The Pianist 76–77
The Plot Against Harry 169
Potash and Perlmutter 11
A Price Above Rubies 189
The Prince of Egypt 185–186
Private Benjamin 100–101
The Producers 91–94

The Rag Man 20–21
Raid on Entebbe 162–163

Schindler's List 73–76
School Ties 73
The Search 63–65
A Serious Man 189–195
Sidney, George 16–17
Silver, Joan Micklin 31–33
Solomon and Sheba 180–181
Sophie's Choice 71–73
Spielberg, Steven 73–76
Steiger, Rod 70–71
A Stranger Among Us 189
Streep, Meryl 71
Street Scene 28
Streisand, Barbra 44, 121–122, 127
The Sunshine Boys 31–32
Sweet Lorraine 144
Sword in the Desert 149
Symphony of Six Million 28–29

Take the Money and Run 105
Taking Woodstock 145–146
The Ten Commandments 178–180
To Be or Not to Be 54–57

The Way We Were 125–128
Wiesel, Elie 79
Wilder, Gene 92, 98–99

The Yellow Ticket 36–37
Yentl 44–47
Yezierska, Anzia 18–19
You Nazty Spy 50

Zanuck, Darryl 24, 59
Zelig 101–102, 105–106
Zionism 35

www.ingramcontent.com/pod-product-compliance
Ingram Content Group UK Ltd.
Pitfield, Milton Keynes, MK11 3LW, UK
UKHW041956140426
5217IPUK00015B/818